AF531525

Preface

Environmental biotechnology is the multidisciplinary integration of sciences and engineering in order to utilize the huge biochemical potential of microorganisms, plants and parts thereof for the restoration and preservation of the environment and for the sustainable use of available resources. The primary role of eco-technology is to develop better approaches for sustainable development and for understanding the basic processes in the natural environment.

Ecological science comprises the study of the effects of anthropogenic and natural materials and activities on organisms at various levels of organization, from sub-cellular through individual organisms to communities and ecosystems. Generally, fish and invertebrates can often be used to indicate the health of an aquatic system because chemicals can accumulate in invertebrates from the water and sediment and in fish from water, sediment, and the food chain. The monitoring of these effects is extremely important to regulate and remediate pollution.

The effects of pollutants on the whole organism can be considered as neuro-physiological, reproductive and behavioural effects. These effects can often be inter-related: neurological changes can affect behaviour; changes in behaviour can affect reproduction and so on. A compound doesn't always put forth an effect on a target organism or a community. It always depends on the concentration of that compound and the time of exposure to it. These effects eventually can be either acute or chronic. Acute toxicity occurs rapidly, are clearly defined, often fatal and rarely reversible. Chronic effects develop after long exposure to low doses or long after exposure and may ultimately cause death. The harmful effects that chemicals have upon individual organisms depend on many different factors. Not only the difference between the freshwater species, but also the form in which pollutants occur, and if the pollutant shows up in lotic or lentic systems.

The present book mainly deals with ecological sciences, eco-technology, environmental toxicology, biotechnological applications and updates the subject matter, illustrations and problems to incorporate new concepts and issues related to eco-technology, environmental toxicology and ecological sciences. The approach to presenting this book is traditional covering of environmental pollution, aquatic ecosystem, environmental toxicology, ecological sciences and biotechnology.

The book includes 11 chapters contributed by outstanding experts and scientists from Nigeria and different parts of India. This book provides comprehensive coverage of the fundamental principles and current practices and trends in the field of ecological sciences, eco-toxicology and eco-technology.

I hope this book will be of benefit to both present and future colleagues, who teach, study and working in the field of eco-technology, freshwater toxicology, aquatic ecosystem, environmental pollution, fisheries, and ecological sciences.

Dr. Pawan Kumar 'Bharti'

E-mail: *gurupawanbharti@gmail.com*

Contents

List of Contributors

Aakansha Goswami; Deptt. of Horticulture, Sardar Vallabhbhai Patel University of Agriculture & Technology, Meerut – 250 110 (India).

Amit Verma; Department of Biochemistry, G.B. Pant University of Agriculture & Technology, Pantnagar, U.S. Nagar, (Uttarakhand) (India).

Anubhuti Sharma; Biochemistry Lab., Vivekanand Parvatiya Krishi Anusandhan Sansthan (ICAR), Almora - 263 601 (Uttarakhand) (India).

A.K. Bhandari; Herbal Research and Development Institute, Mandal, Gopeshwar, (Chamoli) – 246 401 (Uttarakhand) India.

A.K. Prusty; Project Directorate of Farming System Research, Merrut – 250 110 (India).

B. Singh; Deptt. of Horticulture, Sardar Vallabhbhai Patel University of Agriculture & Technology, Meerut – 250 110 (India).

B.K. Behera; Central Inland Fisheries Research Institute (CIFRI), Barrackpore, Kolkata – 700 120 (West Bengal) (India).

Dharmendra Kumar Meena; Central Inland Fisheries Research Institute (CIFRI), Barrackpore, Kolkata – 700 120 (West Bengal) (India).

Emmanuel Ibukunoluwa Moyin-Jesu; Agronomy Department, Federal College of Agriculture, Akure, 340 001, Ondo State, Nigeria.

Gayatri Bhadana; Deptt.of Biotechnology Sardar Vallabhbhai Patel University of Agriculture & Technology, Meerut – 250 110 (India).

Hukum Singh; Department of Plant Physiology, G.B. Pant University of Agriculture & Technology, Pantnagar, U.S. Nagar, (Uttarakhand) (India).

Jayanthi Abraham; Microbial Biotechnology Laboratory, School of Biosciences and Technology, Division of Environmental Biotechnology, VIT University, Vellore – 632 014 (Tamil Nadu) (India).

Jaswant Ray; Institute for Industrial Research & Toxicology, Ghaziabad (U.P.) (India).

J.S. Negi; Herbal Research and Development Institute, Mandal, Gopeshwar (Chamoli) – 246 401 (Uttarakhand) (India).

Kanti Meena; Central Research Institute for Jute & Allied Fibres, Barrackpore, Kolkata – 700 120 (West Bengal) (India).

Manoj Kumar Panda; Lecturer in Zoology, U. P. Sience College, Sheragada, Ganjam (Odisha) (India).

Mayank Dave; Department of Microbiology, Kurukshetra University Kurukshetra (Haryana) (India).

Md. Shahbaz Akthar; Directorate of Coldwater Fisheries Research, Bhimtal – 263 136 (India).

Neelam Garg; Department of Microbiology, Kurukshetra University Kurukshetra (Haryana) (India).

Nermin Adel El Semary; Botany and Microbiology Department, Faculty of Science, Helwan University, Ain Helwan campus, Post code: 11795, Ain Helwan, Helwan, Egypt.

N. Singh; Herbal Research and Development Institute, Mandal, Gopeshwar (Chamoli) – 246 401 (Uttarakhand) (India).

Pronob Das; Central Inland Fisheries Research Institute (CIFRI), Barrackpore, Kolkata – 700 120 (West Bengal) (India).

R.C. Sundriyal; G.B. Pant Institute of Himalayan Environment and Development, Kosi-Katarmal, Almora – 263 643 (Uttarakhand) (India).

Ritika Chauhan; Microbial Biotechnology Laboratory, School of Biosciences and Technology, Division of Environmental Biotechnology, VIT University, Vellore – 632 014, (Tamil Nadu) (India)

S. Kandari; Department of Botany, H. N. B. Garhwal University, Srinagar (Garhwal) – 246 174 (Uttarakhand) (India).

Satendra Kumar; RHS Krishi Vigyan Kendra (Jawaharlal Nehru Krishi Vishwa Vidyalaya) Badgaon, Balaghat – 481 115 (MP) (India).

Sandhya Sharma; Banasthali Vidyapeeth (Rajasthan) (India).

Sekar, M.; Central Institute of Fisheries Education, Mumbai – 400 061 (Maharashtra) (India).

Sivagnanam Silambarasan; Microbial Biotechnology Laboratory, School of Biosciences and Technology, Division of Environmental Biotechnology, VIT University, Vellore – 632 014, (Tamil Nadu) (India).

Smriti Tyagi; Department of Bioscience & Biotechnology, Banasthali University, Banasthali – 304 022 (Rajasthan) (India).

V.K. Bisht; Herbal Research and Development Institute, Mandal, Gopeshwar (Chamoli) – 246 401 (Uttarakhand) (India).

Vibha Bhardwaj; Department of Microbiology, Kurukshetra University Kurukshetra (Haryana) (India).

CHAPTER 1

Comparative Evaluation of Seven Different Spacing Treatments on Weeding Regimes Tuber Yield, Stem and Leaf Biomasses of Cassava (*Manihot esculenta* L)

Emmanuel Ibukunoluwa Moyin-Jesu, *Nigeria*

ABSTRACT

The effect of seven spacing treatments on weeding regimes, tuber yield, stem and leaf biomasses of cassava (*Manihot esculenta,* L) was investigated at Akure in the rainforest zone of Nigeria. The seven spacing treatments were 100 × 100 cm (10,000 plants), 90 × 70 cm (15,000 plants/hectare), 100 cm × 50 cm (20,000 plants/ha), 70 × 50 cm (28,600 plants/ha), 80 × 50 cm (25,000 plants/ha), 65 × 50 cm (30,500 plants/ha), 65 × 50 cm (30,500 plants/ha) and 50 × 50 cm (40,000 plants/ha) with four replications, arranged in a randomized complete design (RCB). A spacing treatment of 100 cm × 100 cm which was conventionally used by farmers served as the control treatment.

The results showed that these spacing treatments significantly (P<0.05) influenced the cassava growth parameters, tuber yield, stem and leaf biomasses and weeding regimes. For the growth parameters, 100 × 100 cm spacing treatment had the highest values of plant height, stem girth and leaf area followed by 100 × 50 cm and 70 × 50 cm. 100 × 100 cm spacing increased the plant height, leaf area and stem girth by 13 per cent, 4.5 per cent and 12 per cent compared to that of 100 × 50 cm spacing. For tuber yield, stem and leaf biomasses of cassava, 100 × 100 cm spacing had second best value for tuber yield and least value of leaf biomass with the highest weeding regime (four times) compared to others. 90 × 70 cm spacing ranked third in term of tuber yield, tuber diameter and population while 100 × 50 cm spacing had the highest tuber weight (57.7t/ha) and second best tuber diameter compared to others. 80 × 50 cm 70 × 50 cm spacing ranked fourth and fifth in terms of tuber weight and diameter performance respectively.

Generally, 100 × 50 cm spacing had good and balanced potentials for cassava root tubers, leaf and stem biomasses. Both 65 × 50 cm and 50 × 50 cm spacing had the least tuber yield performance but had good potentials for stem and leaf biomasses and reduced cost of weeding by 50 per cent compared to 100 × 100 cm. The 50 × 50 cm spacing treatment had the highest gross income, net income gain and BC ratio of 6.343 with the highest contributions from sales of cassava stem cuttings and huge leaf biomass compared to BC 2.92 in 100 × 100 cm spacing treatments respectively. In these experiments, 100 cm × 50 cm, spacing was recommended for tuber yield while 50 × 50 cm spacing was recommended for leaf and stem biomasses.

Key words: Spacing, weeding, cassava tuber, leaf and stem biomasses.

Introduction

Cassava (*Manihot esculentum*) is a major tuber crop grown by farmers for income and as staple foods. In recent times, it has become an important crop for making industrial starch, tapioca, cassava chips and other processed products in Nigeria which helped to enhance export drive for increased foreign exchange, provision of employment opportunities and for meeting local consumption.[1]

In spite of the above mentioned importance of the crop to economic development, the optimum yields of cassava to meet the needs of the society, have not been attained and the fundamental problems are that the present level cultivation of the crops is low and cannot meet up with the local consumption talk less of the cassava processing industries and export drive, coupled with the continued decline in soil fertility and weed competition.

In order to sustain the demand for cassava to meet both local and export needs of the nation, there is need to increase the present cassava plant population per hectare from the present 10,000 plants to between 16,000 and 40,000 plants per hectare as well as maintaining soil fertility.

Interestingly, massive production of cassava at higher plant population will provide substantial leaf biomass for animal production as well as increasing the number of stem cutting available for sustainable cultivation of cassava. A farmer can make between ₦100,000 and ₦300,000 from sales of cassava stem cutting only, in addition to the sales of the tubers.[2]

Having reviewed literature critically, except[3, 4, 5] who worked on the morphology of cassava and plant population densities in cassava/maize mixture, there is scarcity of research reports on determining the best of optimum plant population of cassava that will give good performance of tuber yield, stem cutting and leaf biomass using appropriate spacing, thus, there is justification to look into this research for future development.

The objective of this research are to determine the optimum plant population of cassava using seven spacing treatment that will give the highest tuber yield, leaf biomass and stem cuttings and best weeding regimes for cassava sole cropping in Akure, Ondo State, Nigeria and to determine the economic benefit cost of cassava production under these spacing treatments.

Materials and Methods

Description of the Study Area

The experiment was carried out at Akure in the rainforest zone of Nigeria between August 2004 and September 2005 and was repeated between March 2006 and April 2007 to validate the results. The soil is sandy clay loam, skeletal, kaolinitic, isohyperthermic oxic paleustalf (Alfisol).[5] The annual rainfall is between 1100 and 1500mm while the average temperature is 24°C. The land had been under continuous cultivation for 5 years.

Soil Sampling and Analysis Before Panting

Thirty core samples were collected randomly from 0-15 cm depth on the site using soil auger, mixed thoroughly and the bulk sample was taken to the laboratory, air dried and sieved to pass through a 2 mm screen for chemical analysis. The soil pH (1:1 soil/ water) and (1:2 soil/0.01M $CaCl_2$) solution was determined using a glass calomel electrode system[7] while organic matter was determined by the wet oxidation chromic acid digestion method.[8]

The total nitrogen was determined by the micro kjedahl method[9] while available soil phosphorous was extracted by the Bray P1 extractant and measured by the Murphy blue colouration on spectronic 20[10] while K, Ca, Na were determined with flame photometer while Mg was determined with an atomic absorption spectrophotometer.[11]

The exchangeable acidity (H^+ and $A1^{3+}$) were determined using 0.01M HCl extracts and titrated with 0.1M NaOH[12] while the micronutrient (Mn, Cu, Fe and Zn) were extracted with 0.1M HCl[13] and read on Perkin Elmer atomic absorption spectrophotometer. The mechanical analysis of the soil was done by the hydrometer method.[14]

Field Experiment

The land was cleared, ploughed, harrowed, ridged and laid out into plots. Each individual plot size is 12 × 17m^2 (204m^2) totaling 30 plots. There were discards of 1m × 1m between and within plots for easy accessibility and for carrying out other cultural practices without trampling on the cassava plants. There were seven spacing treatments namely; 90 cm × 70 cm, (15,000 plants/ha), 100 × 50 cm (20,000 plant/ha), 70 × 50 cm (28,600 plant/ha), 80 × 50 cm (25,000 plant/ha), 65 cm × 50 cm (30,800 plants/ha) and 50 cm × 50 cm (40,000 plants/ha with four replications and arranged in a randomized complete block design (RCB). A spacing treatment of 100 cm × 100 cm which was conventionally used by farmers served as the control treatment. Six tonnes/ha of poultry manure was applied basally to the field to supply initial nutrients and allowed 7days to decompose. Planting of viable cassava stem cuttings of 30572 variety into different plots based on the above mentioned spacing started on September 6 and ended on September 13, 2004. Specific labels sharing these spacing treatments were placed on the plots for easy identification and data collection.

The plots were sprayed with pre-emergence herbicides Atrazine and Gramozone to kill weed seeds. The stem cuttings sprouted and the first weeding took place after two months of sprouting. Another three weeding were done for 100 cm x 100 cm while 65 cm x 50 cm, 50 cm x 50 cm and 80 cm x 50 cm spacing treatments had only one extra weeding after the first weeding. At 3 months after sprouting, Avesthrin (Cypermethrin 10% EC) was sprayed at 10ml per 10l of water to control white flies responsible for the widespread of cassava mosaic disease.

Field data collection on the growth parameters (plant height, leaf area and stem girth) were done every week starting from the 3rd week after sprouting till four months after sprouting. Another spraying of Avesthrin (a.i Cypermethrin 10% E.C) to control white flies was done at 6 months after sprouting. The bushes adjourning the cassava plantation was cut back to prevent rodent and grass cutter attack of cassava plants.

At 11 months after sprouting on the field, sampling harvest was done on August 22, 2005 using 3m × 3m for each following parameters were determined which include tuber weight (kg), tuber diameter (cm), tuber population per plant, leaf biomass (weighed of 50 leaves (kg), and number of leaves per plant, weight of plantable stem cuttings (g), number of weeding regimes, estimate cost of weeding (₦12,000 per hectare), weight of litter fall and number of good stem cuttings.

Statistical Analysis

The average data for the 2 years on the growth parameters, tuber, stem and leaf yield parameters of the two experiments were analysed and subjected to ANOVA F-test and their means were separated using Duncan Multiple Range Test at 5 per cent level of significance.[15]

Results

Soil Chemical Composition Before Planting of Cassava

The chemical properties of the soil before planting of cassava are presented in Table 1. Based on the established critical levels for soils in South west Nigeria, the soil was slightly acidic with pH 5.6 and low in organic matter compared to the critical level of 3 per cent O.M.[16] The total nitrogen is less than 0.15 per cent which is considered optimal for most crops.[17]

Table 1.1: Chemical Analysis of the Soil before Planting

Soil Parameters	Values
Soil pH (H_2O)	5.60
Soil pH O.M $CaCl_2$	5.20
Organic matter (%)	0.45
Nitrogen (%)	0.09
Available P (mg/kg)	5.80
K^+ (mmol/kg)	0.15
Ca^{2+} (mmol/kg)	0.11
Mg^{2+} (mmol/kg)	0.09
Na^+ (mmol/kg)	0.08
H^+ (mmol/kg)	4.30
Al^{3+} (mmol/kg)	1.49
Fe (mg/kg)	8.50
Zn (mg/kg)	3.80
Mn (mg/kg)	1.84
Cu (mg/kg)	2.20
Sand (%)	79.50
Silt (%)	14.80
Clay (%)	5.70
Bulk density (mgm^{-3})	1.60
% Porosity	41.81

The available P was less than 10mg/kg P considered as adequate for crop production.[16] The exchangeable K, Ca, Mg and Na were lower than 0.2mmol/kg critical levels[18] while the soil bulk density is high (1.60mgm^{-3}).

Effect of Different Spacing Treatment on the Growth Parameters of Cassava

There were significant increases ($p<0.05$) in the plant height, leaf area and stem girth of cassava under different spacing treatments (Table 1.2). The spacing 100 × 100cm treatment gave the highest values of cassava plant height, leaf area and stem girth followed by 100 × 50cm and 70 × 50cm respectively. For instance, 100 × 100cm spacing treatment increased the plant height, leaf area and stem girth of cassava by 13 per cent, 4.5 per cent and 12 per cent respectively compared to 100 × 50cm spacing. The 65 × 50cm and 50 × 50 cm spacing treatments had the least values of cassava plant height, leaf area and stem girth.

Table 1.2: Effect of Different Spacing Treatments on the Growth Parameters of Cassava

Treatment Spacing (Cm)	Plant Height (Cm)	Leaf Area (Cm^2)	Stem Girth (Cm)
100 × 100	79.66e	327.02g	6.12e
90 × 70	59.40a	258.95a	5.40d
100 × 50	69.70d	312.12f	5.40d
80 × 50	63.95b	294.12d	5.18bc
70 × 50	67.13c	305.00e	5.09b
65 × 50	64.06b	274.35b	4.93b
50 × 50	67.26c	279.93c	4.61a

Treatment means within each group followed by the same letters are not significantly different from other using Duncan Multiple Range Test at 5 per cent level.

Effect of Different Spacing Treatments on the Tuber, Stem and Leaf Biomass Yield of Cassava

There were Significant increases ($p<0.05$) in the tuber, stem and leaf biomass yield of cassava under different spacing treatments (Table 1.3). For 100 × 100cm spacing, the plant population is 10,000 plants. The tuber weight is 54.4 t/ha while the tuber diametre and population values were 5.1cm and 7 respectively. The implication is that the convectional spacing employed by farmers would give an average of 54.4 t/ha tuber but the cost of weeding was at the highest at ₦48,000 which might not give much profit margin (Table 1.4). The weight of 50 leaves sampled and leaf population were 0.11kg and 103 in 100 × 100cm compared to 0.25 kg and 405 in 50 × 50 cm spacing showing that the leaf biomass was the least of all the spading treatments.

Table 1.3: Effect of Different Spacing Treatments on the Tuber, Stem and Leaf Yield of Cassava

Spacing Treatment	Estimated Plant Population per Hectare	Tuber Weight per 3cm × 3cm Plot Size (kg)	Tuber Weight per Hectare (Tonnes/ha)	Tuber Diametre (cm)	Number of Tubers Per Plant	Leaf Biomass		Weight of Plantable Stem Cuttings	Number of Good Stem Cuttings	Number of Weeding Regimes
						Weight of 50 Leaves (kg)	Number of Leaves			
100 × 100 cm	10,000	49f	54.4f	5.1	7c	0.11a	103a	1.06d	22d	4
90 × 70 cm	15,000	47e	52.2e	4.6	5b	0.13b	176c	0.76b	20b	3
100 × 50 cm	20,000	52g	57.7g	4.9	4a	0.15c	155b	0.75b	21c	3
70 × 50 cm	28,600	30c	33.3c	3.1	4.6a	0.12ab	105a	1.30f	22d	3
65 × 50 cm	30,800	26b	28.8b	2.6	7c	0.2e	244d	1.1de	28f	2
80 × 50 cm	25,000	45d	50d	4.5	9d	0.17d	366e	0.91c	25e	3
50 × 50 cm	40,000	24a	26.6a	1.8	5f	0.25f	405f	0.58a	19a	2

Treatment means within each group followed by the same letters are not significantly different from other using Duncan Multiple Range Test at 5 per cent level.

Farmers employing this spacing might not make much money from the export of the leaf biomass, also, the litter fall on the ground was 50g thick compared to 250g of 50 × 50cm. The litter fall on the ground was the least signifying fastest rate of erosion and soil fertility decline than other treatments. In addition, good stem cuttings were obtained from the plots for the planting season.

For 90 × 70cm spacing treatment, it ranked third in term of tuber weight (52.2t/ha) tuber diameter (4.6cm) and tuber population (5). It has a population of 15,900 plants per hectare and the weeding rate was three time at ₦12,000 each (₦36,000:00). The implication is that farmers adopting this spacing for cassava would save at least ₦12,000 from weeding cost compared to 100x100cm, thereby, enhancing higher profit margin.

In addition, the weight of 50 leaves 0.13kg and leaf population is 176, showing higher leaf biomass than the conventional spacing 100 × 100 cm. The litter fall is 121.1g showing that the thickness might influence the rate of erosion and increased soil fertility maintenance. Nevertheless, it has lower weight of plant able stem cuttings than 100 × 100 cm spacing.

The 100 × 50cm spacing treatment, it had the highest tuber weight (57.7t/ha) and second best tuber diameter compared to others. It also had plant population of 20,000 plants per hectare, hence increasing the plant population and also reduced the weeding regimes to three compared to four or more weeding regimes in 100 × 100cm spacing which led to reducing the cost of weeding by ₦12,000.

In term of leaf biomass, the weight of 50 leaves was 0.15 kg and leaf population of 155 which were higher than that of the convectional spacing of 100 × 100cm used by farmers showing that they would make additional income from sales of leaves as source of feed to animals. The litter fall weight was 155.4g showing that the spacing had great potential in reducing soil erosion fertility decline.

Treatment means within each group followed by the same letters are not significantly different from other using Duncan Multiple Range Test at 5 per cent level.

In term of stem biomass, it had on average of 21 good stem cuttings per sampled plants showing that farmers would also make money from sales of stem cuttings (i.e. planting materials). Generally, the 100 × 50 cm had good potentials for root tuber, leaf biomass and stem biomass yield.

Table 1.4: Effect of Different Spacing Treatments on the Weeding Regimes, Cost of Weeding and Litter Fall (g) of Cassava

Spacing Treatments Control	Estimated Plant Population Per Hectare	Number of Weeding Regimes	Estimated Cost of Weeding	Weed Flora	Soil Erosion/ Fertility Litter Fall (g)
100 × 100	10,000	4c	48,000	Elephant grass, Spear Grass *Tridax procumbens*	50.0a
90 × 70	15,900	3b	36,000		112.1b
100 × 50	20,000	3b	36,000		155.4c
70 × 50	28,600	3b	36,000		199.6e
65 × 50	30,800	2a	24,000		200.8e
80 × 50	25,000	3b	36,000		180.0d
50 × 50	40,000	2a	24,000		250.0f

For 70 × 50cm spacing treatment, the plant population is 28,600 plants per hectare. It was fifth in performance in term of tuber weight (33.3t/ha) and tuber diameter (3.1cm). Thus, the increased cassava population also reduced the weeding cost by ₦12,000 for farmers.

The leaf biomass for 50 leaves (0.12kg) and leaf population were slightly higher than that of 100 x 100 cm spacing. Nevertheless, the weight of litter fall of 199.6 g showed that it had great potential in reducing rate of erosion. In addition, this spacing treatment had the highest weight of plantable stem cuttings (22) per sampled plants.

For 80 × 50cm spacing treatment, the plant population is 25,000 per hectare and it was fourth in performance in term of tuber weight 50 tonnes/ hectare and tuber diameter of 4.5 cm compared to that of 100 x 100cm, 100 × 50cm and 90 × 70cm spacing. This showed great potentials in producing good tuber yield, interestingly it had the highest number of tubers (9) per plant. The spacing also reduced the cost of weed by ₦12,000 compared to the convectional spacing of 100 × 100cm used by the farmers.

In terms of leaf biomass, the weight of 50 sampled leaves and leaf population were 0.17g and 366 respectively showing its potential in producing cassava leaves for export or as source of feed to animals or for food consumption.

The weight of litter fall was 180kg showing that the higher plant population reduced the rate of erosion. In term of stem biomass, it had on average 25 good stem cuttings per sampled plants and third best weight of plantable stem cutting implying that farmers using this spacing for cassava would receive additional income from sales of stem cuttings.

For 65 cm × 50 cm spacing, the plant population is 30,800 plants per hectare and its performance was sixth in terms of tuber weight 28.8 tonnes/ hectare (26 kg/9m^2) and tuber diameter of 2.6 cm. This implied that it might not be good for cassava tuber yield production, however, in term of leaf biomass, it had second best weight of sampled 50 leaves (0.2 kg) and an average leaf population of 244.

For the stem biomass, the number of good stem cuttings were 28 per sampled plants and farmers would make additional income from sales of stem cutting. However, the major problem was that the stems were thin in nature caused as a result of etiolation. In term of soil fertility maintenance, the litter fall weight was 200.8 g which effectively checked the rate of erosion and weed growth.

The weeding rate was done two times before total covering of the land by the plants. The implication is that this spacing had reduced the cost of weeding from ₦48,000 in 100 × 100cm spacing to ₦24,000 which is 50 per cent reduction. This is a significant achievement considering the fact that the low cassava tuber yield would have been compensated for by cost of production, high returns on stem cuttings and leaf biomass.

For 50 × 50cm spacing treatment, the plant population is 40,000 plants per hectare and its performance was the least in term of tuber weight (26.6 tonnes/ha or 24kg/9m^2) and tuber diameter of 1.8cm. In term of leaf biomass, it had the highest weight of sampled 50 leaves (0.25kg) and leaf population of 405 implying that this spacing treatment would be the best for farmers wishing to produce cassava for leaves export or as source of feed to animals.

It also had the highest weight of cassava leaf litter fall (250g) showing that it reduced most the rate of erosion and soil fertility decline. This was evident on the field as it had little or no weed growth. This led to low weeding rate of two compared to four or more weeding rates in 100 × 100cm spacing and a benefit cost gain of ₦24,000 from weeding exercise alone.

In term of stem biomass, it had the least number of good stem cuttings of 19 and weight of plant able stem cuttings (0.58 g) because of high population and etiolation. This spacing is also good for those who are interested in setting up cassava starch and tapioca production enterprise because the large number of small sized tubers available which are not lignified.

Economic Cost Benefit for Tuber, Stem and Leaf Biomass Yield Under Different Spacing Treatments

Table 1.5 (*See Table on page No. 12*) presents the yields of tuber, stem and leaf of cassava, the gross income derived from them, the variable cost, net income and benefit cost ratio under different spacing treatments. 100 × 100cm spacing treatment had the least net income gain of ₦567,800 and benefit cost (BC) ratio of 2.92 compared to net income gain of ₦1448,200 and BC ratio of 6.343 in 50 × 50cm spacing (40,000 plants).

The highest contribution to the BC ratio and net gain income in 50 × 50 cm spacing came from the sales of stem cuttings and huge leaf biomass which are at present considered as negligible contributions financially by majority of farmers. For-instance, in 50 × 50cm spacing, leaf biomass/hectare gave about 10t/ha and 1 million naira from sales compared to ₦110,000 in 100 × 100cm spacing.

Therefore, the higher the BC ratio of an enterprise such as cassava farming, the more profitable it is to the farmers. Interestingly, the lower tuber yields in 50 × 50cm, 65 × 50 cm spacing had been effectively compensated for by the high stem and leaf yields.

The 100 × 50cm (20,000 plants/hectare) had good financial returns from the tuber, stem and leaf biomass totaling ₦1192400.00, net income gain of ₦913,400 and BC ratio of 4.27 which ranked fourth after 50 × 50 cm, 80 × 50 cm, 65 × 50 cm spacing treatments respectively.

Discussion

The initial low soil fertility caused as a result of continuous cultivation of land for five years was solved by the general basal application of 6t/ha of poultry manure to the soil before cultivation of cassava. Therefore, the application of the poultry manure had enhanced growth of cassava in all the spacing treatments.

The low plant population of 10,000 in 100 × 100cm encouraged quick growth of weeds, thereby increasing the cost of production compared to 65 × 50cm and 100 × 50cm spacing. The implication is that the high cost of production would reduce the profit margin of farmers hence, the least value of BC ratio. This observation agreed with the views of[19] who reported faster emergence of weeds in Indian spinach plots with wider spacing because of the high isolation rate which encouraged weed competition and high weed density.

The low plant population in 100 × 100cm spacing also reflected in the least values of leaf biomass and liter fall. The implication is that the wider planting spacing between cassava plants exposed the soils to torrential rains and run-off which resulted in fastest rate of erosion and probably fertility decline than other spacing treatments. This observation agreed with[20] who reported that low litter fall in yam/maize rotation resulted in low fertility status and increased the rate of erosion.

Table 1.5: The Economic Cost Benefit for Cultivation of Cassava Under Different Spacing Treatments

Spacing Treatment	Estimated Plant Population Per Hectare	Cassava Tuber Yield Per Hectare (t/ha)	Cost of Tuber Per Tonne at ₦ 12,000 Tonne	Cassava Stem Cuttings		Estimated Leaf Biomass Yield		Gross Income Tuber + Stem + Leaf Yield (□)	Variable Cost (□)	Net Income (□)	Cost-Benefit Ratio (BC)
				Yield/ha Bundles (50 Cutting Each)	Cost of Stem Per Bundle at (□) 500	Weight of Leaves (kg/ha)	Cost of Leaf Biomass at □ 100 Per kg/ha				
100 × 100cm	10,000	54.4	652,800	200	100,000	1,100	110,000	826,800	295000	567,800	2.92
90 × 70cm	15,000	52.2	626,400	320	160,000	2,067	206,700	993,100	279000	714,100	3.56
100 × 50cm	20,000	57.7	692,400	400	200,000	3,000	300,000	1,192,400	279000	913,400	4.27
70 × 50cm	28,600	33.3	399,600	580	290,000	3,432	343,200	1,032,600	279000	753,600	3.70
65 × 50cm	30,800	28.8	345,600	620	310,000	6,160	616,000	1,271,600	271000	1,000,600	4.69
80 × 50cm	25,000	50.0	600,000	500	350,000	4,250	425,000	1,275,000	279000	996,000	4.56
50 × 50cm	40,000	26.6	319,200	800	400,000	10,000	1,000,000	1,719,200	271000	1,448,200	6.34

Note: The difference between the variable costs for different spacing is due to the differences in cost of weeding.

In addition, the second best yield of cassava tubers, presence of good stem, cuttings and good growth parameters in 100 × 100cm could be attributed to the low plant population which encouraged maximum exploitation of nutrients by the cassava crops for big tubers (tuber girth or diametre), good leaf area and stem girth values. This work differed from that of[21] who reported reduction in yield components of intercropped cassava-groundnut mixture at that spacing compared to the corresponding sole crop of cassava.

The increased plant population in 90 × 70cm spacing to 15,000 plants reduced the weeding rate from four in 100 x 100cm spacing to three. The implication is that farmers adopting this spacing for cassava would save ₦12,000 from weeding cost (25% reduction) and consequently, enhanced higher profit margin. This work differed from that of[22] who did not report weeding regimes in his experiment on cassava-maize intercrop.

The increased plant population of cassava in 90 × 70cm, 100 × 50cm, 65 × 50cm, 80 × 50cm and 50 × 50cm can spacing was responsible for higher leaf biomass, litter fall weight, stem cuttings and leaf population compared to the 100 x 100cm. The implication is that farmers adopting these spacing treatments would make additional income from export of leaf biomass hence, they had the highest BC ratio values and there would be a better crop/ livestock enterprise development because of the leaves serving as feeding materials. This observation differed from the previous research work of[23] who did not consider leaf and stem biomass parameters in his experiment on cassava based intercropping system. However, the presence of some etiolated stems of cassava in 65 × 50 cm, 50 × 50 cm spacing could be as a result of intra specific competition among the plants for nutrients, water and air.

The highest tuber weight, moderate tuber diametre, good stem cuttings and leaf biomass in 100 × 50cm compared to 100 × 100 cm, 80 × 50 cm, 65 × 50 cm could be due to its moderate plant population which reduced intra specific competition between them, thereby resulting into good tuber yields, leaf biomass and stem cutting yields and BC ratio of 4.27. This observation agreed with the work of who reported that 20,000 plants in maize/cassava intercrop gave significant tuber and grain yields of both crops compared to low yields in 30,000 plants/hectare, 40,000 plants per hectare and 50,000 plants per hectare respectively. However, his experiment did not consider leaf and stem biomasses components of the work.

Therefore, the low tuber weight and diametre of cassava in 65 × 50cm, 50 × 50 cm and 70 × 50 cm could be due to the intra specific competition between the plants as a result of high plant population. This observation agreed with that of who reported that production of small sized cassava roots was associated with increasing population of maize or cassava in the intercrop, between 30,000 and 50,000 plants, thus there will be decline in quantities of commercially acceptable roots.

However, the production of many small sized tubers from these spacing treatments will help to serve as suitable raw material for starch and tapioca industries. This is because of low lignin content. For-instance, the presence of 40,000 or more small sized tubers will go a long way in meeting raw materials needs of cassava processing industries.

In-addition, the 50 × 50 cm and 65 × 50 cm spacing had the highest leaf biomass, and litter fall which would serve as additional source of income for farmers. This is against the backdrop that farmers only derived maximum benefits from cassava tubers alone and neglected the income to be derived from stem cuttings and leaf biomass. For instance, many East African countries such as Democratic Republic of Congo, Tanzania, Kenya and Rwanda used cassava leaves for soup preparation and also to feed their livestock as observed by.[24]

Furthermore, the weeding regimes in these spacing treatments reduced from four to two signifying a remarkable reduction of ₦24,000 (50%) in weeding cost. This would definitely reduce the cost of production and increase profit margin analyses for the farmers. This observation agreed with the views of who reported that optimal and higher plant density of cassava/ maize mixture covered the ground, thereby, reducing weed density, growth and competition as well as covering the soil against soil erosion.

Also, the highest values of litter fall in 50 × 50cm and 65 × 50cm spacing signified the usefulness in checking the rate of erosion and fertility decline. The higher value for litter fall will preserve the soil physical and chemical attributes for continuous productivity of cassava crop by farmers. This differed from that of[25] who reported decrease in soil organic carbon dynamic and nutrients in cassava based intercropping systems at such higher plant population (30,000 and 40,000 plants per hectare).

The 50 × 50cm spacing had the highest value of BC ratio, gross income, net income gain and this could be due to its highest contributions from sales of stem cuttings and leaf biomass which are at present considered as insignificant by majority of farmers.[26] reported that the higher the BC values of an enterprise, the more profitable it is financially. This should be considered by stakeholders so that maximum financial benefits could be derived from cassava production.

Recommendation and Conclusion

From this experiment, the spacing treatments for cassava at 100 x 50cm (20,000 plants per hectare), 50 × 50cm (25,000 plants) and 90 × 70 cm (15,900 plants per hectare) compared favourably with the convictional spacing

100 × 100cm (10,000 plants per hectare) in term of tuber yield, weeding rate reduction, low cost of production, leaf biomass and litter fall while 65 × 50cm (30,500 plants per hectare) and 50 × 50cm (40,000 plants per hectare) had great potentials for stem and leaf biomass yield of cassava.

These recommendations are that farmers who are interested in commercial cassava tuber yields should adopt 100 × 50cm, 90 × 70cm and 80 × 80cm spacing while those who are interested in leaf and stem biomass yields should adopt 65 × 50cm and 50 × 50cm spacing treatments. This will ensure maximum income benefits from the sales of tubers, stem cuttings and leaf biomass by the farmers compared to the present experience of getting income from cassava tubers alone.

REFERENCES

1. O.N. Adeniyan (2008), Evaluation of NPK Fertilizer and Poultry Manure for Soil Fertility Enhancements and Cassava Production in Two Agro Ecologies of South West Nigeria. Nigeria Jour. of Soil Sci., Vol. 18, 48-53.
2. APAA (2007), Official Bulletin of Ondo State Accelerated Poverty and Agriculture, Agency Vol. (1) 6-7.
3. F. Nweke (1997), Cassava is a Cash Crop in Africa. IITA (International Institute for Tropical Agriculture), Research 14/15, 26-27.
4. B. Osundare (2008), Effect of Increasing Density in a Cassava/Maize (Zea Mays L.) Population Density in a Cassava/Maize Mixture on Major Soil Nutrients and Performance of Cassava (*Manihot esculenta* Crantz) in Southwestern Nigeria. Nigerian Journal of Soil Sci. (18) 60-67.
5. A.Y. Rye (2007), Improving the Productivity of Cassava/Maize Mixture Through the Determination of an Optimal Maize Planting Density. Crops Ecology, 5(2) 222-226.
6. Soil Survey Staff (1999), Soil Taxonomy. A Basic System for Soil Classification for Making and Interpreting Soil Surveys. USDA Handbook No. 436, Washington, D.C. USA.
7. L. Crockford, R. Nowell (1956), Laboratory Manual of Physical Chemistry. Exp 31 and 32, John Wiley and Sons, New York.
8. A. Walkley, I.A. Black (1934), An Examination of Degtajaroff Method for Determining Soil Organic Matter and a Proposed Modification of the Chromic Acid Filtration. Soil Sci. 37, 29-38.
9. AOAC (1970), Official Methods of Analysis 12th ed, Association of Official Analytical Chemists, Arlington, VA.
10. J. Murphy, J.P. Riley (1962), A Modified Single Solution Method for Determination of Phosphate in Natural Water. Analytical Chem. Acta. 27 31-36.
11. M.L. Jackson (1958), Soil Chemical Analysis Englewood Cliffs N.J. 1958. Prentice Hall 57-67.

12. E.O. Mclean (1965), Aluminum P. 927-932 MCA Black (Eds): Methods of Soil Analysis Part 2, Agronomy 9, Amer. Soc. Agron: Madison Wisconsin, U.S.A.

13. J.A. Ogunwale, E.J. Udo (1978), A Laboratory Manual for Soil and Plant Analysis. Agronomy Dept. University of Ibadan, Nigeria 201-206.

14. H. Bouycous (1951), Mechanical Analysis of Soils Using Hydrometer Method. Analytical Chem. Acta. 22 32-34.

15. K.A. Gomez, A.A. Gomez (1984), Statistical Procedures for Agricultural Research 2nd Edition. John Wiley and Sons, New York.

16. A.A. Agboola, and R.B. Corey (1973), Soil Testing N,P,K for Maize in the Soil Derived from Metamorphic and Igneous Rocks of Western State of Nigeria. Nigeria Jour. of West African Sci. Assoc. 17(2) 93-100.

17. R.A. Sobulo, O.A. Osiname (1981), Soils and Fertilizer Use in Western Nigeria. Tech. Bull. No. 11, Institute of Agricultural Research and Training, University of Ife, Nigeria, 8-9.

18. O.O. Folorunso, A.A. Agboola, G.O. Adeoye (1995), Use of Fractional Tecovery (FR) to Calculate the K Needs of Maize (Zea mays). Jour Tech. Educ. 2(1) 65-75.

19. M.A.K. Smith (2002), Seedling Emergence, Growth and Yield Response of Indian Spanish (Basella spp) to Depth of Planting Soil Type and Weed Competition: In Proceeding of the 22nd Annual Conference of Horticultural Society of Nigeria, Ibadan, Nigeria 6-10.

20. F.K. Salako, G. Tian, G. Kirchhof (2008), Soil Chemical Properties and Crop Yield on an Eroded Alfisol Managed with Herbaceous Legumes Under Yam-Maize Rotation. Nigerian Jour of Soil Sci. 18: 1-9.

21. O.P. Aiyelari, H. Tijani-Eniola (2009), Influence of Sowing Density of Groundnut on the Performance of Cassava and Groundnut in an Intercropping System. Applied Trop. Agric. 14 (1, 2) 9-15.

22. C.A. Ogungbe (2004), Investigation of the Traditional Mixed Cropping Systems in South-western Nigeria. Journal of Sustainable Agriculture, 2 (1) 77-81.

23. P.O. Olsa (2006), Evaluation of the Productivity of Cassava-based Intercropping Systems. Cropping Systems Research, 5 (3) 41-44.

24. F.K.N. Cam (2007), Studies on the Effects of Cassava Based Intercropping Systems on Soil Fertility in the Humid Tropics. Soil Fertility Research, 6(6) 801-807.

25. B.T. Kutz (2004), Influence of Cassava-based Intercropping System on Soil Organic Carbon Dynamics in the Tropical Agriculture. Tropical Farming Systems, 3 304-309.

26. J.A. Adegeye (2004), Small Scale Business, you can Start with Little or no Capital Investment. Josadeg Nigeria Limited, Ibadan, Nigeria ISBN 978-2397-059.

CHAPTER

2

Biodegradation of Chlorpyrifos

Sivagnanam Silambarasan, *India*
Jayanthi Abraham, *India*

ABSTRACT

The deleterious effect of pesticides on various strata of ecosystem is well documented for decades. In spite of the dangers caused by pesticides they are still in practice due to the demand for the crop yield every season and to meet the ever growing population. Pesticides undergo variety of transformations a complex pattern of metabolite once they are released in the environment. Biodegradation offers considerable promise as a strategy for detoxifying pesticide wastes. Microbial degradation is often the primary process that regulates the aerobic decay of a pesticide. Pesticides are broken down by microorganisms in the soil through a series of reactions, leading to the eventual production of carbon dioxide, water, and possibly some inorganic products. In the early stages of microbial degradation the parent compound is transformed into one or more new compounds that may have different chemical and physical properties. However, bioremediation of pesticide in agricultural fields require several groups of bacteria to completely mineralize one compound. Individual species isolated in pure culture and given the target compound as a sole carbon source may be found incapable of mineralizing it.

Generally, consortium of microorganisms are best suited for carrying out degradation of pesticide much faster and more efficiently when compared to pure culture. Several organisms may be involved in each step and compete for the pesticide or breakdown products during mineralization. The species suited to the particular environment will predominate. However, compared with the list of widely used pesticides there are few well characterized microbial strains that transform pesticides into less toxic or more labile products at environmentally useful rates. This article reviews recent studies that have focused on actual biodegradation of chlorpyrifos pesticide by using the microorganisms.

Key words: Chlorpyrifos; TCP; Biodegradation.

Introduction

Pesticides are substances or mixture of substances intended for preventing, destroying, repelling or mitigating any pest. In developing countries like India the economy depends on agricultural products and 15-20 per cent of the total harvest is destroyed by pests resulting in uncontrolled use of pesticides by the Indian farmers. Pesticides are considered as some of the most serious environmental pollutants, are frequently used in the control of agricultural and domestic pests. Although they are economically important, pesticides can be harmful to the health of humans and animals, and they can have a detrimental environmental impact. Application of pesticides for improving crop productivity has become necessary in the present day agricultural practices, resulting in entry of these chemicals into soil and water ecosystems. Many of the chemicals used in pesticides are persistent as soil contaminants. The use of pesticides decreases the general biodiversity and quality of the soil.

Nitrogen fixation, which is required for the growth of higher plants, is hindered by pesticides in soil. Pesticides have some direct harmful effect on plant including poor root hair development, shoot yellowing and reduced plant growth. Humans are exposed to pesticides (found in environmental media such as soil, water, air and food) by different routes. Exposure to pesticides results in acute and chronic health problems. Increasing incidence of cancer, chronic kidney diseases, suppression of the immune system, sterility among males and females, endocrine disorders, neurological and behavioural disorders, especially among children, have been attributed to chronic pesticide poisoning. Pesticide pollution to the local environment also affects the lives of birds, wildlife, domestic animals, fish and livestock. In addition to this, discharges from the pesticide manufacturing plants, accidental spills, and natural processes such as dilution, surface run off and leaching are the causes of the occurrence of xenobiotic compounds in surface waters. The presence of these xenobiotics results in greater loss of crop productivity and affects the growth of many beneficial microorganisms (Shetty et al., 2000; Readman et al., 1997; Dua et al., 2002).

Pesticide Mode of Action

Mode of action refers to the mechanism by which the pesticide kills or interacts with the target organism falls broadly into two categories as contact and systematic. Contact pesticides are those whcih kill the target organism by weakening or disrupting the cellular membranes; death can be very rapid. Systemic pesticides must be absorbed or ingested by the target organism to disrupt its physiological or metabolic processes; generally they are slow acting.

How effective the pesticides are at killing the target organisms (efficacy) depends on the properties of the pesticide, soil, formulation, application technique, agricultural management, characteristics of the crop, environmental or weather conditions, nature and behaviour of the target organism.

Fate of Pesticides in the Environment

Ideally, a pesticide stays in the treated area long enough to produce the desired effect and then degrades into harmless materials. Three primary modes of degradation occur in soils:

- *Photochemical* - breakdown by ultraviolet or visible light
- *Chemical* - breakdown by chemical reactions, such as hydrolysis and redox reactions
- *Biological* - breakdown by microorganisms

The rate at which a chemical degrades is expressed as the half-life. The half-life is the amount of time taken for half of the pesticide to be converted into some other compound, or its concentration is half of its initial level. The half-life of a pesticide depends on soil type, its formulation, and environmental conditions (e.g., temperature, moisture). Other processes that influence the fate of the chemicals include plant uptake, soil sorption, leaching, and volatilization. If pesticides move off-site (e.g., wind drift, runoff, leaching), they are considered to be pollutants. The potential for pesticides to move off-site depends on the chemical properties and formulation of the pesticide, soil properties, rate and method of application, pesticide persistence, frequency and timing of rainfall or irrigation, and depth to reach the ground water.

Pesticide Dissipation

The behaviour of a pesticide results from the interactions between the chemical and various components of the environment. Pesticides can undergo various routes of dissipation once applied in the environment. Major routes of pesticide dissipation include adsorption, transfer (i.e. volatilization, runoff, leaching, and absorption) and degradation i.e. photodegradation, chemical degradation, and microbial degradation (Fig. 2.1). Adsorption occurs when the pesticide binds to soil particles. Soil sorption is the affinity a chemical has to adhere to soils. The extent to which a pesticide is adsorbed to soil depends on soil type, soil texture, soil pH, soil moisture and the pesticide itself (Dyson et al. 2002)

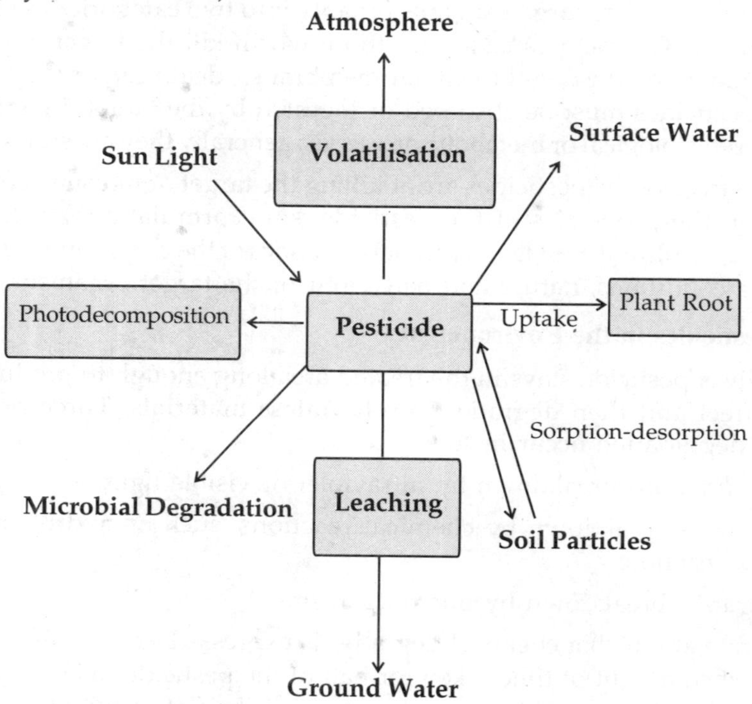

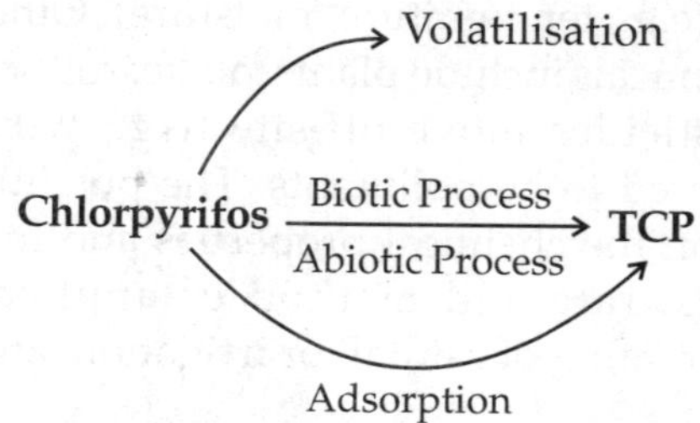

- Biotic transformation – microbial: major route in soils
- Abiotic transformation – e.g., hydrolysis, photolysis: major route in water

Pesticide Dissipation

Pesticide Volatilization

Pesticide volatilization occurs when the solid or liquid form of pesticide is transformed into a gas. The volatilization of pesticide can be influenced by soil moisture content and may be facilitated by a proposed wicking or capillary effect, through which more compounds that are soluble are brought to the soil surface more quickly and compounds that are more volatile disappear from the surface more rapidly. Volatilization can reduce effectiveness of a pesticide by reducing the amount of chemical that makes contact with the intended target. When there is an increase in temperature and air movement, the potential for pesticide loss through volatilization also increases (Yates et al. 2002; Haith et al. 2002). Volatilization rates, which result from the complex interplay between chlorpyrifos sorbed to soil, dissolved in the soil pore water, and present in the soil air spaces, can be quite variable. Pesticide loss in the air can also occur because of spray drift. Drift consists of droplets produced by nozzles of the spray equipment being suspended in air and carried away by air flows before reaching any surface. When applied as a foliar spray, chlorpyrifos volatilized from corn leaves rapidly. In the laboratory, 80 per cent volatilized within 48 hours at 30 °C with a simulated wind speed of 0.8 km/hour (McCall et al. 1985). A field study confirmed the fairly rapid rate of volatilization, with an observed half-life of about 1.5 days on corn and soybean foliage (McCall et al. 1984).

Pesticide Runoff

Pesticide runoff occurs when pesticides are carried away by surface water movement. Typically, if water addition to a field is faster than it can be absorbed into the soil, runoff occurs. Pesticide molecules can move either when dissolved in the water, or through attachment with soil particles or sediments (Bailey et al. 1974). Factors that influence pesticide runoff include the physic-chemical properties of the pesticide, application method, soil property, hillside slope, timing, duration, intensity, climate, and agricultural practices (Chaplot et al. 2003). Losses from runoff can be greatest when it rains heavily soon after a pesticide application. Leaching and runoff from treated fields, pesticide disposal pits, or hazardous waste sites may inadvertently contaminate both groundwater and surface water with chlorpyrifos. Entry into water can also occur from accidental spills, redeposition of atmospheric chlorpyrifos, and discharge of waste water from chlorpyrifos manufacturing, formulation, and packaging facilities.

Pesticide Leaching

Leaching is the downward movement of chemicals in water through the soil. Pesticides that are easily leached have a high potential to reach groundwater. The characteristics of the soil and pesticide play an important role in influencing pesticide leaching. Sandy soils are more prone to leaching than clay textured soils because macropore flow in sandy soil is more extensive than in clay textured soil. When macropore flower is less extensive, adsorption is stronger and leaching potential is lower (Roulier and Jarvis, 2003). Leaching studies have shown chlorpyrifos to have little mobility in soil. Field studies have confirmed this lack of mobility, with chlorpyrifos residues being confined to the upper 12 inches of soils in several trials (Oliver et al. 1987). The leaching and dissipation of the applied ^{14}C-chlorpyrifos in sandy soil under simulated field precipitation, drainage and temperature was less than 0.2 per cent (Fermanich and Daniel 1991). Amounts of chlorpyrifos lethal to termites moved to a depth of at least 30 cm in decomposed granite soil from the Santa Ana River bed in Colton, California, after it was applied at 500 ppm to the top 7.62 cm of soil in a long column of 34 mm diameter and $\approx$130 mL of water was dripped through (Smith and Rust, 1992).

Pesticide Toxicity

The toxicity level of a pesticide depends on the deadliness of the chemical, the dose, the length of exposure, and the route of entry or absorption by the body. Pesticide degradation in soil generally results in a reduction in toxicity; however, some pesticides are degraded (metabolites) into more toxic form than the parent compound. Pesticides are classified according to their potential toxicity to humans and other animals and organisms, as restricted-use (can only be purchased and applied by certified persons who have training in pesticide application), and general use (may be purchased and applied by any person).

Pesticide - Chlorpyrifos

Chlorpyrifos (O,O-diethyl O- (3, 5, 6-trichloro-2-pyridyl) phosphorothioate) (Fig. 2.2) is one of the most widely used organophosphorus insecticides effective against a broad spectrum of insect pests of economically important crops. The characteristic of chlorpyrifos is given in Table 2.1. It is also used for the control of mosquitoes (larvae and adults), flies, termites and various soil and household pests. The half-life of chlorpyrifos in soil is usually between 60 and 120 days, but can range from two weeks to over one year, depending on the soil type, climate, and other conditions (Howard, 1991). The important physical and chemical characteristics which influence the fate and transport of chlorpyrifos in the environment are its low solubility, volatility, and strong affinity for colloidal matter. Abiotic hydrolysis, photodegradation, and biodegradation are all important processes for the transformation and degradation of chlorpyrifos. Chlorpyrifos bioconcentrates to only a limited extent, and has little mobility in most soils. It exists in the atmosphere primarily in the vapor phase, but can partition to particulates. It is not persistent in water, due to volatilization and strong adsorption to particulate matter.

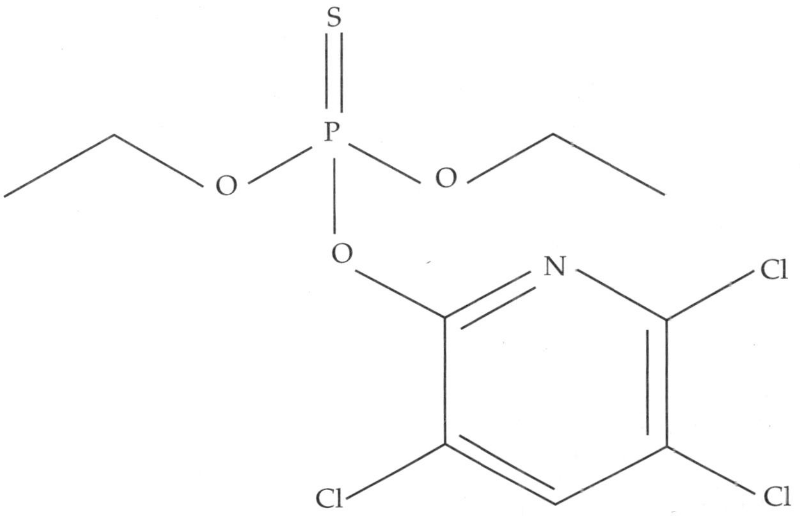

O, O-Diethyl O-3,5,6-trichloropyridin-2-yl phosphorothioate

Fig. 2.2: Chemical Structure of Chlorpyrifos

Table 2.1: Major Characteristics of Chlorpyrifos

Common Name	Chlorpyrifos
IUPAC name	O,O-diethylO- (3,5,6-trichloro-2-pyridyl) phosphorothioate
Molecular Formula	$C_9H_{11}Cl_3NO_3PS$
Molecular weight	350.59 g/mol
Appearance	Colourless crystals
Odour	Mild mercaptan
Melting point	42°C
Solubility in water	0.7 mg/L (20°C)
	2 mg/L (25°C)
Solubility in organic solvents	79% w/w in isooctane
	43 per cent w/w in methanol
Vapour pressure at 20°C	1.87×10^{-5} mmHg
Density	1.398 g/cm3 (43.5°C)

Effect of Chlorpyrifos on Food

Food testing carried out by the U.S. Food and Drug Administration (FDA) found that chlorpyrifos was the fifth most commonly detected pesticide and was found in ten per cent of the samples tested. Between 1990 and 1992, FDA found chlorpyrifos on tomatoes, oranges, peaches, cherries, bananas, and apples. Other food items on which chlorpyrifos residues have been found include broccoli, grapes, orange juice (Hankin and Pylypiw, 1991), tea (Nagayama et al. 1989), and several types of processed oriental foods including noodle soup (Gans et al. 1994). A recent analysis of FDA's tests of commonly eaten produce items for pesticide residues during 1992 and 1993 found illegal chlorpyrifos residues on 16 of the 42 foods. Only one other insecticide, the organophosphate insecticide methamidophos, had illegal residues on more types of food than did chlorpyrifos. Plants when treated with chlorpyrifos by pouring it onto soil around the stem of the plant for protection against the root fly and its soil metabolites were transported from soil into the plant foliage, where it could give a secondary plant protection against the foliage insects.

Effect of Chlorpyrifos on Water and Air

Other exposure to chlorpyrifos comes from drinking contaminated water or breathing contaminated air. Because of its widespread use, chlorpyrifos has been found widely in air and water. In water chlorpyrifos has a tendency to adsorb readily to soil particles, and it is not mobile in soil (Somasundaram et al. 1991); in fact, some researchers have classified it as "immobile" (Racke, 1993). Therefore, it is considered to have a low potential for contaminating ground and surface water. Chlorpyrifos contamination of air close to agricultural applications has been measured. For example, one study found that up to one-half of the chlorpyrifos applied to a Maryland cornfield was volatilized (vaporized) and detected in air samples taken about three feet above the field during a 26 day period (Whang et al. 1993). Volatilization from foliage is even more rapid: almost 80 per cent of chlorpyrifos volatilized from corn foliage in a two day period (Racke, 1993).

Effects of Chlorpyrifos on Soil Quality

The capacity of the soil to filter, buffer, degrade, immobilize, and detoxify pesticides depends on the quality of the soil. The presence and bio-availability of pesticides in soil can adversely impact human and animal health, and beneficial plants and soil organisms. Pesticides can move off-site contaminating surface and groundwater and possibly causing adverse impacts on aquatic ecosystems.

The effects of chlorpyrifos on soil microbial characteristics (including microbial biomass carbon and nitrogen, microbial populations, microbial respiration, enzymatic activities, and nitrogen cycling) have also been frequently studied (Singh et al. 2002; Menon et al. 2004; Adesodun et al. 2005; Menon et al. 2005; Shan et al. 2006). It had been reported that soil microbial biomass was reduced by 25 per cent and 50 per cent after chlorpyrifos treatment at concentrations of 10 and 50 mg/kg, respectively, in an Italian biobed (Vischetti et al. 2007). Menon et al. (2004) reported that nitrogen mineralization in the loamy sand and sandy loam was significantly inhibited after chlorpyrifos application. Shan et al. (2006) also indicated that soil bacterial, fungal, and actinomycete populations were inhibited by chlorpyrifos at a concentration of 10 mg/kg.

Effect Chlorpyrifos on Children

Children are also exposed to chlorpyrifos-contaminated house dust. Because of their low body weight and high dust intake, children appear to be at higher risk than adults from this kind of exposure (Roberts and Camann, 1989). Children are also more exposed to chlorpyrifos in food than are adults because children consume (for their size) more of the fruits and vegetables that contain chlorpyrifos residues. EPA estimates that infants consume about 2.5 times as much chlorpyrifos (again, for their size) as do adults. Children under 6 years of age consume about 2 times as much.

Effects Chlorpyrifos on Beneficial Insects

Chlorpyrifos adversely affects more non target organisms than the pests it is designed to kill. Effects on non-target organisms include both acute and chronic hazards. A common ecological problem with broad spectrum insecticides is that they kill beneficial insects: predators, parasites, and parasitoids of the targeted insect pests. This often results in an increase in the abundance of and damage caused by the pest. Chlorpyrifos is no exception; a review of toxicity to beneficial organisms done by the International Organisation for Biological Control showed that, of 23 beneficial species tested, chlorpyrifos caused over 80 per cent mortality to 17. Mortality of only 4 species was less than 50 per cent. Table 2.3 (*See Table on page 33)* gives examples of beneficial insects affected by chlorpyrifos.

Effect Chlorpyrifos on Fishes

Chlorpyrifos is "very highly toxic to freshwater fish and estuarine and marine organisms". Application rates as low as 0.01 pounds per acre can cause death among fishs. Typically, exposures of about 3 parts per million (ppm) are lethal to fish. Some fish are killed by very much lower concentrations of chlorpyrifos. For example, the median lethal dose for grunion and silversides varies between 0.4 and 6.7 parts per billion (ppb) (Borthwick et al. 1985).

Chlorpyrifos at low concentrations was observed to inhibit acetylcholinesterase (AChE) activity. (Acetyl cholinesterase is an enzyme in the nervous system which is inhibited by all organophosphate insecticides.) For example, AChE inhibition in fathead minnows was measured at a concentration of less than 1 ppb, about 1/10 of the concentration that caused mortality of the fish (Jarvinen et al. 1983). In guppies, concentrations of 1 ppb significantly inhibited AChe activity, which then did not return to normal after two weeks of secluding the test fish in uncontaminated water (Van der Wel and Welling, 1989). In mummichogs, 1 ppb of chlorpyrifos also inhibited AChE, and inhibition was measured for 69 days following application of chlorpyrifos granules (Thirugnanam and Forgash, 1977). Growth of fish is also reduced by low concentrations of chlorpyrifos. For example, less than 2 ppb of chlorpyrifos is sufficient to reduce the weight of grunion fry (Goodman, 1985) and less than 1 ppb reduced length and weight in fathead minnows. The effects on at head minnows were associated with decreases in the abundance of their typical prey, so that the growth reduction was probably due to changes in diet (Brazner and Kline, 1990). Abnormal growth (spinal deformities) occurred at concentrations of 5 ppb in juvenile rainbow trout and at 3 ppb in fathead minnows (Holcombe et al. 1982). Exposure periods of 5 hours were sufficient to cause these deformities (Jarvinen et al. 1988). In tests lasting more for more than one generation, effects of chlorpyrifos on growth occur at even lower doses; in fathead minnows, the growth of the second generation was reduced at concentrations of 0.1 ppb (Jarvinen et al. 1983).

Low concentrations of chlorpyrifos also caused a variety of other adverse effects. For example, in fathead minnows, doses of 0.1 ppb caused a reduction in the number of sexually mature fish (Jarvinen et al. 1983). In catfish, concentrations of 2 ppb caused kidney damage (Srivastava et al. 1990).

Effect Chlorpyrifos on Other Aquatic Organisms

Chlorpyrifos is acutely toxic to a wide variety of aquatic organisms from freshwater, estuarine, and marine habitats. Examples include freshwater algae (Brown and Chow, 1975; Brown et al. 1976); rotifers (Snell, 1991; Ferrando and Andreu-Moliner, 1991); water fleas (Brock et al. 1992); copepod (Johnson, 1978); isopod, amphipod (Brock et al. 1992) and ostracod (Ali and Mulla, 1978); crustaceans; tadpole shrimp (Walton et al. 1990); freshwater crabs (Radhakrishnaiah and Renukadevi, 1990); stoneflies (Day and Scott, 1990); mayflies; damselflies; caddisflies (Siegfried, 1993); larval reef coral (Acevedo, 1991); grass shrimp (Key and Fulton, 1993); and marine diatoms (Walsh, 1983).

Effect of Chlorpyrifos on Humans and Rodents

In humans it causes skin irritation, convulsion, twitching and rapid contraction of muscles, depression, subtle neurological effects, respiratory failures, and death (Sogorb et al., 2004). The acute toxic effects of chlorpyrifos exposure are primarily due to the inhibition of acetyl cholinesterase resulting in excessive accumulation of acetylcholine both in synapses and neuromuscular junctions leading to overstimulation and paralysis of various receptors and ultimately to the failure of the central nervous system (Bicker et al., 2005). The major hydrolysis product of chlorpyrifos, 3,5,6-trichloro-2-pyridinol (TCP) has greater water solubility than chlorpyrifos and it also causes the widespread contamination in soils and in the aquatic environment.

The mechanisms underlying the higher susceptibility of young and developing rodents to CPF have not been fully clarified yet (Testai et al., 2010). Although interactions with targets with different susceptibility in developing organs have been studied, the age-related sensitivity to CPF effects has been partially attributed to toxicokinetic and biotransformation differences, leading to different levels of formation of chlorpyrifos-oxon (CPFO), the actual inhibitor of acetylcholinesterase (AChE), and/or to its detoxicationmetabolites. The desulfuration reaction to CPFO is mediated by cytochrome P450, which can catalyse also CPF dearylation to the inactive 3, 5, 6-trichloro-2-pyridinol (PYRI). Additional detoxifying pathway involving A and B esterases take place in the liver and in plasma (Karanth and Pope, 2000); moreover, CPF and CPFO undergo a very extensive phase II mediated metabolic detoxification leading to GSH-derived conjugates as well as O- and S-glucuronides in human hepatocytes (Choi et al., 2006).

Metabolites of Chlorpyrifos

The major hydrolysis product of chlorpyrifos, 3, 5, 6-trichloro-2-pyridinol (TCP) has greater water solubility than chlorpyrifos and causes the widespread contamination in soils and in the aquatic environment. TCP is not only persistent towards degradation by microorganisms but also limits the biodegradation of chlorpyrifos owing to its antimicrobial activities (Anwar et al. 2009). Chlorpyrifos degrades (breaks down) into a variety of compounds. A primary metabolite in water, air, soil, plants, and animals is 3, 5, 6-trichloro-2-pyridinol. TCP is more readily taken up by plants than is chlorpyrifos (Racke, 1993); it is also more mobile in soil (Somasundaram et al. 1991). TCP is 2 to 3 times more toxic to developing chick embryos than chlorpyrifos (Muscarella et al. 1984). One product, implicated in the death of 50 dairy bulls treated for lice, contained TCP at concentrations about 100 times over typical levels. Chlorpyrifos containing products also contain the impurity sulfotep, an acutely toxic organophosphate insecticide. The concentrations of sulfotep were 3 times higher than typical levels in the product involved in the bull deaths. However, the researchers stated that the TCP was the chemical that was significant from a toxicological standpoint (Allender et al. 1991). Metabolites I, III, IIIa and IIIb, shown in Fig. 2.3, as well as chlorpyrifos were found in fish, and metabolites I, IIIa and IIIb were found in the water (Smith et al., 1966). The major metabolic product in fish is 3, 5, 6-trichloro-2-pyridinol which appears to be slowly broken down by dehalogenation and cleavage of the ring (Smith et al., 1966). Some of the derivatives of 3, 5, 6-trichloro-2-pyridinol which consist of dechlorination forming a series of transient pyridine diols, triols and tetrols (Ia), followed by a series of transient ring diketones (Ib), followed by a breakage of the ring to elemental fragments (carbon dioxide and possibly aliphatic amines).

Degradation of Chlorpyrifos

Pesticide degradation is a process involving three phases. In phase I the process of degradation involves oxidation, reduction, or hydrolysis, which changes the parent compound more water soluble and less toxic degradation product. Oxygenation is the most frequent initial step in the biotransformation of pesticides. Many of these reactions are mediated by oxidative enzymes, e.g., cytochrome P450s, peroxidases and polyphenol oxidases. The second phase involves conjugation of a pesticide or pesticide metabolites to a sugar, amino acid or glutathione, which increases the water solubility and reduces the toxicity compared to parent compound. Generally, metabolites obtained from phase II have little or no toxicity, and may be stored in cellular organelles. Glutathione S-transferase is the enzyme that plays a major role in phase II. It is a homo or heterodimer multifunctional enzyme located in the cytosol, which catalyzes the nucleophilic attack of the sulfur atom of GSH by the electrophilic centre of the substrate. Finally, the third phase involves conversion of phase II metabolites into secondary conjugates, which are also nontoxic (Palanisami et al., 2009).

Initially, degradation of pesticide was observed in alkaline soils and phenomenon was related to its hydrolysis at high pH. However when the high pH soils was rendered, complete inhibition of chlorpyrifos hydrolysis was observed which indicated the involvement of soil microorganisms (Racke et al., 1996). Later, same results were confirmed by Singh et al. (2003). A summary of the available published work on biodegradation of chlorpyrifos and TCP is given in Table 2.2.

Currently there are a number of possible mechanisms for the clean-up of pesticides in soil, such as chemical treatment, volatilization and incineration. Although, chemical treatment and volatilization, are feasible they are problematic as large volumes of acids and alkalis are produced and subsequently must be disposed. Incineration, is a very reliable physical-chemical method for destruction of these compounds, has met serious public opposition, because of its potentially toxic emissions, and its elevated economic costs (Zhang and Quiao, 2002). Overall most of these physical-

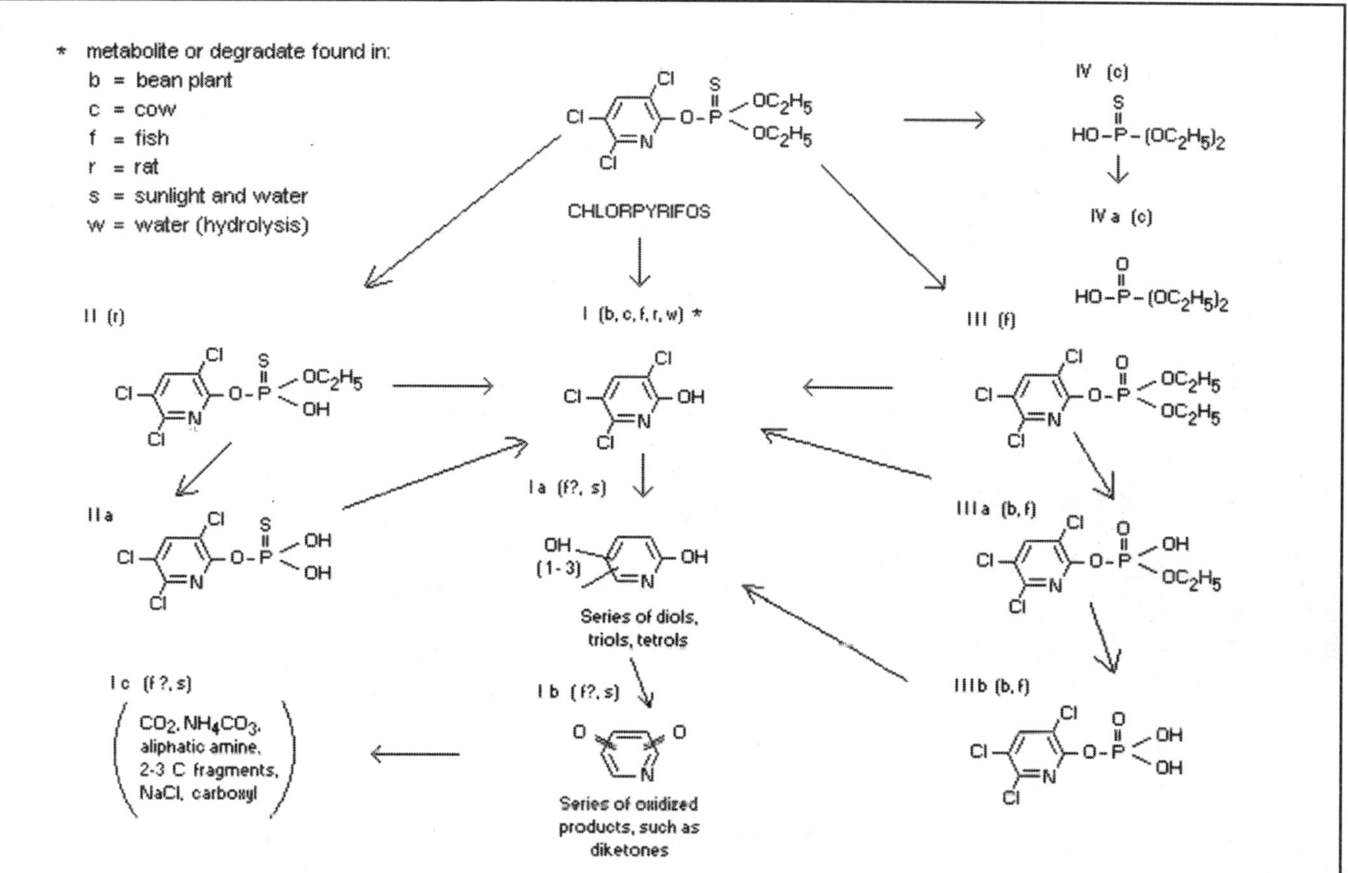

Fig. 2.3: Metabolic Pathway of Chlorpyrifos (Smith et. al., 1966)

chemical cleaning technologies are expensive and rather inefficient because the contaminated soil has to be excavated from the site and moved to a storage area where it can be processed. Due to environmental concerns associated with the accumulation of pesticides in food products and water supplies, there is a great need to develop safe, convenient and economically feasible methods for pesticide remediation (Zhang and Quiao, 2002). For this reason several biological techniques involving biodegradation of organic compounds by microorganisms have been developed (Schoefs *et al.*, 2004). The use of bioremediation to remove pollutants is typically less expensive than the equivalent physical-chemical methods. The complexity of microbial mechanisms for degradation of organopollutants as well as the time period requiring weeks to months, before microbial degradation starts, has made the technology slow to emerge as a viable method of remediation (Nerud *et al.*, 2003). It becomes apparent that more detailed studies on the principles of biodegradation, and the development of efficient methods of decontamination are needed to solve the hazardous waste problem (Nerud *et al.*, 2003).

Biodegradation by Microbes

Pesticide biodegradation involves a wide variety of microorganisms including bacteria and fungi operating under dynamic anaerobic and aerobic conditions. It is suggested that biodegradation of pesticides in soil ecosystems can only take place through the synergistic interactions of a microbial consortium, the activity of which is affected by many soil physical and chemical properties, as well as the nature and extent of the pesticide contamination. A consortium can consist of two or more organisms living in close proximity to other ecosystems which are interacting with each other. A consortium generally implies a positive interation where one group benefits from the actions of the other. Many pesticides have proven resistant to microbial biodegradation and therefore persist in the environments in which they are found. To enhance biodegradation of pesticides in agricultural soils several groups of bacteria may be necessary to completely mineralize one compound. Individual species isolated in pure culture and exposed to the target compound as a sole carbon source may be found to be incapable of mineralizing it. Generally, a consortium of micro organisms are capable of carrying out degradation faster and more efficiently compared to pure culture. Several organisms may be involved in each step and compete for the target compound or breakdown products during mineralization. Khanna and Vidyalakshmi (2004) developed five microbial consortia from chlorpyrifos contaminated sites by selective enrichment. Q1 and Q2 were the promising consortia with degradation efficiency of 72 and 70 per cent respectively. Fifty five isolates were isolated from these consortia by dilution plating and 15 isolates showed degradation between 37 and 76 per cent.

Table 2.2: Summary of the Available Published Work on Biodegradation of Chlorpyrifos and TCP by Soil Microorganisms

Sl. No.	Sample	Microbes	Degradation	References
(1)	(2)	(3)	(4)	(5)
1.	TCP contaminated sludge	*Cupriavidus pauculus* P2	Degradation rate of 10 mg/L h inmineral salt medium amended with TCP (50–800 mg/L).	Cao et al.
2.	Pesticide contaminated cotton field soil	*Bacillus pumilus* C2A1	89% in 15 days (1000 mg/L) of CP and 90% in days (300 mg/l) of TCP	Anwar et al. 2009
3.	Activated sludge sample from pesticide manufacturers	*Paracoccus* sp. TRP	100% in 4 days (50 mg/L) of CP and TCP	Xu et al., 2008
4.	Chlorpyrifos contaminated soil sample	*Pseudomonas aeruginosa*	75–87% in 20 days (50 mg/L) of CP and 67% in 12 h of TCP (2.5 mg/L)	Vidya Lakshmi et al. 2008
5.	Soil sample of chlorpyrifos contaminated paddy field	*Pseudomonas aeruginosa*	84%, in 20 days (50 mg/L) of CP and 100% in 30 days (2.5 mg/L) of TCP	Vidya Lakshmi et al. 2009
6.	Water sample from industrial plant manufacturing chlorpyrifos	Dsp-2 *Sphingomonas* Dsp-4 *Stenotrophomonas* Dsp-6 *Bacillus* sp. Dsp-7 *Brevundimonas*, Dsp1,3,5 *Pseudomonas* sp	Rate (37–100 mg/L/d), 100% in 48 h (100 mg/L) of CP; Dsp 1–4 degrade <30mg/L of TCP	Li et al. 2008
7.	Contaminated agricultural soil	*Enterobacter* strain B-14	100% in 2 days (250 mg/L) of CP	Singh et al. 2004
8.	Contaminated soil around a chemical factory	*Alcaligenes faecalis*	100% in 10 days (100mg/L) of CP and TCP	Yang et al. 2005
9.	Sludge of waste water treatment system of pesticide manufacturer	*Stenotrophomonas* sp.	100% in 24 h (100 mg/L) of CP	Yang et al. 2006
10.	Activated sludge sample of waste water treatment plant	*Klebsiella* sp.	92% CP in 4 days	Ghanem et al. 2007

(Contd...)

(1)	(2)	(3)	(4)	(5)
11.	Activated sludge from the treatment plant of a pesticide unit	*Serratia* and *Trichosporon* sp	100% in 18 h (50 mg/L) of CP byco-culture, 100% within 5 days (50 mg/L) by Trichosporon	Xu et al. 2007
12.	Polluted water samples of chlorpyrifos manufacturing industry	*Sphingomonas* sp. Dsp-2	100% in 24 h (100 mg/L) of CP and 100% within 2 days (20 mg/L) of TCP	Li et al. 2007
13.	Contaminated agricultural soil	*Pseudomonas* sp.	84% in 120 h (0.01 g/L) of CP	Singh et al. 2009
14.	Soil sample	*Verticillium* sp. DSP strain	98.6% in 7 days of (100mg/L) CP	Fang et al. 2008
15.	Algal strains from Indian Agricutural Research Institute, Delhi, India	*Spirulina platensis* ARM 728	Cultured in 80 ppm CP, Alkaline phosphatase degrade 78% of the 100 ppm CP in 1h	Thengodkar and Sivakami, 2010
16.	Axenic culture of *Chlorella vulgaris* taken from IARI, Delhi	*Chlorella vulgaris* grown into BG11 broth medium	68.23% CP was dissipated in 20 days	Mukherjee et al. 2004

Factors that Affect Microbial Activity

Pesticide biodegradation is inanimately tied to the activity of specific microorganisms. Soil temperature and moisture are important factors that influence the activity of soil microorganisms. Numerous studies have examined the effects of soil temperature and moisture on the biodegradation of agrochemicals in soils.

Generally, faster pesticide degradation rates occur with increasing soil temperature up to a temperature that corresponds to the maximal activity of the microorganisms that use the pesticide as a substrate. Once temperature goes beyond an optimum level, degradation rates decline. Soil moisture content plays an important role in influencing microbial degradation of pesticides. At low water content, inhibition of microbial growth is caused by inadequate water activity. At high moisture content, diffusion of air into the soil is reduced and microbial activity may become oxygen limited.

Table 2.3: Examples of Beneficial Insects Harmed by Chlorpyrifos

Beneficial species	Pest Species	Crop	Reference
Parasitoids and Parasites			
Encarsia perniciosi	San Jose scale	Apple,	Masoodi et al. 1988
Teleonemus remus	Spodoptera litura	Tobacco, cabbage, cotton	Mani and Krishnamoorthy, 1986
Aphytis melinus	California red scale	Citrus	Rosenheim and Hoy, 1988
Eucelatoria bryani	Heliothis armigera	Tomato, bean	Mani and Nagarkatti, 1988
Aphelinus perpallidus	Pecan aphid	Pecan	Mizell and Schiffhauer, 1990
Predators			
Spider	Bollworm	Peanut	Funderburk et al. 1990
Spider	Many	Turf	Cockfield and Potter, 1983
Spider	Many	Grapefrui	Mansour, 1987
Carabid beetle	Black cutworm	Corn	Reed et al. 1992
Carabid beetle	Wheat midge	Wheat	Floate et al. 1989
Ant	Fall armyworm, corn leafhopper	Corn	Perfecto, 1990
Chrysoperla rufilabris	Pecan aphid	Pecan	Mizell and Schiffhauer, 1990
Hippodamia convergens	Pecan aphid	Pecan	Mizell and Schiffhauer, 1990
Cycloneda sanguinea	Pecan aphid	Pecan	Mizell and Schiffhauer, 1990
Ollav-nigrum	Pecan aphid	Pecan	Mizell and Schiffhauer, 1990

Soil organic carbon is an important soil constituent that frequently attenuates microbial degradation. Pesticide degradation rates have been found to be positively correlated to soil organic carbon as well as to microbial plate counts.

Bioavailability of Pesticides

While many factors influence pesticide degradation in soil or other porous media, sorption is recognized as a key process regulating pesticide degradation. Adsorption of a chemical by soil reduces its availability to microbial uptake and thus reduces its degradation by microorganisms (Ainsworth et al. 1993). Adsorption and degradation are not fixed properties of a pesticide (Dyson et al. 2002). The effect of sorption on degradation depends on many factors, including soil physical and microbial characteristics and the properties of the chemical being evaluated (Beulke et al. 2005). Soil organic matter is considered to be the single most important soil constituent influencing pesticide sorption in soils (Wauchope et al. 2002; Farenhorst, 2006). In soils, pesticides are initially and predominately sorbed to organic matter that coats soil particles (Park et al. 2003). Generally, the lower the water solubility of a chemical and the higher the amount of organic carbon in the soil, the greater the sorption of a hydrophobic compound (Alexander, 1999).

While sorption generally slows pesticide biodegradation, there are certain occasions where sorption may actually accelerate pesticide biodegradation. One frequently cited example is the increased residence time of pesticides in the root zone where microbial activity is very high at or near the particle surfaces as compared to the underlying stratum (Hance, 1988). Reduced concentrations of oxygen and nutrients can occur inside soil particles due to competition from microorganisms at the surface (Beulke et al. 2005). Thus sorption may provide an opportunity for extended exposure to degrading microorganisms.

Biodegradation of Chlorpyrifos Using Bacteria

A bacterial strain C2A1 isolated from soil was found highly effective in degrading chlorpyrifos and its first hydrolysis metabolite 3,5,6-trichloro-2-pyridinol (TCP). On the basis of morphology, physiological characteristics, biochemical tests and 16S rRNA sequence analysis, strain C2A1 was identified as *Bacillus pumilus*. Role of strain C2A1 in the degradation of chlorpyrifos was examined under different culture conditions like pH, inoculum density, presence of added carbon/nutrient sources and pesticide concentration. Chlorpyrifos was utilized by strain C2A1 as the sole source of carbon and energy as well as it was co-metabolized in the presence of glucose, yeast extract and nutrient broth. Maximum pesticide degradation was observed at high pH (8.5) and high inoculum density when chlorpyrifos was used as the sole source and energy. In the presence of other nutrients, chlorpyrifos degradation was enhanced probably due to high growth on easily metabolizable compounds which in turn increased degradation. The strain C2A1 showed 90 per cent degradation of TCP (300mg L^{-1}) within 8 days of incubation (Anwar et al. 2009). Singh *et al.* (2003) made an attempt to isolate chlorpyrifos degrading bacteria from the soil following successive treatments with chlorpyrifos and several rounds of enrichment in mineral salts medium supplemented with chlorpyrifos as the only source of carbon. The insecticide was rapidly degraded and mineralized to $^{14}CO_2$ by a robust bacterial population that utilized chlorpyrifos as a source of carbon only in soils with a pH 3-6.7.

A bacterium, isolated from activated sludge and named strain TRP, could biodegrade chlorpyrifos and 3,5,6-trichloro-2-pyridinol. Phenotypic features, physiological and chemotaxonomic characteristics, and phylogenetic analysis of 16S rRNA sequence revealed that the isolate belongs to the genus of *Paracoccus*. Strain TRP could also degrade pyridine, methyl parathion and carbonfuran when provided as sole carbon and energy sources. Native-PAGE and enzymatic degradation assay of the cell-free extracts indicated that an alternative degradation mechanism might involve an inducible enzyme. Degradation study of chlorpyrifos by strain TRP was examined by GC–MS and HPLC; no persistent accumulated metabolite was observed (Xu et al. 2008).

Efficacy of soil bacterial communities comprising seven different isolates for biodegradation of chlorpyrifos and TCP (3,5,6-trichloro-2-pyridinol), a degradation product of chlorpyrifos, has been investigated. The concentration of chlorpyrifos has ranged from 25 to 200 mg chlorpyrifos/L, and that of TCP from 25 to 100 mg TCP/L. The average values of Ks and Vmax are found to be different for isolates 1-4, 5-6 and 7 for both chlorpyrifos and TCP. The Ks has ranged from 97 to 142.3 mg/L and Vmax from 7.4 to 12.1 mg/L/d for chlorpyrifos and 103.09 to 148.8 mg/L and 14.9 to 21.2 mg/L/d, respectively, for TCP. Results indicate the high affinity of bacterial community for degradation of both chlorpyrifos and TCP. The 16S rRNA gene sequence analysis has confirmed the genetic relatedness of isolates 1-4 with *Pseudomonas*, isolates 5 and 6 with *Agrobacterium*, and isolate 7 with *Bacillus*. Their degradation potential for chlorpyrifos and TCP has been found to be in the order: *Pseudomonas* > *Agrobacterium* > *Bacillus*. It has been also observed that all seven isolates are more efficient in degrading TCP compared to chlorpyrifos (Maya et al. 2011).

Mallick et al. (1999) reported bacterial degradation of chlorpyrifos (10 ppm) in pure cultures and in soil. *Arthrobacter* sp. degraded the insecticide completely within 24 hrs of incubation while *Flavobacterium* sp. ATCC 27551 effected degradation within 48 hrs of incubation. Under flooded conditions, the soil applied chlorpyrifos was degraded by *Flavobacterium* sp. within 15 days and by *Arthrobacter* sp. within 28 days. Under non-flooded conditions, the soil applied chlorpyrifos was degraded completely within 28 days by *Flavobacterium* sp. While *Arthrobacter* sp. proved to be a slow degrader under these conditions. Kahlon and Saurabh (2003) isolated 43 cultures of bacteria from various soil samples collected from different regions of Punjab and screened for the degradation of chlorpyrifos. Four isolates were found to grow efficiently which were further selected for the bioaugmentation of pesticide degradation in the contaminated soil.

Three aerobic bacterial consortia, AC, BC, and DC, developed from pesticide-contaminated soils of Punjab were able to degrade chlorpyrifos after 21 days of incubation in basal medium by 54, 46, and 61 per cent and chlorpyrifos (50 mg/L) in soil after 30 days by 50, 56, and 64 per cent. *Pseudomonas aeruginosa, Bacillus cereus, Klebsiella* sp, and *Serratia marscecens* obtained from these consortia showed 84, 84, 81, and 80 per cent degradation of chlorpyrifos (50 mg/L) in liquid medium after 20 days and 92, 60, 56, and 37 per cent degradation of chlorpyrifos (50 mg/L) in soil after 30 days. Populations of *Bacillus cereus, Klebsiella sp.*, and *Serratia marscecens* remained steady in soil experiments except for *P. aeruginosa*, where the population showed a substantial increase. Formation of 3,5,6-trichloro-2-pyridinol, the major metabolite of chlorpyrifos degradation, was observed during the degradation of chlorpyrifos by *P. aeruginosa*, which disappeared to negligible amounts (Vidya Lakshmi et al. 2009). The ability of *Enterobacter* strain B-14 isolated by enrichment culture technique to mineralise chlorpyrifos was investigated under different culture conditions (Singh et al., 2004). Studies with ring labelled 14C chlorpyrifos in liquid culture demonstrated that the isolate hydrolysed chlorpyrifos to diethylthiophosphate (DETP) and 3,5,6-trichloro-2- pyridinol and utilised DETP for growth and energy.

From the chlorpyrifos contaminated soil nine morphologically different bacterial strains, one actinomycete and two fungal strains were isolated. Among those isolates four bacterial strains which were more efficient were developed as consortium. The four bacterial isolates namely *Pseudomonas putida* (NII 1117), *Klebsiella* sp., (NII 1118), *Pseudomonas stutzeri* (NII 1119), *Pseudomonas aeruginosa* (NII 1120) present in the consortia were identified on the basis of 16S rDNA analysis. The intracellular fractions of the consortium exhibited more organophosphorus hydrolase activity (0.171 ± 0.003 U/mL/min). The degradation studies were carried out at neutral pH and temperature 37 °C with chlorpyrifos concentration 500 mg L^{-1} LC-mass spectral analysis showed the presence of metabolites chlopyrifos-oxon and Diethylphosphorothioate. These results highlight an important potential use of this consortium for the cleanup of chlorpyrifos contaminated pesticide waste in the environment (Sasikala et al. 2012).

Biodegradation of Chlorpyrifos Using Fungi

Pesticides residues in soils and on vegetables are a public safety concern. Pretreatment with microorganisms degrading pesticides has the potential to alleviate the conditions. For this purpose, the degradation characteristics of chlorpyrifos by an isolated fungal strain *Verticillium* sp. DSP in pure cultures, soil, and on pakchoi (*Brassica chinensis* L.) were investigated. Degradation rate of chlorpyrifos in the mineral salts medium was proportional to the concentrations of chlorpyrifos ranging from 1 to 100 mg l^{-1}. The rate of degradation for chlorpyrifos (1mg l^{-1}) in the mineral salts medium was 1.12 and 1.04 times faster at pH 7.0 than those at pHs 5.0 and 9.0, and the degradation at 35°C was 1.15 and 1.12 times faster, respectively, than those at 15 and 20°C. The addition of the fungal strain DSP into the contaminated soils was found to significantly increase the degradation of chlorpyrifos. Degradation rates of chlorpyrifos in inoculated soils were 3.61, 1.50 and 1.10 times faster in comparison with the sterilized soil, previously chlorpyrifos-untreated soil, and previously chlorpyrifos-treated soil under laboratory conditions. In contrast to the controls, the half-lives of chlorpyrifos were significantly shortened by 10.9 per cent and 17.6 per cent on treated pakchoi, 12.0 per cent and 37.1 per cent in inoculated soils, respectively, in the greenhouse and open field. The results indicate that the fungal strain DSP can be used successfully for the removal or detoxification of chlorpyrifos residues in/on contaminated soil and vegetable (Fang et al. 2008).

Biodegradation of Chlorpyrifos Using Cyanobacteria

Chlorpyrifos degradation by cyanobacterium *Synechocystis* sp. strain PUPCCC 64 was isolated from a rice field. The organism tolerated chlorpyrifos up to 15mg/L. Major fraction of chlorpyrifos was removed by the organism during the first day followed by slow uptake. Biomass, pH, and temperature influenced the insecticide removal and the organism exhibited maximum chlorpyrifos removal at 100 mg protein/L biomass, pH 7.0, and 30°C. The cyanobacterium metabolized chlorpyrifos producing a number of degradation products as evidenced by GC-MS chromatogram. One of the degradation products was identified as 3,5,6-trichloro-2-pyridinol (Singh et al. 2011).

Spirulina is a photosynthetic, filamentous, spiral-shaped, multicellular, blue-green microalga. The two most important species are *Spirulina maxima* and *Spirulina platensis*. *Spirulina* is considered an excellent food, lacking toxicity and having corrective properties against viral attacks, anemia, tumor growth and malnutrition. *Spirulina platensis* grow in media containing up to 80 ppm of the organophosphorous pesticide, Chlorpyrifos. It was found to be due to an alkaline phosphatase (ALP) activity that was detected in cell free extracts of *Spirulina platensis*. This activity was purified from the cell free extracts using ammonium sulphate precipitation and gel filtration and shown to belong to the class of EC 3.1.3.1 ALP. The purified enzyme degrades 100 ppm Chlorpyrifos to 20 ppm in 1 h transforming it into its primary metabolite 3,5,6-trichloro-2-pyridinol (Thengodkar and Sivakami, 2010).

Enzymatic Degradation of Organophosphorus Pesticides

Microorganisms degrading xenobiotic chemicals are equipped with elaborate enzyme systems. Biodegradation of organophosphates involves activities of phosphatase, esterase, hydrolase and oxygenase enzymes. Munnecke (1976) observed that crude cell free extract from a mixed bacterial culture growing on parathion, hydrolysed the same at a rate of 416 n mol/ min/mg of protein. The enzyme phosphotriesterase (parathion hydrolase) was also reported from *Streptomyces lividans* (Rowland *et al.*, 1991). The enzyme cloned from a *Flavobacterium* sp. into *Streptomyces lividans* was secreted at high levels and consisted of a single polypeptide with an apparent molecular weight of 35,000. Biodegradation of organophosphorus pesticides by surface expressed organophosphorus hydrolase was studied by Richins *et al.* (1997). Organophosphorus hydrolase (OPH) was displayed and anchored on to the surface of *Escherichia coli* using an Lpp-Omp A fusion system. More than 80 per cent of the activity was found to be located on the cell surface. The precise conditions for surface targeting or pesticide degradation were further studied by Kaneva *et al.* (1998). Optimum OPH activity was observed when cells were grown in Luria-Bertani buffered medium at 37°C. The resulting culture grown under optimised conditions had an eight fold increase in parathion degradation. Sureshkumar *et al.* (1998) reported that the cell free extract of *Flavobacterium balustinum* hydrolysed a variety of organophosphorus pesticides like fenitrothion, quinalphos and monocrotophos. The enzyme responsible for hydrolysis was identified as a phosphotriesterase. Cho *et al.* (2002) observed that the effectiveness of degradation by OPH varied dramatically ranging from highly efficient with paraoxon to relatively slow with methyl parathion. A solid phase top agar method based on detection of the yellow product Pnitrophenol was developed for the rapid pre-screening of potential variants with improved hydrolysis of methyl parathion. One variant 22AII hydrolysed methyl parathion 25 folds faster than did the wild strain.

Conclusion

Pesticides can be indispensable tools for pest management in agriculture especially when there is no alternative. In many cases pesticides are the first line of control against pest. But the potential environment and public health risks associated with the use of pesticides have become a concern of the general public. Much of the potential risks are to human health. To reduce the risk associated with pesticide use chemical companies have developed and brought to market plant protection chemicals that require much lower rates than historically once used. New agrochemicals also target pests with increased specificity, reducing potential risks to non target organisms, humans and the environment. Integrated pest management (IPM) relies on combination of cultural, biological and chemical practices to control pests.

Biodegradation is a natural way of recycling waste and toxic substances by breaking them with microorganisms either in the presence of oxygen (aerobic degradation) or without oxygen (anaerobic degradation). In soil enriched environments soil conditions such as moisture, temperature, pH and the amount of organic matter affect the rate of microbial degradation due to their direct or indirect influence on microbial growth and microbial activity. Pesticide microbial degradation is the key process in attenuating pesticide fate in the environment. Microbial metabolism is probably the most important pesticide degradative process in soils and is the basis for bioremediation, as the degrading microorganisms obtain C, N or energy from the pesticide molecules. The goal of bioremediation is to at least reduce pollutant levels to undetectable, nontoxic or acceptable levels, i.e. within limits set by regulatory agencies or ideally completely mineralize organopollutants to carbon dioxide. As long as microbial population is not disturbed the degradation of pesticide by microbes is the most environmental friendly method and natural remediation cannot be substituted by any other.

REFERENCES

Acevedo, R. (1991): Preliminary Observations on Effects of Pesticides Carbaryl, Naphthol, and Chlorpyrifos on Planulae of the Hermatypic Coral *Pocillopora damicornis.* Pacific Science, 45(3): 287-289.

Adesodun, J.K., Davidson, D.A., and Hopkins, D.W. (2005): Micromorphological Evidence for Changes in Soil Faunal Activity Following Application of Sewage Sludge and Biocide. Applied Soil Ecology, 29(1): 39-45.

Ainsworth, C. C., Frederickson, J. K., and Smith, S.C. (1993): Effect of Sorption on the Degradation of Aromatic Acids and Bases, Soil Science Society of America, Madison, WI, pp: 125.

Alexander, M. (1999): Biodegradation and Bioremediation, Academic Press, San Diego, pp: 453.

Ali, A., and Mulla, M.S. (1978): Effects of Chironomid Larvicides and Diflubenzuron on Nontarget Invertebrates in Residential-recreational Lakes. Environmental Entomology, 7(1): 21-27.

Allender, W.J. (1991): Determination of Chlorpyrifos and its Major Breakdown Products in Technical Formulations. Bulletin of Environmental Contamination and Toxicology, 46: 313-319.

Anwar, S., Liaquat, F., Khan, Q.M., Khalid, Z.M., and Iqbal, S. (2009): Biodegradation of Chlorpyrifos and its Hydrolysis Product 3,5,6-trichloro-2-pyridinol by *Bacillus pumilus* Strain C2A1. Journal of Hazardous Material, 168: 400-405.

Bailey, G.W., Swank, R.R., and Nicholson, H.P. (1974): Predicting Pesticide Runoff from Agricultural Land: A Conceptual Model. Journal of Environmental Quality, 3: 95-102.

Beulke, S., Beinum, W.V., Brown, C.D., Mitchell, M., and Walker, A. (2005): Evaluation of Simplifying Assumptions on Pesticide Degradation in Soil. Journal of Environmental Quality, 34: 1933-1943.

Borthwick, P.W., Patrick, J.M., and Middaugh, D.P. (1985): Comparative Acute Sensitivities of Early Life Stages of Atherinid Fishes to Chlorpyrifos and Thiobencarb. Archives of Environmental Contamination and Toxicology, 14: 465-473.

Bicker, W., Lammerhofer, M., Genser, D., Kiss, H., and Lindner, W. (2005): A Case Study of Acute Human Chlorpyrifos Poisoning: Novel Aspects on Metabolism and Toxicokinetics Derived from Liquid Chromatography–Tandem Mass Spectrometry Analysis of Urine Samples. Toxicology Letter, 159: 235-251.

Brazner, J.C., and Kline, E.R. (1990): Effects of Chlorpyrifos on the Diet and Growth of Larval Fathead Minnows, Pimephales Promelas, in Littoral Enclosures. Canadian Journal of Fisheries and Aquatic Sciences, 47: 1157-1165.

Brock, T.C.M. (1992): Fate and Effects of the Insecticide Dursban 4E in indoor Elodea Dominated and Macrophyte-free Freashwater Model Ecosystems: I. Fate and Primary Effects of the Active Ingredient Chlorpyrifos. Archives of Environmental Contamination and Toxicology, 23: 69-84.

Brown, J.R., and Chow, L.Y. (1975): The effect of Dursban on Micro Flora in Non-saline Waters. Environmental Quality and Safety, 3: 774-779.

Brown, J.R., Chow, L.Y., and Deng, C.B. (1976): The Effect of Dursban Upon Fresh Water Phytoplankton. Bulletin of Environmental Contamination and Toxicology, 15(4): 437-441.

Brust, H.F. (1966): A Summary of Chemical and Physical Properties of Dursban. Down to Earth, 22: 21-22.

Cao, L., Liu, H., Zhang, H., Huang, K., Gu, T., Ni, H., Hong, Q., and Li, S. (2012): Characterization of a Newly Isolated Highly Effective 3,5,6-Trichloro-2-pyridinol Degrading Strain *Cupriavidus pauculus* P2. Current Microbiology, 65(3): 231-236.

Chaplot, V.A.M., and Bissonnais, Y.L. (2003): Runoff Features for Interrill Erosion at Different Rainfall Intensities, Slope Lengths, and Gradients in an Agricultural Loessial Hillslope. Soil Science Society of America Journal, 67: 844-851.

Chiou, C.T., Freed, V.H., Schmedding, D.W., and Kohnert, R.L. (1977): Partition Coefficient and Bioaccumulation of Selected Organic Chemicals. Environmental Science & Technolnology, 11: 475-478.

Cho, C.M., Mulchandani, A., and Chen, W. (2002): Bacterial Cell Display of Organophosphorus Hydrolase for Selective Screening of Improved Hydrolysis of Organophosphate Nerve Agents. Applied Environmental Microbiology, 68: 2026-2030.

Choi, K., Joo, H., Randy, L., Rose, R.L., and Hodgson, E. (2006): Metabolism of Chlorpyrifos and Chlorpyrifos Oxon by Human Hepatocytes. Journal of Biochemical and Molecular Toxicology, 20: 279-291.

Cockfield, S.D., and Potter, D.A. (1983): Short-term Effects of Insecticidal Applications on Predacious Arthropods and Oribatid Mites in Kentucky Blue Grass Turf. Environmental Entomology, 12: 1260-1264.

Day, K.E., and Scott, I.M. (1990): Use of Acetylcholinesterase Activity to Detect Sublethal Toxicity in Stream Invertebrates Exposed to Low Concentrations of Organophosphate Insecticides. Aquatic Toxicology, 18: 101-114.

Dua, M., Singh, A., Sethunathan, N., and Johri, A.K. (2002): Biotechnology and Bioremediation: Successes and Limitations. Applied Microbiology and Biotechnology, 59: 143-152.

Dyson, J.S., Beulke, S., Brown, C.D., and Lane, M.C.G. (2002): Adsorption and Degradation of the Weak Acid Mesotrione in Soil and Environmental Fate Implications. Journal of Environmental Quality, 31: 613-618.

Fang, H., Xiang, Y.Q., Hao, Y.J., Chu, X.Q., Pan, X.D., Yu, J.Q., and Yu, Y.L. (2008): Fungal Degradation of Chlorpyrifos by Verticillium sp. DSP in Pure Cultures and Its Use in Bioremediation of Contaminated Soil and Pakchoi. International Biodeterioration and Biodegradradation, 61: 294-303.

Farenhorst, A. (2006): Importance of Soil Organic Matter Fractions in Soil-landscape and Regional Assessments of Pesticide Sorption and Leaching in Soil. Soil Science Society of America Journal, 70: 1005-1012.

Felsot, A., and Dahm, P.A. (1979): Sorption of Organophosphorus and Carbamate Insecticides by Soil. Journal of Agricultural and Food Chemistry, 27: 557-563.

Fermanich, K.J., and Daniel, T.C. (1991): Pesticide Mobility and Persistence in Microlysimeter Soil Columns from a Tilled and No-tilled Plot. Journal of Environmental Quality, 20(1): 195-202.

Ferrando, M.D., and Andreu-Moliner, E. (1991): Acute Lethal Toxicity of some Pesticides to *Brachionus calciflorus* and *Brachionus plicatilis*. Bulletin of Environmental Contamination and Toxicology, 47: 479-484.

Floate, K.D. (1989): Field Bioassay to Evaluate Contact and Residual Toxicities of Insecticides to Carabid Beetles (Coleoptera: Carabidae). Journal of Economic Entomology, 82(6): 1543-1547.

Funderburk, J.E., Braxton, L.B., and Lynch, R.E. (1990): Nontarget Effects of Soil-applied Chlorpyrifos on Defoliating Pests and Arthropod Predators in Peanut. Peanut Science, 17: 113-117.

Gans, D.A., Kilgore, W.W., and Ito, J. (1994): Residues of Chlorinated Pesticides in Processed Foods Imported into Hawaii from Western Pacific Rim Countries. Bulletin of Environmental Contamination and Toxicology, 52: 560-567.

Ghanem, I, Orfi, M, and Shamma, M. (2007): Biodegradation of Chlorpyrifos by *Klebsiella* sp Isolated from an Activated Sludge Sample of Waste Water Treatment Plant in Damascus. Folia Microbiology, 52: 423-427.

Goodman, L.R. (1985): A New Early Life-stage Toxicity Test Using the California Grunion (*Leuresthes tenuis*) and Results with Chlorpyrifos. Ecotoxicology and Environmental Safety, 10: 12-21.

Hance, R.J. (1988): Adsorption and Bioavailability. CRC Press, pp: 1.

Hankin, L., and Pylypiw, H.M. (1991): Pesticides in Orange Juice Sold in Connecticut. Journal of Food Protectection, 54(4): 310-311.

Haith, D.A., Lee, P.C., Clark, J.M., Roy, G.R., Imboden, M.J., and Walden, R.R. (2002): Modeling Pesticide Volatilization from Turf. Journal of Environmental Quality, 31: 724-729.

Holcombe, G.W., Phipps, G.L., and Tanner, D.K. (1982): The Acute Toxicity of Kelthane, Dursban, disulfoton, Pydrin, and Permethrin to Fathead Minnows Pimephales Promelas and Rainbow Trout Salmo Gairdneri. Environmental Pollution Series A, 29: 167-178.

Howard, P.H. (1991): Handbook of Environmental Fate and Exposure Data for Organic Chemicals, Pesticides, Lewis Publishers, Chelsea, MI, pp: 5.

Jarvinen, A.W., Nordling, B.R., and Henry, M.E. (1983): Chronic Toxicity of Dursban (Chlorpyrifos) to the Fathead Minnow (*Pimephales promelas*) and the Resultant Acetylcholinesterase Inhibition. Ecotoxicology and Environmental Safety, 7: 423-434.

Jarvinen, A.W., Tanner, D.K., and Kline, E.R. (1988): Toxicity of Chlorpyrifos, Endrin, or Fenvalerate to Fathead Minnows Following Episodic or Continuous Exposure. Ecotoxicology and Environmental Safety, 15: 78-95.

Johnson, C.R. (1978): The Effect of Five Organophosphorus Insecticides on Survival and Temperature Tolerance in the Copepod, Macrocyclops Albidus. Zoological Journal of the Linnean Society, 64: 59-62.

Kahlon, R.S., and Saurabh, G. (2003): To Study the Effect of Bioaugmentation on Pesticides Contaminated Soil by Fluorescent *Pseudomonas*, 44th AMI Conference, November 12-14, Dharwad, pp: 125.

Kaneva, I., Mulchandani, A., and Chen, W. (1998): Factors Influencing Parathion Degradation by Recombinant *Escherichia coli* with Surface-expressed Organophosphorus Hydrolase. Biotechnology Programme 14: 275-278.

Karanth, S., and Pope, C. (2000): Carboxylesterase and A-esterase Activities during Maturation and Aging: Relationship to the Toxicity of Chlorpyrifos and Parathion in Rats. Toxicology Science, 58: 282-89.

Khanna, S., and Vidhyalakshmi, (2004): Chlorpyrifos Degrading Microbes Capable of Bioremediating Contaminated Sites. Microbial Diversity — A Source of Innovation in Biotechnology, National Seminar, May 27-29, TBGRI, Thiruvananthapuram, pp: 84.

Key, P.B., and Fulton, M.H. (1993): Lethal and Sublethal Effects of Chlorpyrifos Exposure on Adult and Larval Stages of the Grass Shrimp, Palaemonetes Pugio. Journal of Environmental Science Health B, 28(5): 621-640.

Li, X., He, J., and Li, S. (2007): Isolation of Chlorpyrifos Degrading Bacterium, *Sphingomonas* sp. Strain Dsp-2, and Cloning of the mpd gene. Research Microbiology, 158: 143-149.

Li, X., Jiang, J., Gu, L., Ali, S.W., He, J., and Li, S. (2008): Diversity of Chlorpyrifos Degrading Bacteria Isolated from Chlorpyrifos Contaminated Samples. International Biodeterioration Biodegradation, 62: 331-335.

Mallick, K., Bharati, K., Banerji, A., Shakil, N.A., and Sethunathan, N. (1999): Bacterial Degradation of Chlorpyrifos in Pure Cultures and in Soil. Bulletin of Environmental Contamination and Toxicology, 62: 48-54.

Mani, M., and Krishnamoorthy, A. (1986): Susceptibility of Telenomus Remus Nixon, an Exotic Parasitoid of *Spodoptera litura* (F.), to Some Pesticides. Tropical Pest Management, 32(1): 49-51.

Mani, M., and Nagarkatti, S. (1988): Response of the Parasitoid, *Eucelatoria bryani Sabrosky* (Diptera: Tachinidae) to Different Pesticides. Entomology, 13(1): 25-28.

Mansour, F. (1987): Effect of Pesticides on Spiders Occuring on Apple and Citrus in Israel. Phytoparasitica, 15(1): 43-50.

Maya, K., Singh, R.S., Upadhyay, S.N., and Dubey, S.K. (2011): Kinetic Analysis Reveals Bacterial Efficacy for Biodegradation of Chlorpyrifos and its Hydrolyzing Metabolite TCP. Process Biochemistry, 46: 2130-2136.

Masoodi, M.A., Bhat, A.M., and Koul, V.J. (1988): Toxicity of Insecticide to Adults of *Encarsia perniciosi*. Indian Journal of Agricultural Science, 59(1): 50-52.

McCall, P.J., Oliver, G.R., and McKellar, R.I. (1984): Modeling the Runoff Potential and Behaviour of Chlorpyrifos in a Terrestrial-aquatic Watershed. Rep. GH-C 1694. Dow Chemical U.S.A., Midland, Michigan.

McCall, P.J., Swann, R.L., and Bauriedel, W.R. (1985): Volatility Characteristics of Chlorpyrifos from Soil. Rep. GH-C 1782. Dow Chemical U.S.A., Midland, Michigan.

Munnecke, D.M. (1976): Enzymatic Hydrolysis of Organophosphate Insecticides, a Possible Pesticide Disposal Method. Applied Environmental Microbiology, 32: 7-13.

Menon, P., Gopal, M., and Parsad, R. (2005): Effects of Chlorpyrifos and Quinalphos on Dehydrogenase Activities and Reduction of Fe^{3-} in the Soils of Two Semi-arid Fields of Tropical India. Agriculture Ecosystems & Environment, 108(1): 73-83.

Menon, P., Gopal, M., and Parsad, R. (2004): Influence of Two Insecticides, Chlorpyrifos and Quinalphos, on Arginine Ammonification and Mineralizable Nitrogen in Two Tropical Soil Types. Journal of Agricultural and Food Chemistry, 52(24): 7370-7376.

Mizell, R.F., and Schiffhauer, D.E. (1990): Effects of Pesticides on Pecan Aphid Predators *Chrysoperla rufilabris* (Neuroptera: Chrysopidae), *Hippodamia convergens, Cycloneda sanguinea* (L.), Olla v-nigrum (Co-leoptera: Coccinellidae) and *Aphelinus perpallidus* (Hymenoptera: Encyrtidae). Journal of Economic Entomology, 83(5): 1806-1812.

Mukherjee, I., Gopal, M., and Dhar, D.W. (2004): Disappearance of Chlorpyrifos from Cultures of *Chlorella vulgaris*. Bulletin of Environmental Contamination and Toxicology, 73: 358-363.

Muscarella, D.E., Keown, J.F., and Bloom, S.E. (1984): Evaluation of the Genotoxic and Embryotoxic Potential of Chlorpyrifos and its Metabolites *in vivo* and *in vitro*. Environmental Mutagen, 6: 13-23.

Nagayama, T. (1989): Residues of Organophosphorus Pesticides in Commercial Tea and Their Leaching into Tea. Journal of Pesticide Science, 14(1): 39-45.

Neely, W.B., Branson, D.R., and Blau, G.E. (1974): Partition Coefficient to Measure Bioconcentration Potential of Organic Chemicals in Fish. Environmental Science and Technology, 8: 1113-1115.

Nerud, F., Baldrian, J., Gabriel, J., and Ogbeifun, D. (2003): Nonenzymic Degradation and Decolorization of Recalcitrant Compounds. Problems and Solutions, pp: 29.

Oliver, G.R., McKellar, R.L., and Woodburn, K.B. (1987): Field Dissipation and Leaching Study for Chlorpyrifos in Florida Citrus. Rep. GH-C 1870. Dow Chemical U.S.A., Midland, Michigan.

Palanisami, S., Prabaharan, D., Uma, L. (2009): Fate of Few Pesticide-metabolizing Enzymes in the Marine Cyanobacterium *Phormidium valderianum* BDU 20041 in Perspective with Chlorpyrifos Exposure. Pesticide Biochemistry and Physiology, 94: 68-72.

Park, J.H., Feng, Y., Ji, P., Voice, T.C., and Boyd, S.A. (2003): Assessment of Bioavailability of Soil-sorbed Atrazine. Applied Environmental Microbiology, 69: 3288-3298.

Perfecto, I. (1990): Indirect and Direct Effects in a Tropical Agroecosystem: The Maize-pest-ant System in Nicaragua. Ecology, 71(6): 2125-2134.

Racke, K.D. (1993): Environmental Fate of Chlorpyrifos. Reviews of Environmental Contamination & Toxicology, 131: 1-151.

Racke, K.D., Steele, K.P., Yoder, R.N., Dick, W.A., and Avidov, E. (1996): Factors Effecting the Hydrolytic Degradation of Chlorpyrifos in Soil. Journal of Agricultural and Food Chemistry, 44: 1582-1592.

Radhakrishnaiah, K., and Renukadevi, B. (1990): Size and Sex Related Tolerance to Pesticides in the Freshwater Field Crab. Environmental Ecology, 8(10): 111-114.

Readman, J.W., Albanis, T.A., Barcelo, D., Galassi, S., Tronczynski, J., and Grabrielidesi, G.P. (1997): Fungicide Contamination of Mediterranean Estuarine Waters: Results from a MED POL Pilot Survey. Marine Pollution Bulletin, 34: 259-263.

Reed, J.P., Hall, F.R., Krueger, H.R. (1992): Contact and Volatile Toxicity of Insecticides to Black Cutworm Larvae (Lepidoptera: Noctuidae) and Carabid Beetles (Coleoptera: Carabidae) in Soil. Journal of Economic Entomology, 85: 256-261.

Richins, R.D., Kaneva, I., Mulchandani, A., and Chen, W. (1997): Biodegradation of Organophosphorus Pesticides by Surface-expressed Organophosphorus Hydrolase. Nature Biotechnology, 15: 984-987.

Rigterink, R.H., and Kenaga, E.E. (1966): Synthesis and Insecticidal Activity of some 0, 0-diakyl 0-(3,5,6-trichloro-2-pyridyl) Phosphates and Phosphorothioates. Journal of Agriculural and Food Chemistry, 14: 304-306.

Roberts, J.W., and Camann, D.E. (1989): Pilot Study of a Cotton Glove Press Test for Assessing Exposure to Pesticides in House Dust. Bulletin of Environmental Contamination and Toxicology 43: 717-724.

Rosenheim, J.A., and Hoy, M.A. (1988): Sublethal Effects of Pesticides on the Parasitoid Aphytis Melinus (Hymenoptera: Aphelinidae). Journal of Economic Entomology, 81(2): 476-483.

Roulier, S., and Jarvis, N. (2003): Modeling Macropore Flow Effects on Pesticide Leaching: Inverse Parameter Estimation Using Microlysimeters. Journal of Environmental Quality, 32: 2341-2353.

Rowland, S.S., Speedie, M.K., and Pogell, B.M. (1991): Purification and Characterization of a Secreted Recombinant Phosphotriesterase (Parathion Hydrolase) from *Streptomyces lividans*. Applied Environmental Microbiology, 57: 440-444.

Sasikala, C., Jiwal, S., Rout, P., and Ramya, M. (2012): Biodegradation of Chlorpyrifos by Bacterial Consortium Isolated from Agriculture Soil. World Journal of Microbiology and Biotechnology, 28: 1301-1308.

Schoefs, O., Perrier, M., and Samson, R. (2004): Estimation of Contaminant Depletion in Unsaturated Soils Using a Reduced-order Biodegradation Model and Carbon Dioxide Measurement. Applied Microbiology and Biotechnology, 64: 256-261.

Shan, M., Fang, H., Wang, X., Feng, B., Chu, X.Q., and Yu, Y.L. (2006): Effect of Chlorpyrifos on Soil Microbial Populations and Enzyme Activities. Journal of Environmental Science, 18(1): 4-5.

Shetty, P.K., Mitra, J., Murthy, N.B.K., Namitha, K.K., Savitha, K.N., and Raghu, K. (2000): Biodegradation of Cyclodiene Insecticide Endosulfan by *Mucor thermohyalospora* MTCC 1384. Current Science, 79: 1381-1383.

Siegfried, B.D. (1993): Comparative Toxicity of Pyrethroid Insecticides to Terrestrial and Aquatic Insects. Environmental Toxicology Chemistry, 12: 1683-1689.

Singh, D.P., Khattar, J.I.S., Nadda, J., Singh, Y., Garg, A., Kaur, N., and Gulati, A. (2011): Chlorpyrifos Degradation by the Cyanobacterium *Synechocystis* sp. Strain PUPCCC 64. Environmental Science Pollution Research, 18: 1351-1359.

Singh, P.B., Sharma, S., Saini, H.S., and Chadha, B.S. (2009): Biosurfactant Production by *Pseudomonas* sp. and its role in Aqueous Phase Partitioning and Biodegradation of Chlorpyrifos. Letters Applied Microbiology, 49: 378-383.

Singh, B.K., Walker, A., Morgan, J.A.W., and Wright, D.J. (2004): Biodegradation of Chlorpyrifos by *Enterobacter* Strain B-14 and its Use in Bioremediation of Contaminated Soils. Applied Environmental Microbiology, 70: 4855-4863.

Singh, B.K., Walker, A., Morgan, J.A., and Wright, D.J. (2003): Effects of Soil pH on the Biodegradation of Chlorpyrifos and Isolation of a Chlorpyrifos-degrading Bacterium. Applied Environmental Microbiology, 69: 5198-5206.

Singh, B.K., Walker, A., and Wright, D.J. (2002): Degradation of Chlorpyrifos, Fenamiphos, and Chlorothalonil Alone and in Combination and Their Effects on Soil Microbial Activity. Envrionmental Toxicology Chemistry, 21: 2600-2605.

Singhal, V. (2003): Indian Agriculture 2003, Published by Indian Economic Data Research Centre, New Delhi, pp: 85.

Smith, J.L., and Rust, M.K. (1992): Activity and Water-induced Movement of Termiticides in Soil. Journal of Economic Entomology, 85(2): 430-434.

Smith, G.N., Watson, B.S., and Fischer, F.S. (1966): The Metabolism of (^{14}C) O, O-diethyl O-(3,5,6-trichloro-2-pyridyl) phosphorothioate (Dursban) in fish. Journal of Economic Entomology, 59(6): 1464-1475.

Snell, T.W. (1991): Acute Toxicity Tests Using Rotifers. Ecotoxicology and Environmental Safety, 21: 308-317.

Sogorb, M.A., Vilanova, E., and Carrera, V. (2004): Future Application of Phosphotriesterases in the Prophylaxis and Treatment of Organophosphorous Insecticide and Nerve Agent Poisoning. Toxicology Letter, 151: 219-233.

Somasundaram, L. (1991): Mobility of Pesticides and Their Hydrolysis Metabolites in Soil. Environmental Toxicology Chemistry, 10: 185-194.

Srivastava, S.K., Tiwari, P.R., and Srivasta, A.K. (1990): Effects of Chlorpyrifos on the Kidney of Freshwater Catfish. *Heteropneustes Fossilis*. Bulletin of Environmental Contamiantion and Toxicology, 45: 748-751.

Sureshkumar, C., Anuradha, C.M., and Dayananda, S. (1998): Detoxification of Organophosphorus Pesticides by Bacterial Phosphotriesterase. In 39th AMI Conference, December 5-7, Jaipur, pp: 236.

Testai, E., Buratti, F.M., and Di Consiglio, E. (2010): Chlorpyrifos in 'Hayes' Handbook of Pesticide Toxicology, Elsevier Inc., USA, pp: 1505.

Thengodkar, R.R.M., and Sivakami, S. (2010): Degradation of Chlorpyrifos by an Alkaline Phosphatase from the Cynobacterium *Spirulina platensis*. Biodegradation, 21: 637-644.

Thirugnanam, G., and Forgash, A.J. (1977): Environmental Impact of Mosquito Pesticides: Toxicity and Anticholinesterase Activity of Chlorpyrifos to Fish in a Salt Marsh Habitat. Archives of Environmental Contamiantion and Toxicology, 5: 415-425.

Van der Wel, H., and Welling, W. (1989): Inhibition of Acetylcholinesterase in Guppies (*Poecilia reticulata*) by Chlorpyrifos at Sublethal Concentrations: Methodological Aspects. Ecotoxicology and Environmental Safety, 17: 205-215.

Vidya Lakshmi, C., Kumar, M., and Khanna, S. (2009): Biodegradation of Chlorpyrifos in Soil by Enriched Cultures. Current Microbiology, 58: 35-38.

Vidya Lakshmi, C., Kumar, M., and Khanna, S. (2008): Biotransformation of Chlorpyrifos and Bioremediation of Contaminated Soil. International Biodeterioration and Biodegradation, 62: 204-209.

Vischetti, C., Coppola, L., Monaci, E., Cardinali, A., and Castillo, M.D. (2007): Microbial Impact of the Pesticide Chlorpyrifos on Swedish and Italian Biobeds. Agro Sustainable Development, 27(3): 267-272.

Walsh, G.E. (1983): Cell Death and Inhibition of Population of Marine Unicellular Algae by Pesticides. Aquatic Toxicology, 3: 209-214.

Walton, W.E. (1990): Impact of Selected Synthetic Pyrethroids and Organophosphorus Pesticides on the Tadpole Shrimp, Triops Longicaudatus. Bulletin of Environmental Contamination and Toxicology, 45: 62-68.

Wauchope, R.D., Yeh, S., Linders, J.B., Kloskowski, R., Tanaka, K., Rubin, B., Katayama, A., Kordel, W., Gerstl, Z., Lane, M., and Unsworth, J.B. (2002): Pesticide Soil Sorption Parameters: Theory, Measurement, Uses, Limitations and Reliability. Pesticide Management Science, 58: 419-445.

Whang, J.M. (1993): Volatilization of Fonofos, Chlorpyrifos, and Atrazine from Conventional and no Till Surface Soils in the Field. Journal of Environmental Quality, 22: 173-180.

Xu, G.M., Li, Y.Y., Zheng, W., Peng, X., Li, W., and Yan, Y.C. (2007): Mineralization of Chlorpyrifos by Co-culture of *Serratia* and *Trichosporon* spp. Biotechnology Letters, 29: 1469-1473.

Xu, G., Zheng, W., Li, Y., Wang, S., Zhang, J., and Yan, Y. (2008): Biodegradation of Chlorpyrifos and 3,5,6-trichloro-pyridinol by a Newly Isolated *Paracoccus* sp Strain TRP. International Biodeterioration Biodegradation, 62: 51-56.

Yang, C., Liu, N., Guo, X., and Qiao, C. (2006): Cloning of mpd Gene from a Chlorpyrifos Degrading Bacterium and Use of this Strain in Bioremediation of Contaminated Soil. FEMS Microbiology Letter, 265: 118-125.

Yang, L., Zhao, Y.H., Zhang, B.X., Yang, C.H., and Zhang, X. (2005): Isolation and Characterization of a Chlorpyrifos and 3,5,6-trichloro-2-pyridinol Degrading Bacterium. FEMS Microbiology Letter, 251: 67-73.

Yates, S.R., Wang, D., Papiernik, S.K., and Gan, J. (2002): Predicting Pesticide Volatilization from Soils. Environmetrics, 13: 569-578.

Zhang, J., and Chiao, C. (2002): Novel Approaches for Remediation of Pesticide Pollutants. International Journal of Environmental Pollution, 18(5): 423-433.

CHAPTER 3

Effect of Lead Toxicity on the Reproductive System

Smriti Tyagi, *India*
Anubhuti Sharma, *India*

Introduction

The living organisms are always come in the exposure of many environmental contaminants in their every stage of life. Majority of these contaminants are various chemicals which are hazardous for the life. One of these chemicals is lead which has been recognized as ubiquitous environmental pollutants (Goyer, 1990; Needleman and Jackson, 1992). Environmental pollution by lead is a widespread problem. Lead toxicity is known to humanity since ancient times and mentioned in documents left by the Greeks, Romans and Arabs, and even the Egyptians reported by Ahmad, *et al.*, (2003). Lead is an oldest harmful agent to mankind. Lead is an environmental and industrial pollutant that has been detected in every facet of environmental and biological systems.

Properties of Lead

Lead is a p block element, comes in 14th group. Its atomic number is 82, atomic mass is 207. Its electronic configuration is $6S_{2,}$ $6P_{2.}$ It shows two valancy +2 and +4. Lead is a heavy soft metal, occurs in nature as an oxide or salts for eg. Galena (PbS). It has been one of the most useful metals known to man, mainly because of its physical properties like malleability and resistance to corrosion. Lead became popular because of its dense, ductile, malleable and corrosion resistant properties (Florea, *et al.,* 2006).

Uses of Lead

The major modern uses have been for electric storage batteries, paint, pigment, gasoline additives various metals products and cable sheathing.Mining, smelting, refining, manufacturing of lead containing compound and goods give rise to lead emission. Organic lead emission from combustion of leaded gasoline is 61 per cent of the total emission of lead into the envioument from anthropogenic sources. Other sources of lead dispersion the abrasive action of automobile traffic on lead painted lines on street and highways, resuspension of lead by high speed cars, welding of lead painted structure, or other steel and weathering of lead painted surface with resultant flaking and distribution of lead bearing particle in the atmosphere. The incineration of leaded plastics and secondary smelting of old battery cases, a lead pipe causes lead air pollution.

Lead appears in homes in many forms as lead piping, lead-containing solders, paints, ceramic glazes, base metal utensils and fixtures. Also, cream powder, lipstick and hair colour have lead. Agricultural soil contamination may be responsible for lead found in many herbal medicines and cigarettes.

How Lead Reach into the Body

Lead enters into the body generally gastrointestinal tract (ingestion) and respiratory tract (inhalation). Ingestion occurs via drinking and eating of contaminated improperly glazed vessels whereas inhalations through direct contact or by lead containing automobile emission. In children's lead enters into the body through eating or licking lead bearing residential paints toys and furniture. In both cases the quantity of lead absorbed very important. Absorption from the atmosphere is depending on the particle size, length of exposure and respiration rate. Oral absorption is depending on the source of lead and the nature of diet. Significant quantities of lead transfers to the developing fetus, however the placenta appeared to greatly limit the passage of lead. These factors range from indirect effects of lead on maternal nutritional or hormonal status before and during pregnancy that could affect parental fertility in both sexes. Various studies provided information on congenital anomalies, length of gestation, birth weight, and stillbirth or miscarriage (McMichael, *et al.,* 1986) and on neurobehavioral development (Baghurst *et al.,* 1987; Vimpani, *et al.,* 1985).

Nearly 10-20 per cent of ingested lead is absorbed in body and is extracted through faeces. Once it enters in the body it causes deleterious effect in the organ systems.

Toxic Effect of Lead

Many of studies shows the detrimental effects on physiological, biochemical, and behavioural dysfunctions in animals and humans by several investigators (Goyer, *et al.*, 1979; Ruff, *et al.*1996,)

Lead is a very toxic agent for the human being. It causes potential brain damage, mental impairment and several behavioural aspects besides this is also have an adverse influence on the renal , hepatic, nervous and the reproductive system sharma *et al* .,(2009). It is very toxic to children. It interfere the nervous system of children and causing permanently learning disorders. Symptoms of lead toxicity are abdominal pain, headache, anemia, irritability, and in severe cases coma and death. Lead can shortened the life span of RBC, by this it can damage red blood cells. It also reduces the erthropoitic capacity of bone marrow.

Lead can damages the nervous system by damaging brain cells. It affects the ability to learn. By damaging the brain cells it can make you miserable, irritable, absentminded, and clumsy. At very high doses, lead poisoning can cause hallucinations, swelling of the brain, coma, and even death. It also damages the ability of your nerves to give and receive messages. It can damage the nerves that go to fore limbs and hind limbs. When this nerve damage it can cause your hands to shake; and in severe cases, it can cause your hand or foot to become weak and drop. If wrist drop or foot drop develops, you may never have full use of your hand or foot again. Lead can also affect the children. It causes behaviour problems in children. Some studies have linked learning disabilities, such as attention deficit disorder (ADD).

Lead can be stored in bone tissue for more than 30 years. Lead also competes with calcium in the bone. Calcium is released from bone tissue as our bodies need it. If lead is there instead of calcium, then lead is released into the blood. The bones and teeth store 95 per cent of the lead in the body. In stress condition of body the lead is released from bone to the blood, via blood it enters into the organs. A body is under stress during illness, over activity, pregnancy, or during times of anxiety. If the lead goes from the bone back into the blood, then other body systems are exposed, and problems can begin all over again. Lead that stays in your body is called a *"body burden"*. The more lead you are exposed to, the higher your lead body burden is. The lead body burden is not easy to measure because it is mostly found in your bone tissue. Samples of bone tissue are difficult to get.

A child's tooth can be tested for lead when it falls out. The tested tooth can tell you how much lead is in the child's bones—that is, the child's lead body burden. A special X-ray machine can measure shin bone lead to tell us body burden, but these machines are used for research only.

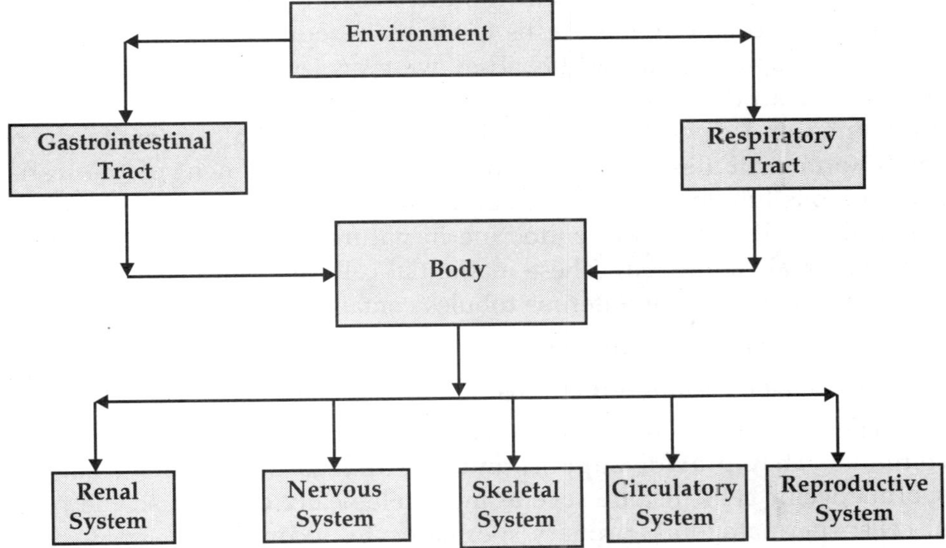

Fig. 3.1: Environment and Various Systems of Human Body

Sign and Symptoms of Lead Poisoning

- Weakness
- Loss of appetite
- Laziness
- Headache
- Depression
- Clumsiness
- Metal taste in mouth
- Infertility
- Constipation
- Stomach ache
- Decreased concentration

Effect of Lead on Male Reproductive System

In humans, there is increasing evidence that the birth sex ratio is altered in areas close to industry and exposed to environmental and industrial chemicals. It is well known that Pb influence biological enzyme system and it can be assumed that multiple mechanism of interaction is yet to be elucidated. The regulatory mechanisms of development of male reproductive system are very complex.

Male reproductive system includes testis, seminal vesicles, vas deferences, and epididymis. Testis is the main reproductive organ for the sexual development and fertility. They were present in scrotal sac, soft in consistency and well vascularised. Each testis is surrounded by Tunica albugenea and divided into 250 lobules. Each lobule is made up of seminiferous tubules. These are the structural component of the testis. Seminiferous tubules were embedded in loose interstitial connective tissue containing cells which are endocrine in nature and secrets testosterone hormone (male androgen). These interstitial cells are called leydig cells or interstitial cells. The seminiferous tubules contain two types of cells:

(a) the spermatogenic cells; and

(b) the somatic or supporting cells.

The supportive cells are also called sertoli cell, they are large and columner. They provide support and nutrition to the spermatozoa. The spermatogenic cells include several morphologically distinguishable types of cells: spermatogonia, primary spermatocyte, secondary spermatocytes, spermatids and spermatozoa. Seminiferous tubules are surrounded by basement membrane (BM) made up proteins (Tung, et al., 1984) which seperates the seminiferous tubules (Fig 3.A Ragini Sharma and Umesh garu, 2011)

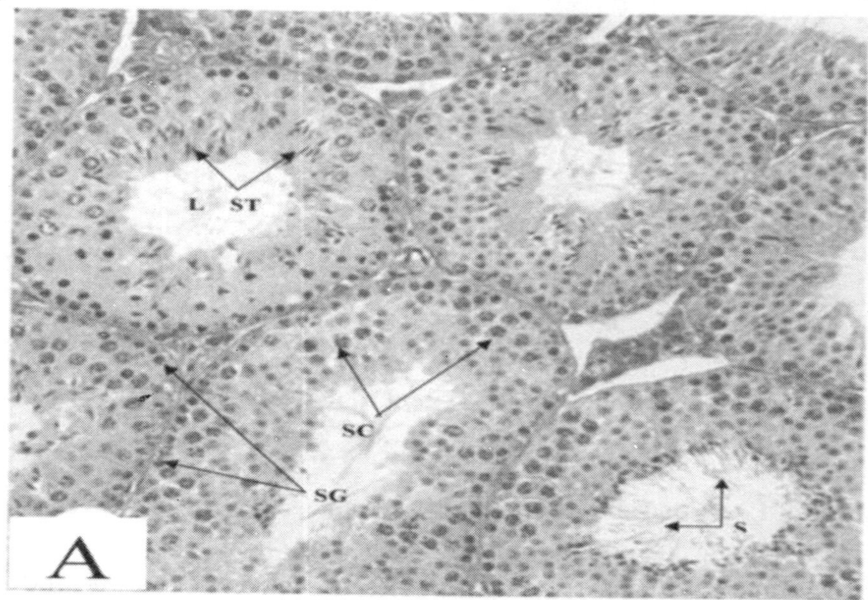

Fig. 3.A: T.S of Testis: Showing Normal Histology of Semniferous Tubules, (L) Luman, (ST) Sertoli Cells, (SC) Sermatocytes, (SG) Spermatogonia, (S) Sperms

Lead was the first metal recognized which have adverse effect on male fertility. The number and quality of sperms in lead workers less than the normal persons. The life span and motility of sperms is decreased in these workers (Xuezhi *et al.*, 1992). It was supported by Telisman *et al*. (2000) who stated that moderate exposure to lead (blood lead <400 _g/l) can significantly reduce semen quality.

The effect of environmental lead on the male reproductive system has been a major area of concern for several years by which the testicular spermatogenesis and spermatozoa within the epididymis are the major targets for lead action to produce toxicity on reproduction (Wadi and Ahmad, 1999). They reported that the major function of testes is spermatogenesis and hormone synthesis to produce spermatozoa. So when the testicular tissue is damaged by the toxic effects of lead, the process of spermatogenes is would be impaired and sperm production rate will also reduced.

Histological observation of toxicity of lead shows germ cell disorganisation in testis. According to Adhikari *et al.*, (2001) high doses of lead cause apoptosis of germ cells which is the common toxic effect of various toxicants.

Lead has an adverse effect on sperm count and retarded the activity of live sperm reported by Chowdhury (2009). Other metals such as arsenic, selenium, chromium also destruct the sperm morphology,sperm count and motility. Allouche, *et al.*, (2009) found that there were no changes in body weight gain and in absolute or relative weight of testes, epididymis and seminal vesicles. In lead poisoned animals tunica albugenia was thickened and blood vessels were sparsed and collapse. Al-Omar, *et al.*, (2000) reported that lead causes decrease in seminiferous tubules diameter in adult rats. They were slightly shrunken and had more or less wavy outline. The basement membrane was thickened and hyalinized. Debris of shaded cells occupied most of the lumen of the seminiferous tubules. It has been shown that lead acetate intoxication during spermatogenesis can delay spermiation as well as release of immature spermatogenic cells in the tubules of testes (Corpas, *et al.*, 2002).They also showed that lead acetate causes decrease in the diameter and epithelial thickness of rat seminiferous tubules. Most of the spermatogonia and spermatocytes were large in size and contained darkly stained nuclei. In some of them nuclear membrane ruptured. Some of the tubules contained only spermatogonia, which were scanty in number, bigger in size and had eccentrically placed dark nuclei. Similarly McGivern *et al.*, (1991) observed a decrease in the intra testicular sperm count in rats prenatally exposed to 0.1 per cent acetate supplemented to drinking water and attributed that to the dysfunction of the Sertoli cells as these cells are responsible for the environment of germ cell proliferation and maturation. Interstitial cells of leydig were also reduced in number and their charterstic tendency to clumping together to form groups were also reduced. Nuclei of these were decreased in size. Thus it shows the atrophy of the testis.

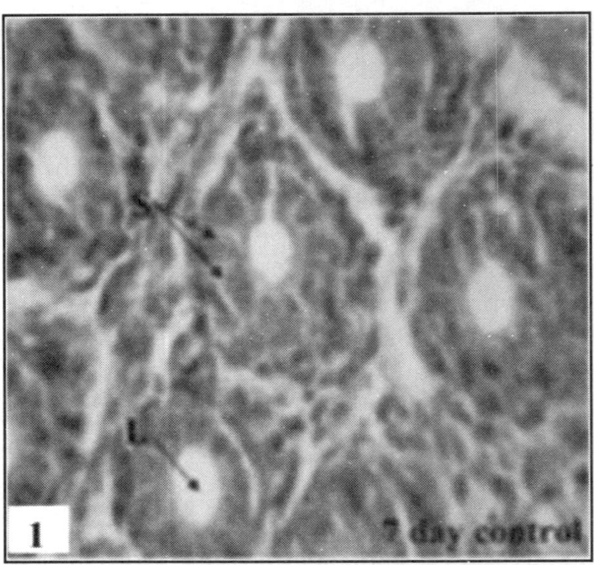

Fig. 3.2: Photomicrograph of Control Mice Testis Showing Normal Development and Seminiferous Tubules at PND 7. Eosin and Haematoxylin stain. X10. (S= Spermatogonia, L=Lumen)

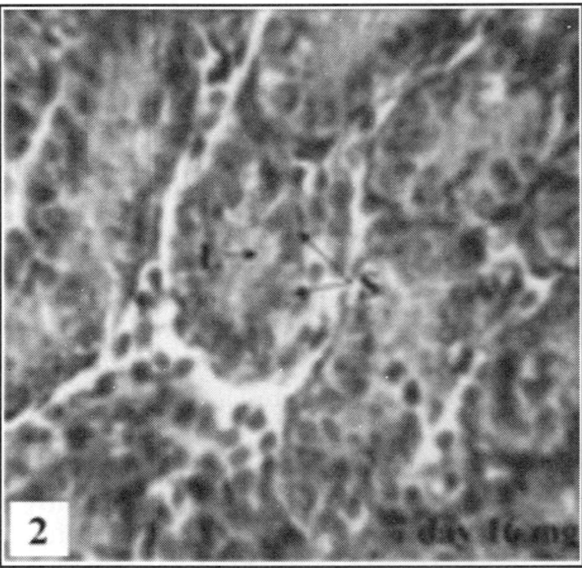

Fig. 3.3: Photomicrograph of Lead Treated (16mg) Mice Testis Showing Altered Distribution and Development of Seminiferous Tubules at PND 7. Eosin and Haematoxylin Stain. X10. (S= Spermatogonia, L= Lumen)

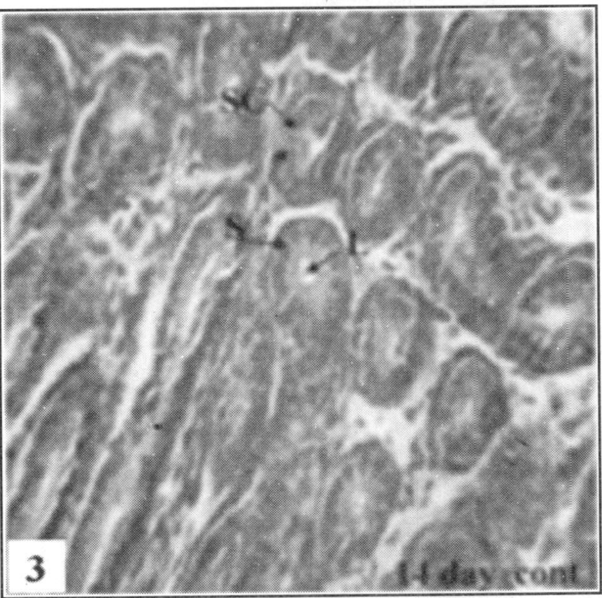

Fig. 3.4: Photomicrograph of Control Mice Testis Showing Normal Development of Spermatocytes and Development of Seminiferous Tubules at PND 14. Eosin and Haematoxylin stain. X10. (S= Spermatogonia, L= Lumen, SC= Spermatocytes)

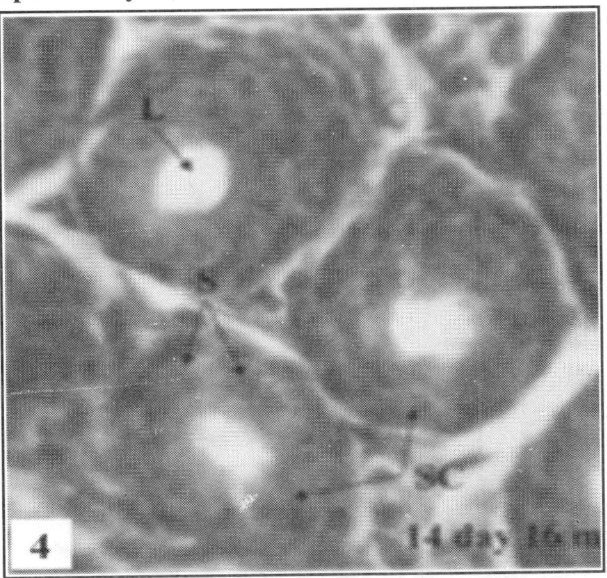

Fig. 3.5: Photomicrograph of Lead Treated (16mg) Mice Testis Showing Altered Development of Spermatocytes and Distribution of Seminiferous Tubules at PND 14. Eosin and Haematoxylin Stain. X10. (S= Spermatogonia, L= Lumen, SC= Spermatocytes)

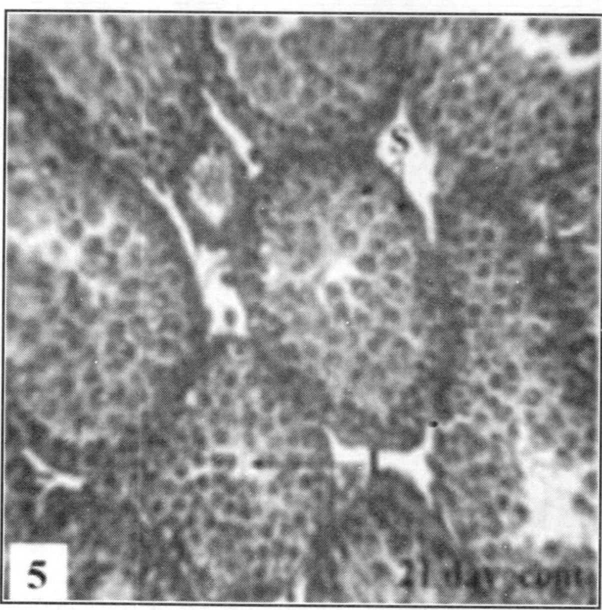

Fig. 3.6: Photomicrograph of Transverse Section of 21day Control Mice Testis Showing Normal Structure and Round Shape of Seminiferous Tubules at PND 21. Spermatogonial Cells are Well Define and Small Interstitial Space in Between Seminiferous Tubules. Eosin and Haematoxylin stain. X10. (S= Spermatogonia, L= Lumen)

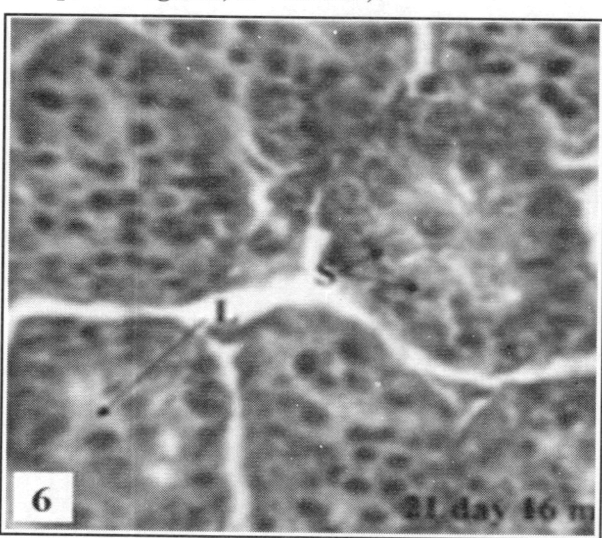

Fig. 3.7: Photomicrograph of Transverse Section of 21day Lead Treated (16mg) Mice Testis Showing Reduction Number in the Spermatogonial Cells and Regular Arrangement is Disturb in Seminiferous Tubules. Eosin and Haematoxylin stain. X10. (S= Spermatogonia, L= Lumen)

Effect of Lead on Female Reproductive System

The female reproductive system consists of a pair of ovaries, a pair of fallopian tubes, uterus, vagina, external genitilia or vulva. Ovary is the main reproductive organ of the females. They are about 3 cm long, 1.5 cm wide and 1 cm thick. Each ovary is suspended from the dorsal abdominal wall by a mesentry called mesovarium. Each ovary is attached to the uterus by a double fold of peritoneum, known as ovrian ligament. They produce female sex hormone (estrogen and progesterone). After menopause, the ovaries become small and lose follicles.

Internally each ovary is a compact organ or solid organ consisting of an outer cortex and inner medulla. The stroma of cortical region is made up of fibroblast cells. Cortex is covered by tunica albugenea. Outside the tunica albugenea, the germinal epithelium is present which is made up of squamous or cuboidal epithelium.

There are number of small, oval and rounded developing primary or ovrian follicles in different stages of oogenesisin the medullary region of the ovary. Every month, a primary follicle transforms into mature or Graafian follicle under the stimulation of FSH (Follicle stimulating hormone) of anterior pituitary.

Lead poisoning is very dangerous to the female reproductive system. Exposure of heavy metal during pregnancy has an adverse effect on fetus. It can make women less fertile and can cause abnormal menstrual cycles and affect menopause. The rate of abortion is also higher in the lead treated women. If pregnant females exposed to lead, it gets enter into the fetus through the blood of the mother. This lead could cause brain damage and even death to the fetus. It could also cause miscarriages and premature (early) birth. It causes abnormal menstrual cycles, decreased sex drive and decreased fertility. In lead exposed females the incidence of polymenorrhea, prolonged and abnormal menstruations, hypermenorrhea were significantly higher. In Polymenorrhea the menstruation cycle was shorter and it is repeated after 21 days. In Oligomenorrhea the cycle becomes longer than 35 days. Prolonged menstruation was defined as menses longer than 7 days and consumption more than three sanitary suspensories per day. The dark-red menstrual blood with blood clots was defined as abnormal menstruation. In females the menstruation cycle was maintained by the gonadotropins. These gonadotropins are follicle stimulating hormone (FSH) and lutinizing hormone (LH). FSH controls the transformation of young primary follicle into Graafian follicle; maturation of ovum and secretion of estrogen by its follicular cells. The LH (lutinizing hormone) of anterior pituitary regulates the ovulation from the Graafian follicle; transformation of empty Graafian follicle intopous yellowish, conical corpous luteum and secretion of progesterone hormone from the corpous lutuem. Growth and function of secondary sex organs are regulated by estrogen and progesterone. Estrogen controls the growth, maintenance and functioning of secondary sex organs of females. Progestrone suspends ovulation during pregnancy, promotes implantation of foetus on the endometrium and development of foetus in the uterus.

Foster, (1996) showed that chronic exposure of lead decreases the concentration of FSH, LH, estrogen and progesterone. Camoratto, (1993) also said that the exposure to a low level of lead can also reduce pituitary responsiveness to a hypothalamic stimulus. Some data showed that many of the exposed lead workers had lower plasma levels of follicle stimulating hormone, luteinizing hormone and cortisol, and a decrease in plasma selenium level Gustafson *et al.*, (1989)

It is clear that when lead is exposed during gestation and lactation it causes several damages in embryo. Prenatal exposure to lead may cause toxic effects in the human fetus, including an increased risk of premature delivery, low birth weight and impaired mental development Falcón *et al.*, (2003). The libido is decreased upto 10 per cent in lead treated females which is significant reduction. However it is nonsignificant in normal females.

1. Decreased fertility
2. Number, life span and motility of sperm decreased
3. Decreased sex derive
4. Atrophy of Testis
5. Miscarriage in female partner

1. Decreased fertility
2. Abnormal masturbation cycle
3. Abortion
4. Premature birth
5. Decreased fertility
6. Decreased libido

Effect of Lead on Reproductive System

Protective Effect of *Tinospora cordifolia*

Tinospora cordifolia is the herb widely used in Ayurvedic medicinal system. It is a large deciduous climbing shrub belonging to family Menispermacea(Anoymous, 1976 ; Nadkami and Nadkami, 1976). Stem of *Tinospora cordifolia* is succulent with long filiform fleshy aerial roots from branching. Bark is grey, brown and warty. Leaves are membranous and cordate. Flowers are yellow and seeds are curved. (Kirtikar and Basu, 1975; Anon ymous,1976).

It has a tremendous healing power. Its whole plant is used as a medicine (root, stem and leaf).Its stem is bitter and stimulates bile secretion. It is used to cure jaundice, skin diseases, diabetes, vaginal and urethral discharge and spleen enlargement (Aiyer and Kolammal, 1963; Raghunathan and Mittra, 1982; Nayampalli *et al.*, 1988).A variety of constituents have been isolated from the root and stem of the *Tinospora cordifolia* belonging to different classes such as alkaloids, glycosides, steroid, sesquiterpenoids. It contains clerodane, furanditerpenes i.e columbin which is the bitter principle, tinosporaside. It has tinosporin, tinisporic acid and tinosporol. It has been reported that it contain various anti oxidants including vitamin C, GSH, and polyphenols (Rawal *et al* 2004).The dry bark of it anti-spasmatic, anti-pyretic, anti-allergic, anti-inflammatory and anti-leprotic properties (Raj and Gupta 1966; Pendse *et al.*, 1977). The aqueous extract it is bradycardic and causes temporary fall in blood pressure. It also reduces blood glucose and brain lipids (Staneley *et al.*, 2000). *Tinospora cordifolia* also increases the immunity. It protects the cholistatic patients against E.Coli infection. Leaves are rich in calcium, protein and phosphorous (Khosa and Prasad, 1971; Zhao *et al*, 1991).It increase body resistance in various diseases (Bhatt and Bhatt, 1996).Lead exposed animals led to significant fall in WBC, RBC, Hb and PCV level as compared to respective controls. It is evident that presences of lead in an organism decreases the level of iron and thus decrease the Hb concentration. The decreased in PCV value in blood indicated the increased destruction of erythrocytes i.e decrease in RBC count. *Tinospora cordifolia* leaf and stem extract significantly increased Hb and PCV levels and at some extent it retained the normal architecture of testis. These extract were unable to protect testis completely. When the extract of *Tinospora cordifolia* along with lead was administered together, it decreases the toxic effect of lead in blood. Oral administration of *Tinospora cordifolia* stem and leaf extract with lead increased the protein, calcium and iron level and decreased the glucose level. Significant decreased in blood glucose level with both extract of *Tinospora cordifolia* suggests its insulin like action.

Conclusion

Lead is a very harmful metal for human beings. Weather it is not present in the free form, it present in the form of ores in the environment. Many of things are made up of Lead. It enters into the body by gastrointestinal tract or Respiratory Tract. It affects our Renal system, skeletal system, Digestive system, Reproductive system etc. It affects male, female and children. In children it reduces the mental growth and affects the learning ability.

Good Nutrition reduces the Lead absorption. A diet with enough iron and calcium prevents worse lead poisoning. vitamin C, zinc, and protein—found in a well-balanced diet—appear to decrease lead absorption. Foods with a lot of fat, such as fried foods, appear to increase lead absorption. *Tinospora cordifolia* also reduces the effect of lead at some extent.

REFERENCES

Adhikari, N., Sinha, N., Narayan, R. and Saxena, D. K. 2001. Lead Induced Death Cell in Testis of Young Rats. *J. of Applied Toxicology.*, 21:275-277.

Ahmad, I., Sabir, M. and Yasin, K. F. 2003. Study of The Effects of Lead Poisoning On The Testes In Albino Rats. *Pak. J. Med. Res.*, 42: 97-101.

Allouche, L., Hamadouche, M. and Touabti, A. 2009. Chronic Effects of Low Lead Levels on Sperm Quality Gonadotropins and Testosterone in Albino Rats. *Exp. Toxicol.Pathol.*, 61: 503-510.

Al-Omar, M.A., Abbas, A.K. and Al-Obaidy, S. A. 2000. Combined Effect of Exposure to Lead and Chlordane on The Testicular Tissues of Swiss Mice. *Toxicol. let.*, 10: 1-8.

Anonymous, 1976. Wealth of India. Raw materials. Vol. X. New Delhi. CSIR.

Baghurst, P. A., Robertson, E. F. and McMichael, A. J. 1987. The Port Pirie Cohort Study Lead Effects on Pregnancy Outcome and Early Childhood Development. *Neurotoxicology.*, 8: 395-401.

Bhatt, A.D., and Bhatt N.S. 1996. Hepatitisc : 9 Major Health Problem of India. *J. Gastro*, 15, 63-67.

Camoratto A, White L.M, Lau Y.S, Ware G.O, Berry W.D, Moriarty C.M. 1993. Effect of Exposure to Low Level Lead on Growth and Growth Hormone Release in Rat. *Toxicol*; 83(1-3): 101-14.

Chowdhury, A. R., Rao, R. V. and Gautam, A. K. 1986. Histochemical Changes in The Testes of Lead Induced Experimental Rats. *Folia. Histochem. Et. Cytobiol.*, 24: 233-238.

Corpas, I., Castillo, M., Marquina, D. and Benito, M. J. 2002. Lead Intoxication in Gestational and Lactation Periods Alters The Development of Male Reproductive Organs. *Ecotoxicol. Environ. Saf.*, 53: 259-266.

Florea, A. M. and Busselberg, D. 2006. Occurrence Use and Potential Toxic Effects of Metals and Metal Compounds. *Biometals.*, 19: 419-27.

Foster WG. 1992. Reproductive Toxicity of Chronic Lead Exposure in the Female Cynomolgus Monkey. *Reprod Toxicol*; 6(2): 123-31.

Goyer R.A. 1990. Lead Toxicity: Overt to Subclinical to Subtle Health Effects. *Enviour. Heith.Perspect*, 86: 177-81.

Goyer, R. A. and M. G. Cherion, M. G. 1979. Ascorbic Acid and EDTA Treatment of Lead Toxicity in Rats. *Life Science.*, 24: 433-438.

Gustafson A, Hender P, Schütz A, Skerfvings S. *Occupational Lead Exposure and Pituitary Function*. Intl Arch Occup Environ Health 1989; 61(4): 277-81.

Khosa R.L and Prasad S. 1971. Pharmacognostical Studies on Guduchi (Tinospora Cordifolia). *J.Res. Ind.Med.* 6. 261-9.

Kirtikar K.R and Basu B.D. 1975. Indian Medicinal Plants Vol. 1 and 2nd ed. New Connaught Place. Dehradun : M/S Bisher Singh, Mahendra Pal Singh.

McGivern, R. F., Sokol, R. Z. and Berman, N. G. 1991. Prenatal Lead Exposure in The Rat During The Third Week of Gestation: Long-term Behavioural, Physiological, and Anatomical Effects Associated with Reproduction. *Toxicol.Appl. Pharmaco.,* 110: 206-215.

McMichael, A. J., Vimpani, G. V. and Robertson, E. F. 1986. The Port Pirie Cohort Study Maternal Blood Lead and Pregnancy Outcome. *J. Epidemiol. Community.,* 40: 18-25.

Nadkami K.M and Nadkami A.K. 1976. Indian meteria meica. Vol. 13. Mumbai: M/s popular Prakashan Pvt. Ltd.

Needleman H.L and Jackson R.L.1992. Lead Toxicity in the 21st Century: Will We Still be Treating It? Padiatrics, 89: 678-80.

Ragini Sharma and Umesh Garu. 2011. Effects of Lead Toxicity on Developing Testes in Swiss Mice. *Universal Journal of Environmental Research and Technology,* Vol : 390-398.

Ruff, H.A., Markowitz, M.E., Bijur, P.E. and Rosen, J.F. 1996. Relationships Among Blood Lead Levels, Iron Deficiency and Cognitive Development in 2-year-Old Children. *Environ. Health Perspect.,* 104: 180-185.

Sharma V, Kansal L, Sharma A. 2009. Prophylactic Efficacy of *Coriandrum sativum* (Coriander) of Testis of Lead Exposed Mice. *Biol Trace Elem Res;* 136(3): 337-354.

Tung, P. S., Skinner, M. K. and Fritz, I. B. 1984. Cooperativity Between Sertoli Cells and Peritubular Myoid Cells in The Formation of The Basal Lamina in The Seminiferous Tubule. *Ann. N. Y. Acad. Sci.,* 438: 435-446.

Vimpani, G. V., Wigg, N. R. and Robertson, E. F. 1985. The Port Pirie Cohort Study Blood Lead Concentration and Childhood Developmental Assessment. *Presented at Lead Environmental Health,* Current Issues, May, Duke University, Durham NC.

Wadi, S. A. and Ahmed, G. 1999.Effect of Lead on Male Reproductive System in Mice. *J.Toxicol. Environ. Health.,* 40: 170-176.

Xuezhi J, Youxin L, Yilan W. 1992. Studies of Lead Exposure on Reproductive System: A Review of Work in Chaina. *Biomed. Environ. Sci.* 5: 266-275.

CHAPTER

4

Saponins
Isolation, Identification, Characterization Properties and Biosynthesis

J.S. Negi, *India*; **V.K. Bisht**, *India*; **A.K. Bhandari**, *India*
N. Singh, *India*; **S. Kandari**, *India*; **R.C. Sundriyal**, *India*

ABSTRACT

Naturally occurring saponins are glycosides of steroids, alkaloids and triterpenoids. They are widely distributed in nature and reported to be present in 500 genera of plants. A wide variety of plants belonging to family Liliaceae, Dioscoreaceae, Solanaceae, Sapindaceae and Agavaceae are the major source of saponins. On hydrolysis, saponins gave aglycone and sugar. Saponins are amorphous substances having high molecular weight. They are soluble in water and alcohol to produce foam but organic solvents inhibit their foaming property. Plants saponins are generally extracted in to butanol through liquid-liquid partition and separated through column chromatography using silica gel as adsorbent and chloroform: methanol as mobile phase. HPLC, GC, Sephadex LH-20 Chromatography, DCCC, preparative paper chromatography and TLC were also used for the separation and isolation of saponins. The structures of saponins were determined by several spectroscopic techniques, viz, UV, IR, ^{1}H NMR, ^{13}C NMR and Mass spectroscopy. Saponins possess a variety of biological activities such as anti-oxidant, immunostimulant, antihepatotoxic, antibacterial, anticarcinogenic, antidiarrheal, antiulcerogenic, antioxytocic, antihypoglycemic, anticytotoxic and antimolluscicidal. Saponins are biologically synthesized by C5 isoprene units through cytosolic mevalonate pathway. 2,3-Oxidosqualene gives β-amyrin or triterpenoid skeletons on cyclization through isoprenoid pathway. The triterpenoid backbone then undergoes various modifications to form saponins.

Introduction

Saponins are plant glycosides which are recognized by their ability to produce a soapy lather when shaken with water. They are widely distributed in the nature and have been reported to be present in at least 500 genera of plants. All saponins are polar in nature thus they are freely soluble in water but insoluble in non polar solvents. They are glycosides of triterpenoid or steroid aglycones with a varying number of sugar side chains. A wide variety of plants belonging to family Liliacae, Sapindaceae and Agavaceae are major source of saponins. Saponins on hydrolysis yield an aglycone known as "sapogenin" and glycone known as sugar. The structure of sugar moiety is generally determined by mild acidic or alkaline hydrolysis of the permethylated glycosides. The individual methylated sugars are then identified either by direct chromatographic comparison with standard or by gas chromatography. Saponins have been classified into two groups (neutral and acidic sapogenin) based on the chemical structure of their aglycones.

Saponins occur in plants of families Liliaceae, Dioscoreaceae, Solanaceae, Sapindaceae and Agavaceae, However, a few neutral saponins have been isolated and characterized from animal resources. Neutral saponins/ sapogenins possess cholesterol like skeleton (C-27). In most of the cases the cholesterol ring is oxygenated at 16, 22 and 26 carbon. This group of compounds is divided into two groups.

1. Steroidal saponins/sapogenins
2. Alkaloids saponins/sapogenins

Steroidal Saponins/Sapogenins

Steroidal saponins are widely distributed in nature and exhibit various biological activities. The aglycone of steroidal saponins is usually a spirostanol or its modification. They are found in oats, capsicum, peppers, aubergine, tomato seed, alliums, asparagus, yam, fenugreek, yucca and ginseng. Dehydration with various reagents e.g. sulphur, selenium or zinc dust, steroidal saponins afford 3'methyl-1,2-cyclopenteno-phenanthrene which contain a terracyclic cholane skeleton related to the steroid type compounds. Some examples of steroidal saponins/sapogenins are digitonin, gitonin, tigonin, sarsasaponin, dioscin trillarin and trillin (*See Fig. 4.1 on page 65*).

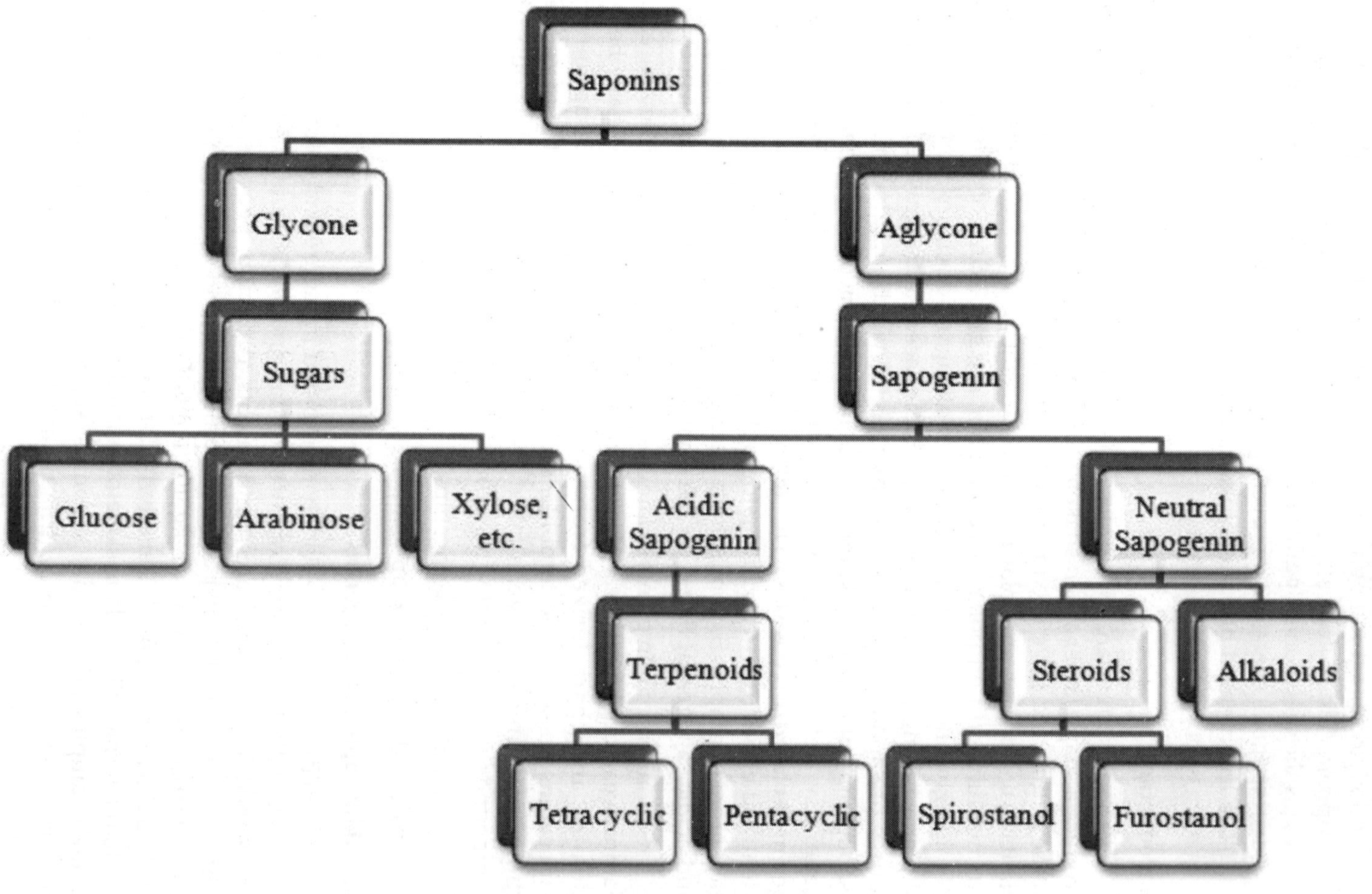
Saponins
Glycone
Aglycone
Sugars
Sapogenin
Glucose
Arabinose
Xylose, etc.
Acidic Sapogenin
Neutral Sapogenin
Terpenoids
Steroids
Alkaloids
Tetracyclic
Pentacyclic
Spirostanol
Furostanol

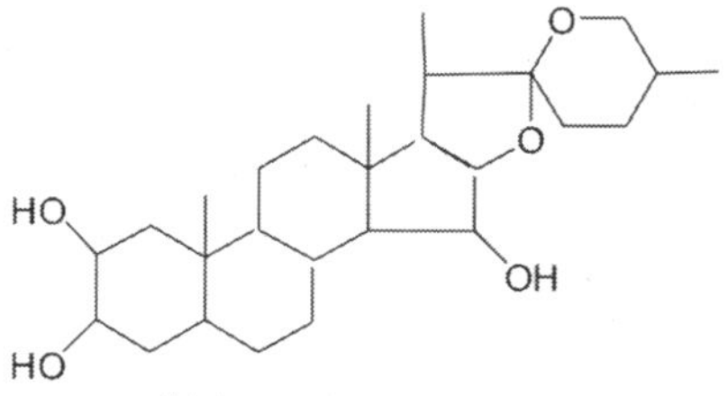

Digitogenin

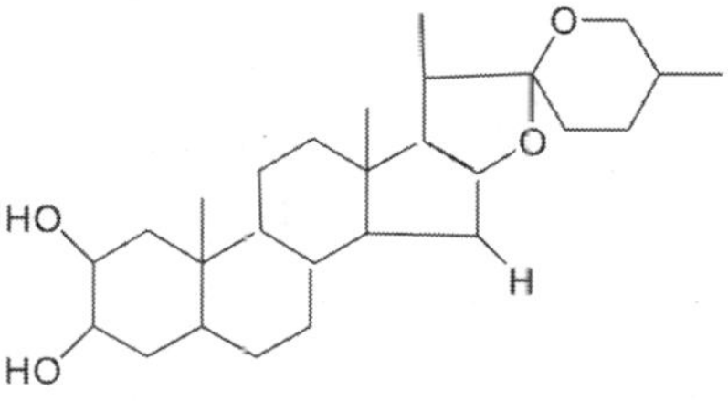

Gitogenin

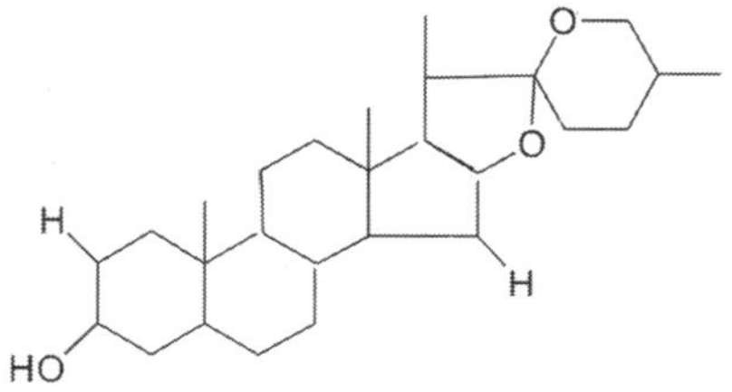

Sarsasapogenin

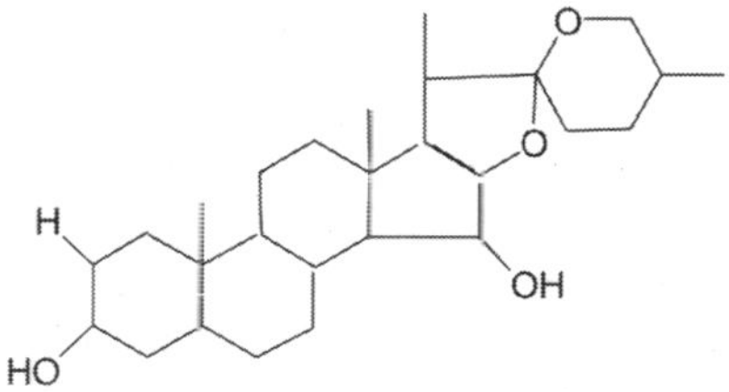

Tigogenin

Fig. 4.1: ***Steroidal sapogenins***

Alkaloids Saponins/Sapogenins

In these saponins, aglycone carry N atom as a bridge between two rings e. g. solanidine (Ripperger and Schreiber 1981) or ring F carring –NH or $-NCH_3$ e.g. Hapepunine in Fig. 4.2 (Kaneko et al. 1981).

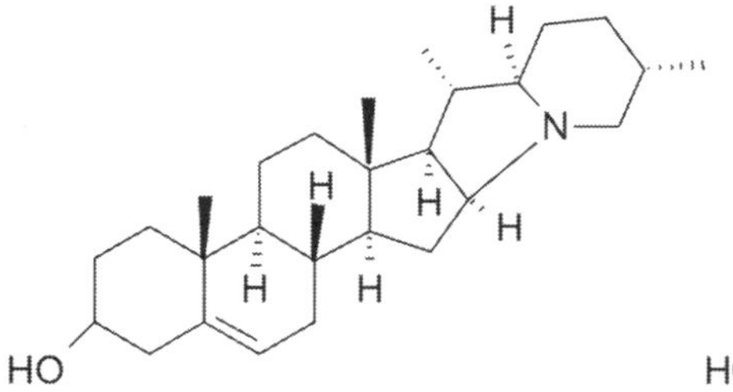

Solenidine

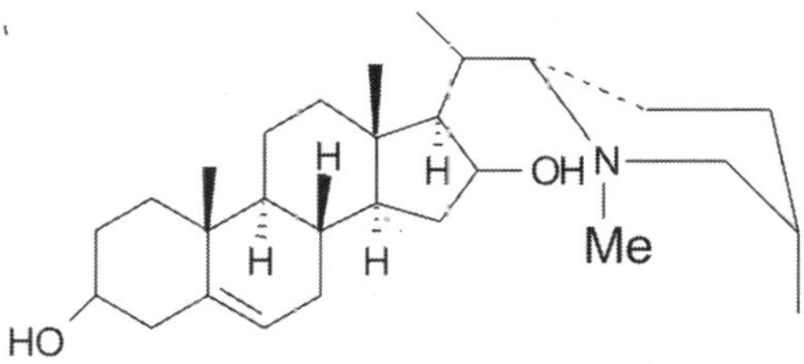

Hapepunine

Fig. 4.2: ***Alkaloidal sapogenins***

Triterpenoid saponins (glycosides of acidic sapogenins) are *triterpene* based glycosidic compounds. Most of the triterpenoid compounds in adaptogenic plants are found as saponin glycosides which refers to the attachment of various sugar molecules to the triterpene unit. These sugars can be easily cleaved off in the gut by bacteria, allowing the *aglycone* (triterpene) to be absorbed (Yosioka et al. 1966). The alternative techniques of cleaving the sugar moiety are also reported. A photochemical procedure for cleaving the arabinoside linkage has also been reported (Kitagawa et al. 1977). Lead tetra-acetate oxidation in alkali medium was found to be effective for selective cleavage of the glucuronide linkage in saponins. The cleavage of sugar moiety containing glucuronic acid consists of anodic oxidation followed by treatment of alkali (Kitagawa et al. 1980). The sapogenins of these glycosides are tetracyclic or pentacyclic triterpenoids which on selenium dehydrogenation give naphthalene, phenanthrene hydrocarbons, mainly sapotalene (1,2,7-teimethoxynaphthalene). Triterpenoids generally occur in family Leguminosae, Hippocastanaceae, Ranunculaceae, Symplocaceae, Euphorbiaceae, Verbenaceae and Araliaceae etc. The aglycone in triterpenoids contains thirty carbon atoms based on six isoprene units. However, some substances which contain more or less than thirty carbon atoms and do not strictly follow isoprene rule have also been isolated and characterized as triterpenoids (Kulshreshtha et al. 1972). Most of the triterpenoid sapogenins, with few exceptions, belong to â-amyrin group and are usually simple alcohol and acids. Occasionally sapogenin is encountered having aldehydic and lactone functional groups. The chemical structure of α- and β-amyrin are shown in Fig. 4.3a. Some examples of β-amyrin group triterpenoid aglycones are cincholic acid, oleanolic acid, gypsogenin, hederagenin gummosogenin, erythrodiol and cochalic acid (Fig. 4.3b) and α-amyrin group are centoic acid, brahmic acid, quinovic acid and asiatic acid shown in Fig. 4.3c.

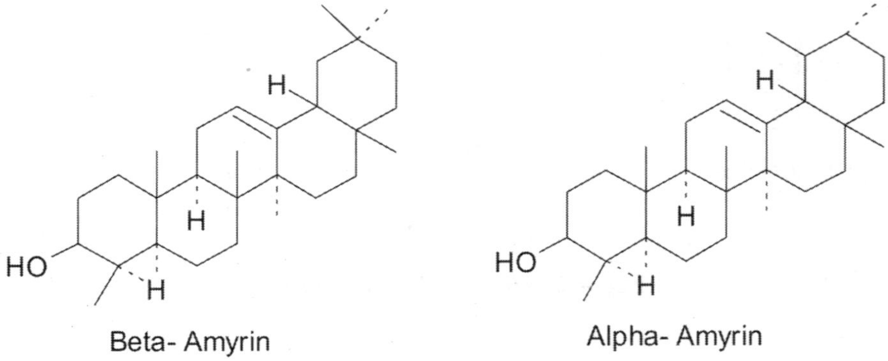

Beta- Amyrin

Alpha- Amyrin

Fig. 4.3a: ***Chemical structure of α- and β-amyrin***

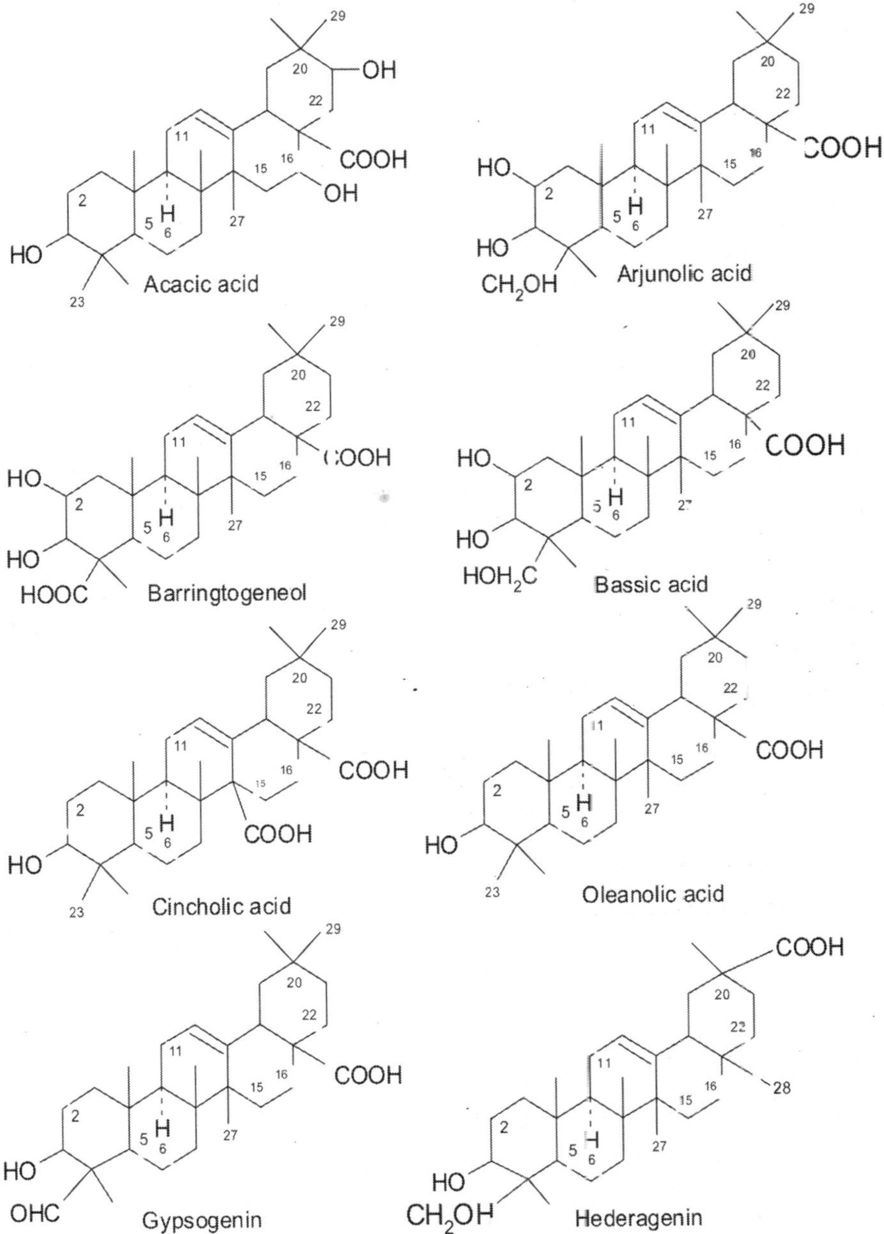

Fig. 4.3b: ***Structures of β-amyrin group sapogenins***

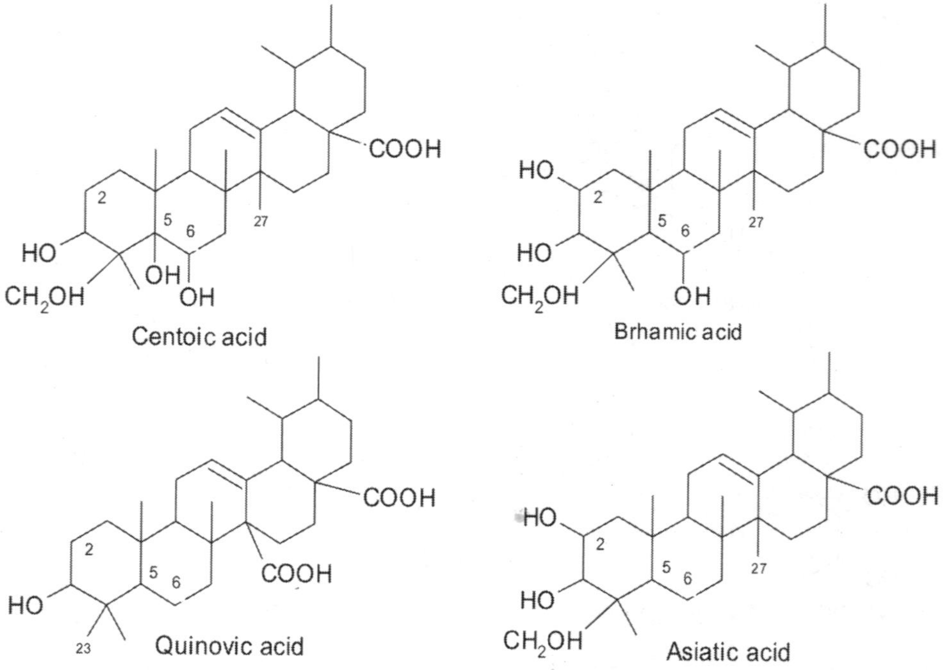

Centoic acid

Brhamic acid

Quinovic acid

Asiatic acid

Fig. 4.3c: ***Structures of α-amyrin group sapogenins***

The tetracyclic triterpenoid genins (Fig. 4.4) have also been reported, there are five examples namely panaxadiol, bryogenin, bacogenins, gratiogenin and cucurbitacins (Basu et al. 1967).

General Properties of Saponins

The structural complexity of saponins results in a number of physical, chemical, and biological properties. Saponins are usually amorphous substances having high molecular weight. They are soluble in water and produce foam but organic solvent like chloroform, acetone and ether inhibit their foaming property. Solubility of saponins is also affected by the properties of the solvent (as affected by temperature, composition, and pH), while water and alcohols (methanol, ethanol) are the most common extraction solvents for saponins. Due to the presence of a lipid-soluble aglycone and water soluble sugar chain in their structure (amphiphilic nature), saponins are surface active compounds with detergent. In aqueous solutions surfactants form micelles above a critical concentration called critical micelle concentration (cmc). Saponins, including soybean saponins, saponins from *Saponaria officinalis* and *Quillaja saponaria*, form micelles in aqueous solutions, whose size and structure are dependent on type of saponin. The micelle forming properties [(cmc and the aggregation number (number of monomers in a micelle)] were affected

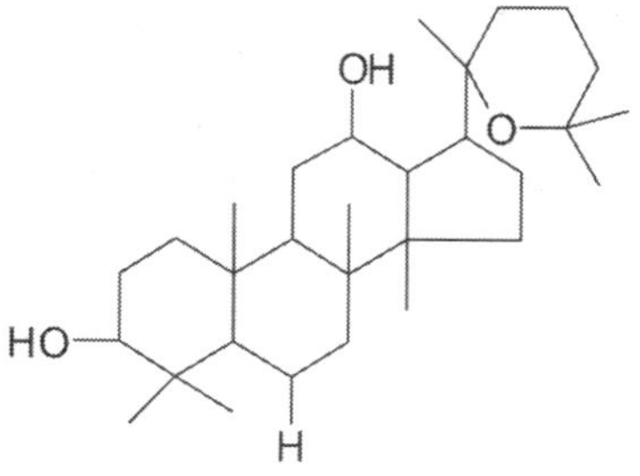

Panaxadiol

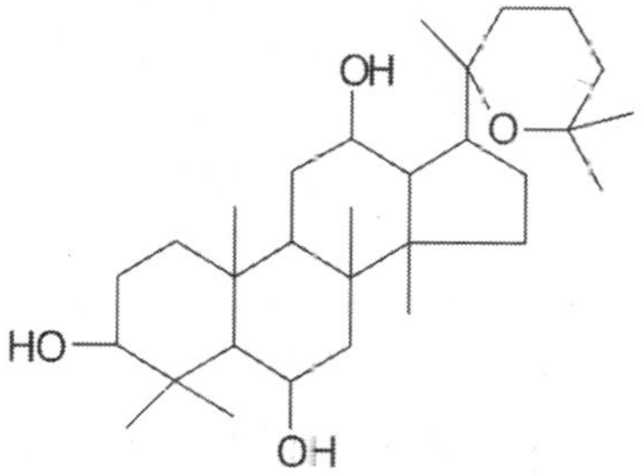

Panaxatriol

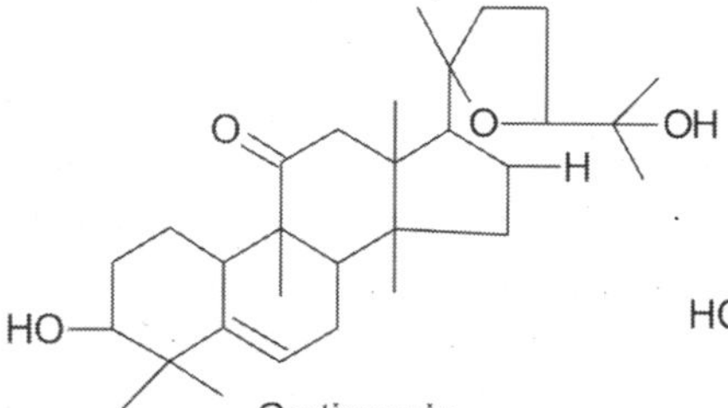

Gratiogenin

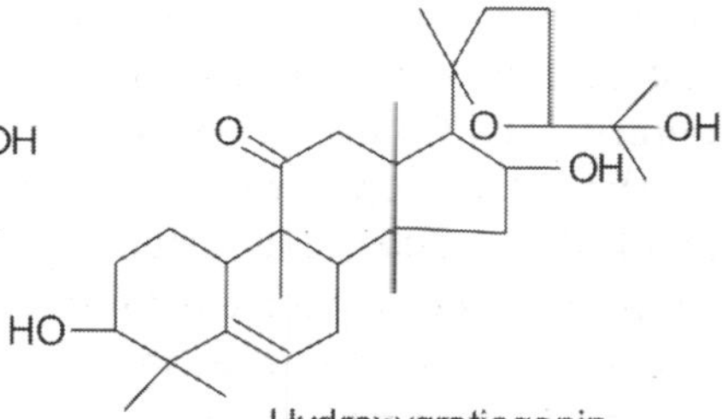

Hydroxygratiogenin

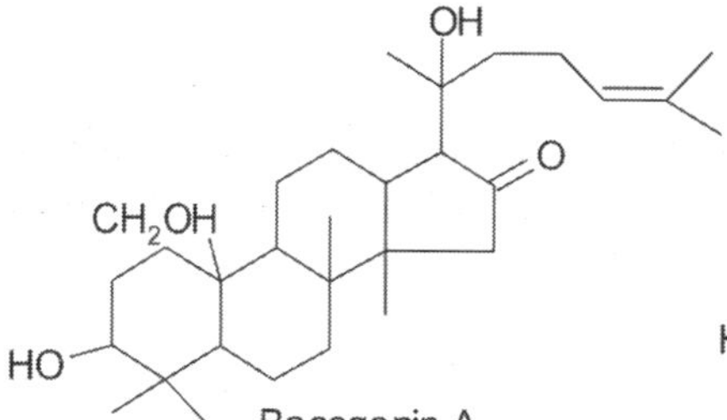

Bacogenin A_1

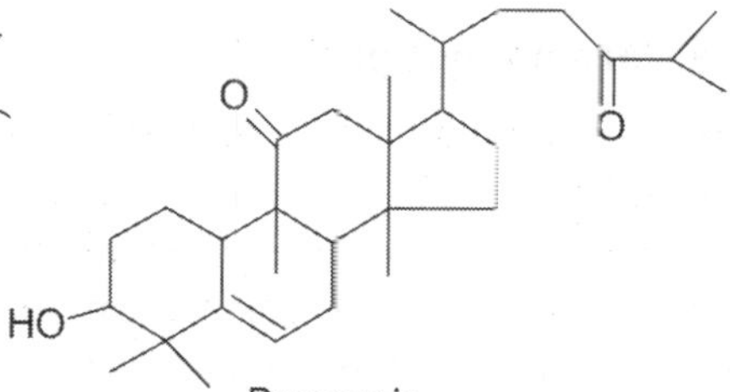

Bryogenin

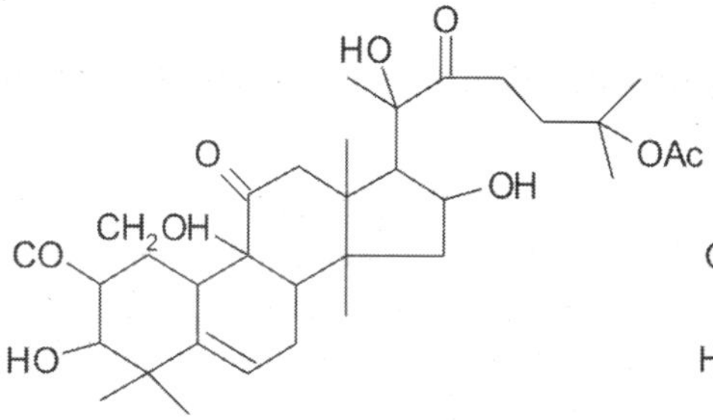

Cucurbitacin A

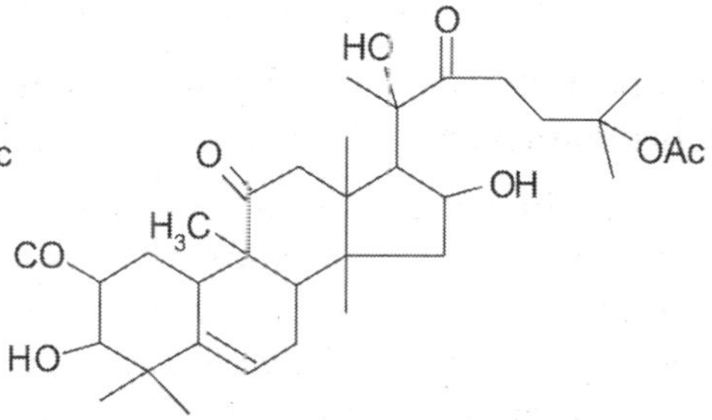

Cucurbitacin B

Fig. 4.4: ***Structures of tetracyclic triterpenoid sapogenins***

by temperature, salt concentration, and pH of the aqueous phase (Mitra and Dangan 1997). The incorporation of cholesterol into the saponin micelles increased their cmc, size, viscosity, and the aggregation number (Mitra and Dangan 2000) resulting in the solubility enhancement of cholesterol. Purified saponins or saponin mixtures may also have a solubilizing effect on other saponins. The extent of the enhancement is dependent on the structure of the monodesmoside saponin, and the composition or concentration of the saponin bidesmosides. They are optically active due to the presence of asymmetric carbon atoms.

Extraction, Separation and Isolation of Saponins

Traditionally saponins are extracted into water/ethanol mixtures, after which the ethanol is removed by distillation and the saponins extracted from the water phase into 1-butanol through liquid-liquid partition (Brimer et al. 2007). Supercritical CO_2 extraction in combination with modifiers such as methanol, ethanol or aqueous methanol has proven successful (Guclu-udtundag and Mazza 2007). High performance liquid chromatography is the most important method of choice for the separation of saponins. Both normal phase and reverse phase columns have been used. However, RP-HPLC with C18 columns and gradient elution seems to be the most preferred method. There are several strategies available for the isolation of saponins.

Column Chromatography (CC)

The extractions of plant material are usually done in aqueous methanol or ethanol. Processing of the extracts is carried out after evaporation under reduced pressure, dissolution in small amount of water and phase separation in to n-butanol. It is currently recognized that only those saponins extracted in to ·butanol which have short oligosaccharide side chain. Saponins are separated by column chromatography on silica gel with mobile phase composed of $CHCl_3$-MeOH with increasing polarity.

Sephadex LH-20 Chromatography & Droplet Counter-Current Chromatography (DCCC)

Sephadex LH-20 has been successfully used for the separation of steroidal saponins. A typical isolation procedure involving silical gel CC and Sephadex LH-20 for the separation of furostanol glycosides of *Asparagus cochinchinensis* has been reported. The technique of DCCC has been applied successfully for the separation of saponins (Ogihara et al. 1976). This technique is based on the difference of distribution coefficients of compounds in liquid-liquid phase such as counter current distribution. Only those solvent systems which form two immiscible layers are used for the separation of saponins by this method. In Sephadex LH-20 chromatography the plant extracts are partially purified by silical gel CC methods before subjecting them to DCCC. This method is useful for qualitative and quantitative determination of saponins; however, it is time taking process.

High Performance Liquid Chromatography (HPLC)

HPLC is liquid chromatography which has been optimized to provide rapid high resolution and separations. HPLC utilizes a liquid mobile phase to separate the components of a mixture. These components (analytes) are first dissolved in a solvent, and then forced to flow through a chromatographic column under a high pressure. In the column, the mixture is resolved into its components. The interaction of the solute with mobile and stationary phases can be manipulated through different choices of both solvents and stationary phases. As a result, HPLC acquires a high degree of versatility not found in other chromatographic systems and it has the ability to easily separate a wide variety of chemical mixtures. The time at which a specific analyte elutes is called the retention time and is considered a reasonably unique identifying characteristic of a given analyte. Different HPLC methods are reported for the separation, identification and quantification of saponins.

Paper Chromatography (PC)

Paper chromatography is a technique for separating mixtures into the components in order to analyze, identify, quantify, and purify the mixture. In this chromatography the stationary phase is the filter paper and the mobile phase is the mixture of solvents. The filter paper holds the components until the solvent dissolves them and carries them up the filter paper The solvent travels up in the filter paper by capillary action. The solvent's attraction to itself pulling it up is greater than the force of gravity pulling it down. The separation of components depends on their solubility with the solvent and their affinity to the solvent and filter paper. The distance travelled relative to the solvent is called the R_f value. For each compound it can be worked out using the formula, R_f=distance traveled by compound/distance traveled by solvent. According to Hultin, (1967) ethyl formate, formic acid and water (75:10:15) is a suitable solvent mixture for the separation of saponins by paper chromatography. Paper Chromatography (PC) of triterpene saponin from *Chenopodium ficifolium* has been reported using Whatman filter paper No 1 and solvent mixtures consisted of butanol, benzene, pyridine and water (4:1:3:3, v/v using aniline hydrogen phthalate as spray reagent (Gohara et al. 2002).

Thin Layer Chromatography (TLC)

TLC is a liquid-solid adsorption technique where the mobile phase ascends the thin layer of stationary phase coated onto a backing support such as glass by capillary action. TLC is a rapid method for determining solvent composition for separations. It is supporting technique in the analysis of saponin fractions obtained from column. This has also been used for confirmation of purity and identity of isolated compounds. Silica gel, DC card, silica gel 60F and RP-18 were used as adsorbent and n-BuOH: HOAc: H_2O (60:15:25), Petrolium ether: EtOAc (8.5:1.5), $CHCl_3$: MeOH: HOAc: H_2O (15:8:3:2) and MeOH: H_2O (8.5:1.5) as mobile phase (Yoshikawa et al. 2002; Radwan et al. 2004; Hadded et al. 2003) for the separation of saponins. Different reagents were used for visualization such as 5 per cent H_2SO_4 and Carrprice reagent i.e. 20 per cent antimonychloride in chloroform (Nandhakumar et al. 2007).

Gas Chromatography (GC)

In the GC instruments the sample was first vaporized and then various components are separated and analyzed. Each component ideally produces a specific spectral peak. The time elapsed between injection and elution is called the retention time. This can help to differentiate between some compounds. The size of the peaks is proportional to the quantity of the corresponding substances in the specimen analyzed. GC analysis of saponins has been carried out with a GC-17A gas chromatograph (Shimadzu, Japan) fitted with a DB-1 column (0.25 mm i.d.×30 m) at 50-230°C column temperature and Helium at a flow rate of 50 mL/min as carrier gas, Shimadzu GC-7A with silicone OV-17 on Uniport HP (80-100 mesh) 3 mm i.d.×2.1 m column at 122°C, N_2 carrier gas at 40 mL/min flow rate was also used. GC of saponins was also carried out on a Tsvet-110, using a glass column (0.3×150 cm) with 1.5 per cent QF-1 as stationary liquid phase. GC-MS of saponins have also been reported using a LKB 9000S apparatus and a glass column (0.3×300 cm) with 1.5 per cent QF-1 as stationary liquid phase and He as the carrier gas at 50 mL/min.

Methods of Identification of Saponins

Colour Reactions

➢ ***Libermann-Burchart Test***

When saponins or sapogenins react with acetic anhydride and concentrated sulfuric acid (1:1 v/v), a characteristic bluish pink colour usually begins to appear immediately (Van Atta and Guggolz 1958).

➢ ***Noller's Reagent***

Triterpenoid saponins when chromatographed on Al_2O_3 impregnated filter paper and sprayed with 1 per cent $SnCl_4$ in pure $SOCl_2$, red colour is developed (Pasich 1958).

➢ *Ehrlich's Reagent*

Steroidal saponins (furostanol glycosides) when sprayed with dimethylamino-benzaldehyde in 60 ml of 95 per cent ethanol, 60 ml of 12N HCl and heated at 110°C for 5 min to develop bright red colour (Konishi et al. 1985).

➢ *Sannie's Reagent Test*

Mixture of sapogenin when treated with 1 per cent ethanolic cinnamaldehyde and mixture of acetic anhydride and sulphuric acid (12:1) or alcohol, phosphoric acid and perchloric acid (30:50:0.5) gives yellow colour on heating (Sannie *et al.*, 1951).

➢ *Antimonychloriden Test*

A drop of saponins solution is applied on the filter paper and sprayed with antimony chloride solution prepared in chloroform, sulphuric acid and acetic anhydride followed by hêating produced orange colour (Stahl 1969).

➢ *4-Dimethylaminobenzaldehyde Reagent Test*

The steroidal sapogenins give brown colour on spraying with a solution of 4-dimethylaminobenzaldehyde in ethanol, phosphoric acid and perchloric acid followed by heating.

➢ *Tetranitromethane Test*

This test is specific for steroidal saponins containing olefinic unsaturation. The dilute solution of saponins in chloroform developed yellow colour with tetranitromethane (Paech and Tracey 1955).

➢ *Anthrone (9,10-dihydro-8-oxoanthracene) Reagent Test*

Anthrone in concentrated sulphuric acid when sprayed on developed TLC plates, exhibits greenish-blue spot of saponins (Kamat and Kawale 1987).

➢ *Chlorosulphonic Acid Reagent Test*

The chromatograms of steroidal saponins and sapogenins showed brown colour on spraying with solution of chlorosulphonic acid and acetic acid (1:2) followed by heating at 110°C.

Hydrolysis

Saponins on hydrolysis cleaved to the sapogenin aglycone and sugar or polysaccharide. Hydrolysis can be done in the presence of acid, base or enzymes.

➢ *Alkaline hydrolysis of the saponins*

Kirmizigul et al. (1995) have reported alkaline hydrolysis of saponins by dissolving the saponins in MeOH (5 mL) pH was adjusted to 12-13 with dry methanolic NaOMe, and the mixtures were left overnight at room temperature. After neutralization with 2M HCl the mixtures were concentrated to dryness under vacuum and extracted with butanol giving hydrolyzed compound prosapogenin.

➢ ***Acid hydrolysis of saponins***

Solutions of saponins in 5 mL 80 per cent MeOH: benzene (1:1) was refluxed for 6 h at 95°C with 2M HCl (5 mL). The organic layers were evaporated under reduced pressure. H_2O was added to each mixture and aglycones were extracted using $CHCl_3$ as Hederagenin. Acidic hydrolysis of *Asparagus plumosus* saponin afforded yamogenin and diosgenin (Sati and Sharma 1985)

➢ ***Enzymatic hydrolysis of saponins***

Enzyme hydrolysis of *Agave serulata* gave hecogenin, manogenin and small quantities of the 9(11)-dehydro analogs of both sapogenins, Yucca species, Dioscorea species gave diosgenin (Krider and Wall, 1952) and *Asparagus* species gave sarsasapogenin (Sati and Pant 1985).

Characterization of Saponins

Ultra Violet (UV) Spectroscopy

UV (200-400 nm) is helpful in the determination of functional groups and unsaturation in the molecule. The unit of the molecule that is responsible for the absorption is called the chromophore, of which the most common are C=C (π to π^*) and C=O (n to π^*) systems. The carbonyl group in steroidal saponins absorbs UV light in the range of 280-300 nm and ethylenic double bond appears at 195-198 nm. Due to lack of strong chromophore in some sapogenins they do not absorb UV light.

Infra Red (IR) Spectroscopy

IR spectra of saponins and sapogenins provided valuable information about the various functional groups and also stereochemistry of molecules to some extent. Spirostane derivatives showed absorptions in between 1350-875 cm^{-1}. The relative intensities of absorptions around 920-950 cm^{-1} and 900-884 cm^{-1} permit a choice of 25 R or 25 S compounds. In 25 S the former is more intense than the latter whereas it is vice versa in 25 R configuration. In Hopane triterpenoids IR spectra is useful for the determination of the substitution patterns of hopane 6α-, 15α-, 22α-, 7β-, 22, 24-triol. Peak at 1700-1702 cm^{-1} indicates the presence of C-12 carbonyl group whereas at 1660-1680 cm^{-1} suggest the conjugated carbonyl group.

Nuclear Magnetic Resonance (NMR) Spectroscopy

^{1}H NMR spectrum of saponin peracetate or permethylate is helpful in determination of mode of sugar linkages. The signals of anomeric proton in the spectrum are assignable to that of a D-glucopyranose (or L-arabinopyranose) unit, the sugar may be regarded as having β-configuration. The J value suggests trans-diaxial relationship of the proton at C1 and C2 of the pyranose residues. When anomeric proton signal appears with J= 1-3 Hz suggesting the equatorial-equatorial or axial-equatorial orientation of C1 and C2 proton. However, the anomeric proton signal of α-D-glucoside, α-D-manoside, α-L-rhamnoside and β-L-arabinoside appears generally at lower field (δ 5.0-6.0) than those of corresponding α and β anomers respectively (δ 4.5-5.0). This difference is also helpful in the differentiation of the anomeric structure (Mahato et al. 1981). In both 25 R and 25 S series, the 27-methyl protons resonated upfield than the 21-methyl protons. Moreover, 27-methyl signal in 25 R appears upfield than in 25 S, hence these two isomers can be distinguished (Kutney 1963).

^{13}C NMR spectroscopy is very useful tool for the structure elucidation of saponins. The chemical shift values for sugar moieties and for few steroidal sapogenins have been reported. The points of linkages are confirmed by the glycosylation shift rules (Kasai et al. 1979) according to which α- and β- carbon of the aglycones as well as sugar moieties undergo characteristic shifts on glycosylation. The α-C is shifted 6-9 ppm downfield whereas the β-C signals move slightly upfield. If 27-CH_3 is axial a small á effect is observed in C-25 signal. This signal appears 3-4 ppm upfield in 25 S neoyonogenins than that of 25 R yonogenin. The difference of deoxytigogenin and tigogenin is reflected in the C-3 signal appearing 45 ppm downfield due to the electronegativity of oxygen in tigogenin. The presence of double bond at C-5 has remarkable effect on the chemical shift of C-5 and C-6 in diosgenin and tigogenin. The signal intensity of the carbonyl carbon is always very low and it is recorded in the range of 200-220 ppm. This can be explained by comparing hecogenin with tigogenin. The C-12 signal is recorded dowfield at ä 213 ppm in hecogenin due to the influence of the doubly bonded oxygen. The C-11 and C-13 signals are also recorded downfield by 16.4 and 14.4 ppm, respectively, in hecogenin. Acetylated C-3 OH group causes a downfield shift of about 2.2 ppm for C-3 (α-effect) and upfield shift of 4 ppm for C-2 and C-4 signals (β-effect).

Mass Spectroscopy

Electron ionization mass spectroscopy (EI-MS) has been shown to be a very useful method for identification, determination of purity and structure elucidation of saponins (Kasai et al. 1977). Saponins containing more than four sugars do not give molecular ions, even when derivatized. However, MS has limited application in the field of underivatized oligosaccharides because it required volatilization and ionization of the sample. Ionization and volatilization are coupled in one process in *field desorption mass spectrometry*

(FD-MS). FD-MS of underivatized steroidal and triterpenoidal saponins have been reported. The spectra show the intense ions formed by attachment of alkali cation to the neutral molecule. A new technique of plasma desorption mass spectrometry (PD-MS) has also been used for molecular weight determination of underivatized steroidal saponins (Hostettmann et al. 1978). The positions of various substituents in the sapogenin are determined by estimating the shifts in the masses of the characteristic fragments with relation of the peaks of the standard. The mass spectrum of deoxytigogenin showed molecular ion peak at m/z 400 and prominent fragment ions at m/z 341, 331, 328, 286, 257, 139, 122 and 115 (Fig. 4.5). These peaks are usually shifted equivalent to the increase or decrease in the molecular weight caused by a particular substituents, provided that this substituent falls in any of these fragments e. g. tigogenin the peak corresponding to 357, 347, 344, 302 and 273 are recorded at 16 mass units more (Faul and Djerassi 1970). All the spirostanols with unsubstituted ring E and F display characteristic fragment at m/z 115 and 139, the former retains both the spiroketal oxygen atoms while the latter the F ring oxygen (Budzikiewicz et al. 1964). In these genins such as igagenin, the peak recorded at m/z 375, 363, 360, 300 and 289 have been rationalized to be formed by the partial or complete loss of spiroketal side chain.

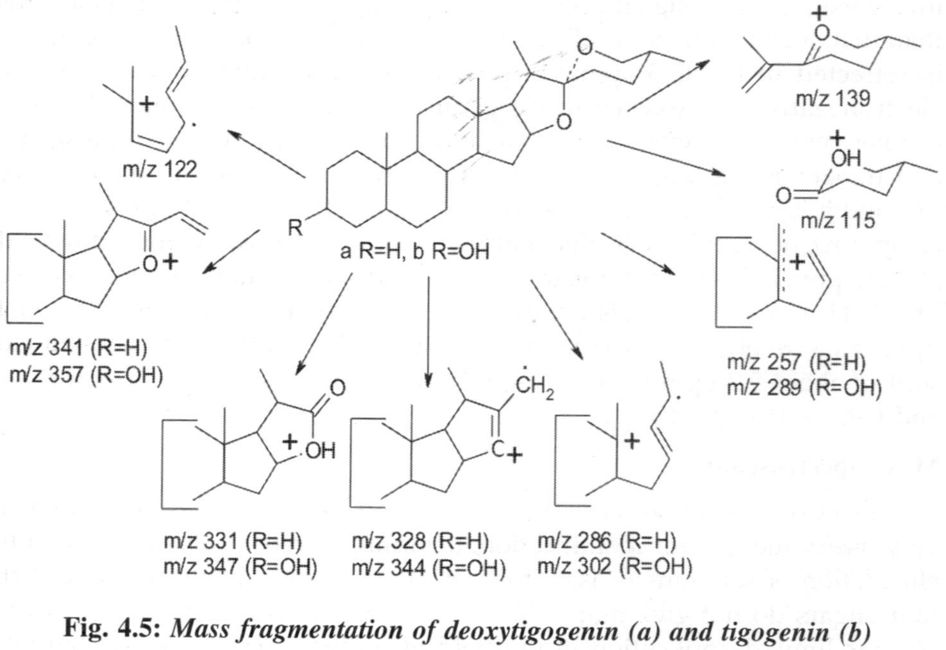

Fig. 4.5: ***Mass fragmentation of deoxytigogenin (a) and tigogenin (b)***

Biological Activities of Saponins

Saponins possess a variety of biological activities viz antioxidant, immunostimulant, antihepatotoxic, antibacterial, anticarcinogenic, antidiarrheal, antiulcerogenic, antioxytocic and useful in diabetic retinopathy and reproduction. Many saponins are known to be antimicrobial to inhibit mould and to protect plants from insects. They may be considered as defense system and have been included in a large group of protective molecules found in plants named phytoanticipins or phytoprotectants. Saponins have been known to have a lytic action on erythrocyte membranes and this property has been used for their detection. Saponin rich plant has been found to improve growth, feed efficiency and health in ruminants (Mader and Brumm 1987).

Saponins from a variety of sources have also been shown to have a range of biological activities and potential health benefits such as hypocholesterolemic, anti-coagulant, hepatoprotective, hypoglycemic, neuroprotective, antiinflammatory, inhibition of dental caries and platelet aggregation (Rao and Gurfinkel 2000; Guclu-ustundag and Mazza 2007). Saponins are known as pharmacodynamic group of natural products with wide range of biological activities few of them are described here.

➢ **General Toxicology and Hazard Assessment for Humans**

Due to the great structural diversity within the saponins group, a large variation is seen in their biological activities. Besides the general action of many saponins their aglycones also cause specific systemic toxicity and cause haemolysis (Francis et al. 2002).

➢ **Saponins as Adjuvant**

Saponins have been shown to act as adjuvant which was first shown for rabies vaccine in mice (Maharaj et al. 1986) and has further been explored by adding cholesterol and phospholipids to the matrix in order to reduce the toxicity of the final vaccine. Saponins have unique ability to stimulate the immune system as well as enhance antibody production.

➢ **Hypoglycemic Activity**

Saponins isolated from *phellodendron cortex* and *Aralia cortex* (Kim et al. 1998), *Pueraria thunbergiana* (Lee et al. 2000) and *Calendula officinalis* (Yashikawa et al. 2001) have been shown to have hypoglycemic effects.

➢ **Effect on Animal Reproduction**

The negative effects of saponins on animal reproduction have been known and ascribed to their abortifacient, antizygotic and anti implantation properties (Tewary et al. 1973; Stolzenberg and Parkhurst 1977).

- **Action on Cardiovascular System**

  A herbo-mineral formulation "Abana" containing 10 mg *Asparagus racemosus* extract per tablet was found to have significant hypocholesterolaemic effect, therefore, used as potential cardio-protective agent (Kharına et al. 1991).

- **Cytotoxic Activity**

  Saponins isolated from different plants and animals have been shown to inhibit the growth of cancer cells *in vitro*. Diosgenin glycoside isolated from Chinese herbal drug "Yunnan Bai Yao" showed significant cytotoxicity (Ravikumar et al. 1987). Saponins isolated from Starfish (*Certonardoa semiregularis*) have good cytotoxicity against a small panel of human solid tumor cell lines. They showed selective cytotoxicity against the SK-MEL-2 skin cancer cell line with an ED_{50} 2.67 µg/mL (Wang et al. 2005).

- **Molluscicidal Activity**

  The molluscicidal activity of the saponins may be due to their characteristic detergent effect on the soft body membranes of the molluscs. The purified *Sesbania sesban* saponins at 2-25 mg/kg (Dorsaz et al. 1988) and *Maesa lanceolata* at above 5 ppm (Sindambiwe et al. 1998) have been found to be active against *Biomphalaria glabrata*. Monodesmodic triglycosides from fruits of *Sapindus rarak* (Hamburger et al. 1992), spirostanol glycoside from the *Yucca aloifolia*, steroidal saponins from *Asparagus plumosus* (Sati et al. 1984) and sarsasapogenin glycosides from *Cornu florida* were found to exhibit strong molluscicidal activity.

- **Antiinflammatory Activity**

  Saponins and sapogenins (saponosides, prosapogenins and ruscogenins) isolated from *Ruscus aculeatus* and *Asparagus pubescence* (Nwafor and Okwuasaba 2003) have been reported for their antiinflammatory activity.

- **Antimicrobial Activity**

  Saponins are generally good antifungal and antibacterial agents. The antifungal activity is found to be more effective with saponins than sapogenins. Digitonin has a considerable fungistatic activity (Assa et al. 1972). Eupteleosides from *Euptelea polyandra* possess intense antimicrobial activity (Goto et al. 1970) against *Saccharomyces cerevisiae* and *piricularia oryzae* as well as some phytopathogenic fungi. *Asparagus* saponins from leaves of *Asparagus officinalis* have antifungal activity in concentrations of 0.5-8.0 µg/ml (Shimoyamada et al. 1990).

- **Antidiarrheal Effect**

  According to WHO diarrhea is estimated to kill about 2.2 million people globally each year, a majority of them are infants and children below the age of 5 year. It is found that shatavari is effective in the treatment of diarrhea, dysentery and gastritis. Ethanolic and aqueous roots extract of *Asparagus racemosus* exhibited significant antidiarrheal activity against castor oil induced diarrhea in rats (Venkatesan et al. 2005).

Biosynthesis of Saponins

The sequence of enzyme catalyzes reactions by which complex molecules in living cells are formed from nutrients with relatively simple structures are known biosynthesis. Triterpenes belong to a large group of compounds arranged in four or five ring configurations of 30 carbons with several oxygens attached. These are formed by assembly of C5 isoprene units through the cytosolic mevalonate pathway to make C30 compounds. They are synthesized via the isoprenoid pathway by cyclization of 2,3-oxidosqualene to give primarily oleanane (β-amyrin) or dammarane triterpenoid skeletons. The triterpenoid backbone then undergoes various modifications (oxidation, substitution and glycosylation), mediated by glycosyltransferases and other enzymes. The cyclization of 2,3-oxidosqualene to lanosterol and cycloartebik skeleton is initiated by participation of a neighbouring π-bond via protosteryl C-20 cation. This cation then undergoes a series of 1,2-methyl and hydride shifts with proton elimination to yield either lanosterol or cycloartenol skeleton. The cyclisation of 2,3-oxidosqualene to sterols and triterpenoids represents a bridge point between primary and secondary metabolism (Henry et al. 1992).

In lanosterol biosynthesis two 1,2-hydride shifts take place from protosteryl cation from C-17, the H-17β goes to C-20, and the H-13α becomes H-17α. Then two 1,2-methyl shifts occur from 14β to 13β and from 8α to 14α accompanied by elimination of C-9β proton. The mechanism of cyclization of oxidosqualene in to cycloartenol is the same as lanosterol except the final 9β, 19-cyclopropane ring closure instead of C-9 hydrogen migration (Fig. 4.6). The steroidal sapogenins are spiroketals having same configuration at C-22 but stereoisomerism at C-25 as in cholesterol. 26 (25R)- Hydroxycholesterol was shown to be the first intermediate (Fig. 4.7) which was converted to diosgenin and diosgenin on reduction is converted to tigogenin (Tschesche et al. 1968; Tschesche et al. 1970) but not to yamogenin. However, yamogenin obtained from 27 (25S)-hydroxycholesterol. Yamogenin converted into neotigogenin on reduction. 27 (25S)-hydroxycholesterol was shown to be the key intermediate in the formation of neotigogenin (Ronchetti et al. 1975).

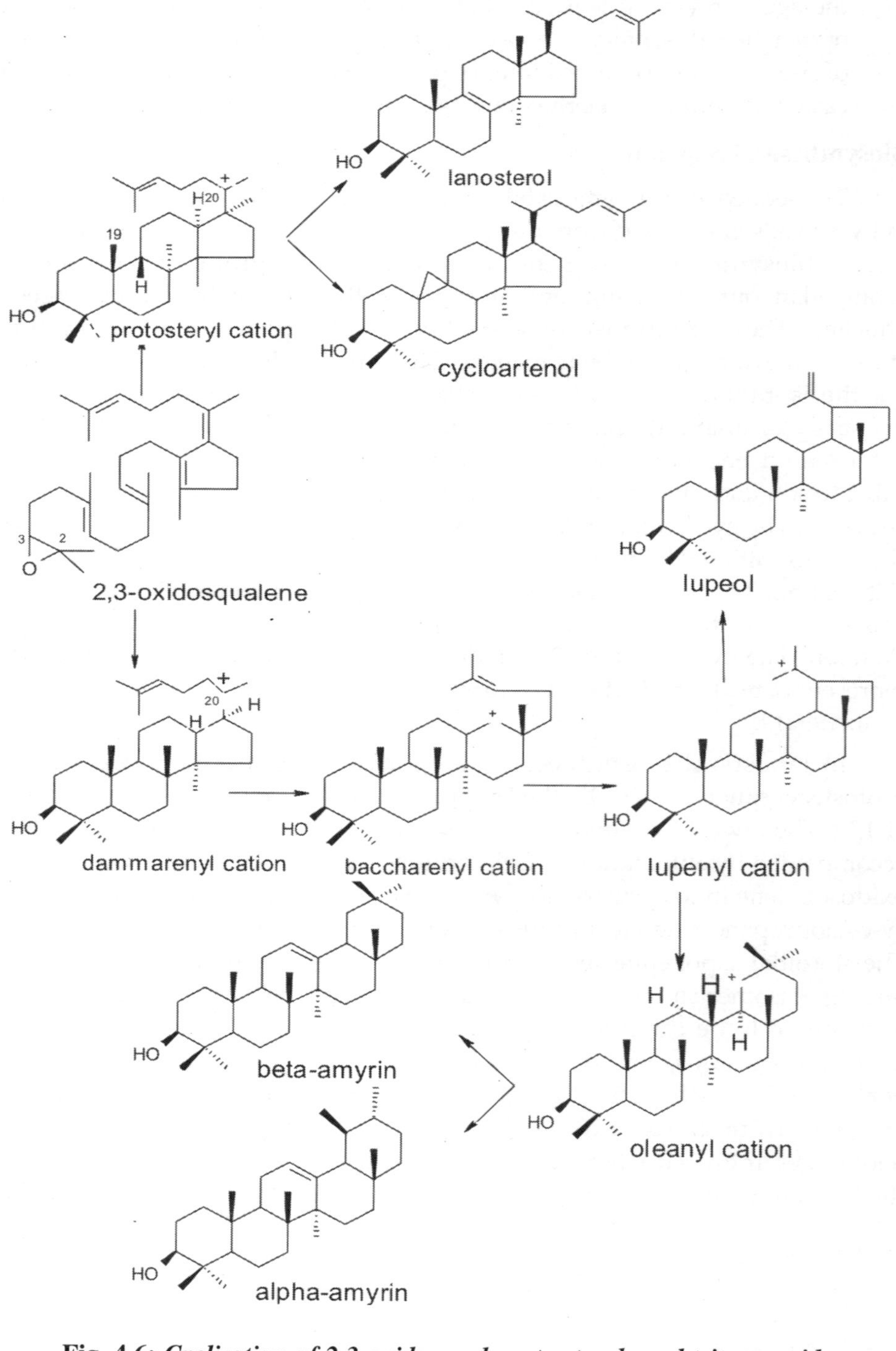

lanosterol

protosteryl cation

cycloartenol

2,3-oxidosqualene

lupeol

dammarenyl cation

baccharenyl cation

lupenyl cation

beta-amyrin

oleanyl cation

alpha-amyrin

Fig. 4.6: ***Cyclization of 2,3-oxidosqualene to sterols and triterpenoids***

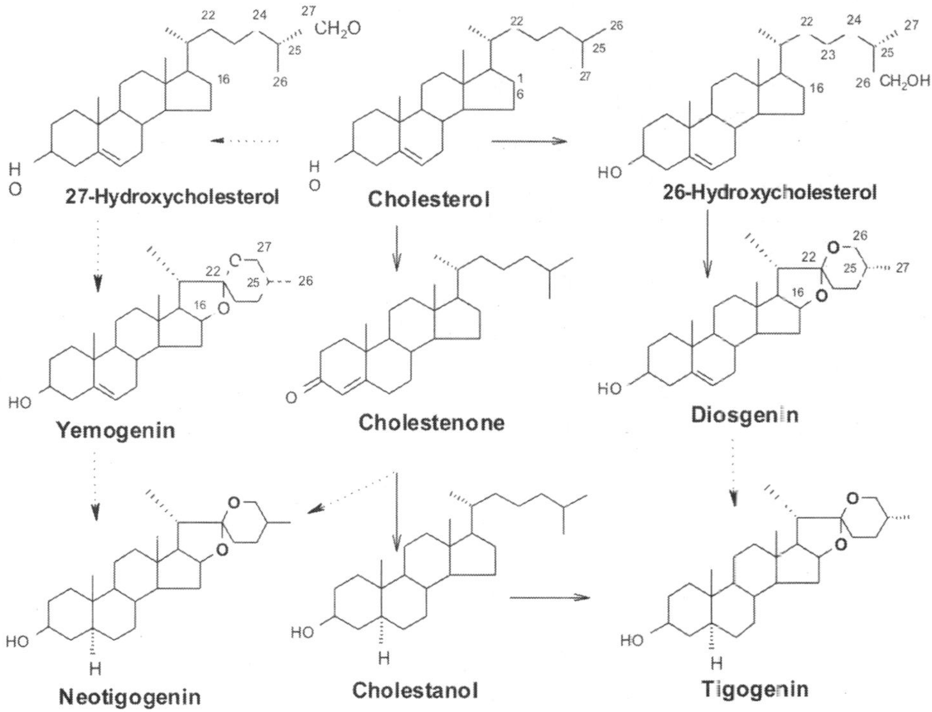

Fig. 4.7: ***Biosynthesis of C_{27} sapogenins***

REFERENCES

Assa, Y., Gestetner, B., Chet, I. and Henis, Y.(1972): Fungistatic Activity of Lucerne Saponins and Digitonin As Related to Sterols. Life Science II, 11(13): 637-647.

Basu, N. and Rastogi, R.P. (1967): Triterpenoid Saponins and Sapogenins. Phytochemistry, 6: 1249-1270.

Breimer, L., ElSheikh, S.H. and Furu, P. (2007): Preliminary Investigation of the Disposition of the Molluscicidal Saponin Deltonin from Balanites Aegyptiaca in a Snail Species (Biomphalaria glabrata) and in Mice. Journal of Pesticide Science, 32: 213-221.

Budzikiewicz, H., Djerasi, C. and Williams, D.H. (1964): Structure Elucidation of Natural Products by Mass Spectrometry, Holden-Day, Inc. San Francisco.

Dorsaz, A.C., Hostettmann, M. and Hostettmann, K. (1988): Molluscicidal Saponins from Sesbania Sesban. Planta Medica, 54: 225-227.

Faul, W.H. and Djerassi, C. (1970): Mass Spectrometric Fragmentations of Steroidal Sapogenins. Organic Mass Spectrometry, 3(9): 1187.

Francis, G., Kerem, Z., Makkar, H. P. and Becker, K. (2002): The Biological Action of Saponins in Animal Systems: A Review. British Journal of Nutrition, 88(6): 587-605.

Gohara, A.A., Maatooqa, G. T., Niwab, M. and Yoshiakib, T. (2002): A New Triterpene Saponin from Chenopodium Ficifolium. Z. Naturforsch, 57(7-8): 597-602.

Goto, M., Murata, T., Imai, S. and Fujioka, S. (1970): Anti-microbial Glycosides of Euptelea Polyandra Sieb. et Zucc. I. Isolation, Constitutions and Anti-microbial Activities of Eupteleside A and eupteleoside B. Yakugaku Zasshi, 90: 736-743.

Guclu-ustundag, O. and Mazza, G. (2007) : Saponins: Properties, Applications and Processing. Food Science & Nutrition, 47: 231-258.

Hadded, M., Miyomato, T., Laurens, V. and Lacaille-Dubois, M. A. (2003): Two New Biologically Active Triterpenoidal Saponins Acylated with Salicylic Acid from Albizia Adianthifolia. Journal of Natural Products, 66(3): 372-377.

Hamburger, M., Slacanin, I., Hostettmann, K., Dyatmiko, W. and Sutarjadi (1992): Acetylated Saponins with Molluscicidal Activity from Sapindus Rarak: Unambiguous Structure Determination by Proton Nuclear Magnetic Resonance and Quantitative Analysis. Phytochemical Analysis, 3(5): 231-237.

Henry, M., Rahier, A. and Taton, M. (1992): Effect of gypsogenin 3,O-glucuronide Pretreatment of Gypsophila Paniculata and Saponaria Officinalis Cell Suspension Cultures on the Activities of Microsomal 2,3-oxidosqualene Cycloartenol and Amyrin Cyclases. Phytochemistry, 31: 3855-3859.

Hostettmann, K., Hostettmann, Kaldas, M. and Nakanishi, K. (1978): Molluscicidal saponins from Cornus florida L. Helvetica Chimica Acta, 61(6): 1990-1995.

Hultin, E. (1967): Securidaca-saponin. Acta Chemica Scandinavica, 21: 1714-1720.

Kamat, S. S. and Kawale, G. B. (1987): Anthrone as a reagent for the detection of glycosides and saponins by thin layer chromatography. Current Science, 56(16): 818-820.

Kaneko, K., Nakaoka, U., Tanaka, M., Yoshida, N. and Mitsuhashi, H. (1981): Two steroidal alkaloids, hapepunine and anrakorinine, from the mature Fritillaria camtschatcensis. Phytochemistry, 20: 157-160.

Kasai, R., Matsuura, K., Tanaka, O., Sonada, S., Shoji, J. (1977): Mass Spectra of Trimethylsilyl Ethers of Dammarane-type Ginseng-sapogenins and Their Related Compounds. Chemical and Pharmaceutical Bulletin, 25: 3277-3282.

Kasai, R., Okihara, M., Asakawa, J., Mizutani, K. and Tanaka, O. (1979): 13C NMR Study of á- and â-anomeric pairs of D-mannopyranosides and L-rhamnopyranosides. Tetrahedron, 35: 1427-1432.

Khanna, A. K., Chander, R., Kapoor, N. K., Khanna, A. K., Chander, R. and Kapoor, N. K. (1991): Hypolipidaemic Activity of Abana in rats. Fitoterapia, 62: 271-275.

Kim, S. J., Kim, Y.Y., Ko, K.H., Hong, E.K., Han, Y.B., Kang, B.H. and Kim, H. (1998): Butanol Extract of 1:1 Mixture of Phellodendron Cortex and Aralia Cortex Stimulates PI3-kinase and ERK2 with Increase of Glycogen Levels in HepG2 Cells. Phytotherapy Research, 12: 255-260.

Kirmizigul, S., Anil, H. and Rose, E. M. (1995): Triterpenoid Glycoside from Cephalaria Transsylvanica. Phytochemistry, 39: 1171-1174.

Kitagawa, I., Im , K. S. and Fusimoto, Y. (1977): Sapcnin and Sapogenol. XXI. Photochemical Cleavage of Glycoside Linkage in Triterpenoidal and Steroidal Arabinoside and Galactoside via Ultraviolet Irradiation of Their 2′-keto Derivatives. Chemical and Pharmaceutical Bulletir., 25: 1977, 800-808.

Kitagawa, I., Kamiguchi, T., Ohmori, H. and Yoshikawa, M. (1980): Saponin and Sapogenol. XXIX. Selective Cleavage of the Glucuronide Linkage in Oligoglycosides by Anodic Oxidation. Chemical and Pharmaceutical Bulletin, 28: 3078-3086.

Konishi, T., Kiyosawa, S. and Shoji, J. (1985): Studies on the Colouration Mechanism of Furostanol Derivatives with Ehrlich Reagent. II. On the Reaction of Furostanol Glycoside with Ehrlich Reagent. Chemical and Pharmaceutical Bulletin, 33: 591-597.

Krider, M.M. and Wall, M. E. (1952): Steroidal Sapogenins Enzymatic Hydrolysis of Steroidal Saponins. Journal of American Chemical Society, 74 (12): 3201.

Kulshreshtha, M.J., Kulshreshtha, D.K. and Rastogi, R.P. (1972): The Triterpenoids. Phytochemistry, 11: 2369-2381.

Kutney, J.P. (1963): An NMR Study in the Steroidal Sapogenin Series. The Stereochemistry of the Spirokeial System. Steroids, 2: 225-235.

Lee, K.T., Sohn, I.C., Kim, D.H., Choi, J.W. and Kwon, S.H. (2000): Hypoglycemic and Hypolipidemic Effects of Tectorigenin and Kaikasaponin III in the Streptozotocin-Induced Diabetic Rat and Their Antioxidant Activity in vitro. Archives of Pharmacal Research, 23: 461-466.

Mader, I. L. and Brumm, M. C. (1987): Effect of Feeding Sarsasaponin in Cattle and Swine Diets. Journal of Animal Science, 65: 9-15.

Maharaj, I., Froh, K. J. and Campbell, J. B. (1986): Immune Responses of Mice to Inactivated Rabies Vaccine Administered Orally: Potentiation by Quillaja Saponin. Canadian Journal of Microbiology, 32: 414-420.

Mahato, S. B., Sahu, N. P., Ganguly, A. N., Miyahara, K. and Kawasaki, T. (1981): Steroidal Glycosides of Tribulus Terrestris. Linn. Journal of Chemical Society Perkin Trans, 1: 2405-2410.

Mitra, S. and Dangan, S. R. (1997): Micellar Properties of Quillaja Saponin. Effects of Temperature, Salt, and pH on Solution Properties. Journal of Agricultural and Food Chemistry, 45(5): 1587-1595.

Mitra, S. and Dangan, S. R. (2000): Micellar Properties of Quillaja Saponin. 2. Effect of Solubilized Cholesterol on Solution Properties. Colloidals and Surfaces B : Biointerfaces, 17(2): 117-133.

Nandhakumar, J., Sethumathi, P. P., Malini, A., Sengottuvelu, S., Duraisamy, R., Karthikeyan, D. and Shivakumar, T. (2007): Anti-diabetic Activity of Methanol Leaf Extract of Costus Pictus D. DON in Alloxan-induced Diabetic Rats. Journal of Health Science, 53(6): 655-663.

Nwafor, P.A. and Okwuasaba, F.K. (2003): Anti-nociceptive and Anti-inflammatory Effects of Methanolic Extract of Asparagus Pubescens Root in Rodents. Journal of Ethnopharmacology, 84(2-3): 125-129.

Ogihara, Y., Inoue, O., Otsuka, K., Kawai, K. I., Tanimura, T. and Shibata, S. (1976): Dipole Counter Current Chromatography for the Separation of Plant Products. Journal of Chromatography, 128: 218-223.

Pasich, B. (1958): Detection of Triterpenoid Acids on Paper Chromatograms. Nature, 181: 765.

Peach, K. and Tracey, M. V. (1955): Modern Methods of Plant Analysis, Springer Verlag, Berlin, 1st Edition, pp. 64-65.

Radwan, M. M., Farooq, A., El-Sebakhy, N. A., Asaad, A. M., Toaima, S. M. and Kingston, D. G. I. (2004): Acetals of Three New Cycloartane-type Saponins from Egyptian Collections of Astragalus Tomentosus. Journal of Natural Products, 67: 487-490.

Rao, A.V. and Gurfinkel, D.M. (2000): The Bioactivity of Saponins: Triterpenoid and Steroidal Glycosides. Drug Metabolism and Drug Interactions, 17: 211-235.

Ravikumar, P.R., Soman, R., Chetty, G.L., Pandey, R.C. and Sukhdev, (1987): Chemistry of Ayurvedic Crude Drugs: Part VIa-(Shatavari-l): Structure of Shatavarin-IV. Indian Journal of Chemistry, 26(B): 1012-1017.

Ripperger, H. and Schreiber, K. (1981): Solanum Steroid Alkaloids. In: Manske, R.H.F., Rodrigo, R.G.A. (Eds.), The Alkaloids. Chemistry and Physiology, Academic Press, New York, pp. 81-92.

Ronchetti, F., Russo, G., Ferrara, G., and Vecchio, G. (1975): The Role of (25 S)-5α-cholestan-3β, 26-diol and (25 S)-5α-furostan-3β, 26-diol in the Biosynthesis of tomatidine and neotigogenin. Phytochemistry, 14 (11): 2423-2425.

Sannie, C., Heitz, S. and Lapin, H. (1951): Paper Partition Chromatography of Sterolic Sapogenins. Comptes Rendus Hebdomadaires des seances de l'Academie des sciences, 233: 1670-1672.

Sati, O.P. and Pant, G. (1985): Spirostanol Glycosides from Asparagus Plumosus. Phytochemistry, 24: 123-126.

Sati, O.P. and Sharma, S.C. (1985): New Steroidal Glycosides from Asparagus Curillus (roots). Pharmazie, 40: 417-418.

Sati, O.P., Pant, G. and Hostettmann, K. (1984): Potent Molluscicides from Asparagus. Pharmazie, 39: 581.

Shimoyamada, M., Suzuki, M., Sonta, H., Maruyama, M. and Okubo, K. (1990): Antifungal Activity of the Saponin Fraction Obtained from Asparagus Officinalis L and its Active Principle. Agricultural and Biological Chemistry, 54(10): 2553-2557.

Sindambiwe, J.B., Calomme, M., Geerts, S., Pieters, L., Vlietinck, A. J. and Vanden Berghe, D.A. (1998): Evaluation of Biological Activities of Triterpenoid Saponins from Maesa lanceolata. Journal of Natural Products, 61: 585-590.

Stahl, B. (1969): Thin Layer Chromatography, 2nd Edition Springer Verlag, Berlin, pp. 857.

Stolzenberg, S. J. and Parkhurst, R. M. (1977): Blastocidal and contraceptive Actions by an Extract and Compounds from Endod (Phytolacca dodecandra). Contraception, 14: 39-51.

Tewary, P. V., Chaturvedi, C. and Pandey, V. B. (1973): Antifertility Activity of Costus Speciosus Sm. Indian Journal of Pharmacology, 35: 114-115.

Tschesche, R., Fritz, R. and Josst, G. (1970): Vergleich der spirostanolbiogenese aus cholestanol und cholestanon. Koprostanol ist keine vorstufe für cardenolide oder sapogenine. Phytochemistry, 9: 371-376.

Tschesche, R., Hulpke, H. and Fritz, R. (1968): Zur biosynthese von steroidderivaten im pflanzenreich-X : Zur spirostanol-biogenese aus Δ4-cholestenon und aus anderen möglichen vorstufen. Phytochemistry, 7: 2021-2026.

Van Atta, G. R. and Guggolz, J. (1958): Forage Constiuents, Detection of Saponins and sapogenins on paper chromatograms by liebermann-burchard reagent. Journal of Agricultural and Food Chemistry, 6: 849-850.

Venkatesan, N., Thiyagarajan, V., narayanan, S., Arul, A., Raja, S., Kumar, S.G.V., Rajarajan, T. and Perianayagam, J.B. (2005): Anti-diarrhoeal Potential of Asparagus Racemosus Wild Root Extracts in Laboratory Animals. Journal of Pharmacology and Pharmaceutical Sciences, 8: 39-45.

Wang, W., Jang, H. and Hong, J. (2005): New Cytotoxic Sulfated Saponins from the Starfish Certonardoa Semiregularis. Archives of Pharmacal Research, 28(3): 285-289.

Yashikawa, M., Murakami, T., Kishi, A., Kageura, T. and Matsuda, H. (2001): Medicinal Flowers III. Marigold. (1): Hypoglycemic, Gastric Emptying Inhibitory, and gastroprotective Principles and New Oleanane-type Triterpene Oligoglycosides, calendasaponins a, b, c, and d, from Egyptian Calendula officinalis. Chemical and Pharmaceutical Bulletin, 49: 863-870.

Yoshikawa, M., Morikawa, T., Nakano, K., Pong-Priyadacha, Y., Murakami, T. and Matsuda, H. Characterization of New Sweet Triterpene Saponins from Albizia myriophylla. Journal of Natural Products, 65: 1641-1642.

Yosioka, I., Fujio, M., Osamura, M. and Kitagawa, I. (1966): A Hotel Cleavage Method of Saponin with Soil Bacteria, Intending to the Genuine Sapogenin: On Senega and Panax Saponins. Tetrahedron Letters, I: 6303-6308.

CHAPTER 5

Ameliorating Effects of Vitamin E and C on Lead Acetate Induced Swiss Mice

Manoj Kumar Panda; *India*

ABSTRACT

Lead (Pb) is a ubiquitous environmental pollutant, which enters into the biological system mainly through anthropogenic activities and manifests pathologic conditions in a various tissues of human beings. Mechanistically, a good number of metals including lead can induce the generation of singlet oxygen species in cells which are crucial in damaging the structure and function of tissues. On the contrary, intracellular defense systems including both enzymatic and non-enzymatic antioxidants are known to safe guard the tissues against metal induced oxygen toxicity. However, the increased or decreased activity of the antioxidants fairly depends on the quantum of oxygen radicals generated due to metal catalysis. Sometimes extraneous supplementation of antioxidant vitamins becomes necessary under conditions of inhibition of intracellular defense by the noxious oxygen radicals. Keeping the information in view, lead acetate injected Swiss mice (5mg/kg b.w.) through intraperitoneal route, were utilized to assess the adverse effects of lead in liver and testis tissues. Lead induced oxidative stress was measured in the respective tissues at 5th-8th weeks of post treatment. Lipid per-oxidation, an index of oxidative stress, was found to increase significantly in the above tissues in lead treated group of mice compared to the vehicle injected controls. Catalase and peroxidase enzymes, as a part of enzymatic antioxidant system and the concentration of ascorbic acid (vit. C), the non-enzymatic antioxidant vitamin, were assessed to evaluate the quantum of lead induced oxidative stress in the concerned tissue. Results of the present study indicated the significant declinein vit. C content of lead induced mice compared to controls; while the enzymatic parameters were significantly increased with respect to the control mice, indicating the adaptive response conferred by the antioxidant defense system to tissues under metal induced oxidative stress. However, extraneous supplementation of vitamins likes vitamin C, vitamin E and vit. (E+C) to the lead-induced mice groups could ameliorate the oxidative stress by declining lipid per-oxidation, increasing the level of ascorbic acid and antioxidative enzymes.

Key words: Lead acetate; Lipid peroxidation; Oxidative stress; Liver; Testis; Catalase; Peroxidase; VitC; VitE.

Introduction

Human beings are exposed to the heavy metal lead from different sources like contaminated water, air and food (Alphen, 1999). Since, lead is not known to serve any biological function; its mere presence in the body can lead to toxic manifestations even in lower quantities (Wang et al., 2006). Almost all of the organs in humans (Adonylo and Oteiza, 1999; Stohs and Bagchi 1995; Soldin et al., 2003; Mishra and Acharya, 2004; Hernandez-Ochoa et al., 2006) are susceptible sites for lead toxicity. Lead generates Reactive Oxygen Species (ROS) (Gurer et al., 1999; Ercal et al., 2000, 2001; Ding et al., 2001) which are instrumental in degrading cellular macromolecules (Stohs and Bagchi, 1995) and finally initiate pathologic conditions.

In order to safeguard the tissues from oxidative injury, cells are generally equipped with intracellular defense system comprising of both enzymatic and non-enzymatic antioxidants which capably scavenge or quench the Reactive Oxygen Species (ROS) and protect the cells from oxidative injury (Heffner and Repine, 1989; Halliwell and Gutteridge, 1992). Under normal physiological conditions, the concentrations of these antioxidants are maintained properly. In presence of stressors including metal ions, chemicals, radiations, pesticides and xenobiotics, the concentration of these antioxidants are increased to scavenge the ROS and, thus, the toxicity is combated. Extraneous supplementation of vitamins, to stressed cells accelerates the functioning of the enzymatic antioxidants, can recycle activity of some vitamins and/or terminate the irreversible lipid per-oxidation (Sies, 1991).

Experimental evidence indicates that lead ions are able to induce the generation of ROS in tissues like liver and testis (Stohs and Bagchi, 1995; Acharya and Acharya 1997). Liver, in vertebrates play a fundamental role in biotransformation process of toxic substances and happen to be the most adequate organ for evaluating response against most environmental pollutants. Testes, on the other hand, the male reproductive organ and is the site of formation of spermatozoa. Moreover, lead is variously reviewed as a metal that exhibits reproductive toxicity and carcinogenicity (Landrigan et al., 2000). Spermatogonial cells, the precursor of spermatozoa, are sensitive to many metals including lead and thus are altered both structurally and functionally (Acharya et al., 1997).

Keeping this information in view, the present study has been undertaken to evaluate the toxic effects of lead on liver and testes. The protective role of extraneous supplementation of vitamins on certain cellular antioxidant defense in combating the metal toxicity is also evaluated.

Materials and Methods

Test Animal

Male Swiss mice (*Mus musculus*) 9-10 weeks old, procured from a live animal supply farm (M/S Ghosh Enterprises, Kolkata, India) and were employed as test animals in the present study. Mice were acclimated to laboratory conditions with regular temperature control ranging from 23±2°C with balanced diet and water *ad libitum.*

Test Chemicals

1. Lead acetate (Pb) is a known mutagen and carcinogen manufactured by BDH and marketed by Merck, India, Ltd., was used as the test chemical. The chemical formula of lead acetate is $Pb(C_2H_8O_6)_2.3H_2O$.
2. Tochopheryl acetate (vit. E) bearing the chemical formula (á-tochopherol, $C_{29}H_{50}O_2$) manufactured by E-merck India Ltd., Mumbai, was tested here for its efficiency in protecting mice from genotoxic effects of lead acetate.
3. L-Ascorbic acid (vitC) bearing the chemical formula $C_6H_8O_6$, a widely tested antioxidant in genotoxic studies, manufactured by Loba Chemicals, India was used in the study.

End Points Selected for Study

1. Evaluation of lipid peroxidation potential of testes and liver from week five to eight.
2. Estimation of protein content of liver and testes in Pb-treated, Pb+vit.C, Pb+vit.E and Pb+vit.(E+C) treated mice.

3. Estimation of Ascorbic acid content of liver and testes of mice.
4. Estimation of catalase and peroxidase enzymes in the above tissues.

Experimental Protocol

Hundred-twenty healthy male Swiss mice ranging from 15 to 20g body weight were selected and randomly divided into five groups (twenty-four mice/group). The first group of mice was injected with distilled water. The second group was injected with lead acetate (5mg/kg body weight) only; while the third group of mice was injected simultaneously with lead acetate + vitC (10mg/kg body weight), fourth group of mice was injected with lead acetate + vitE (100mg/kg body weight) and the fifth group was injected with lead acetate + vitE + vitC. All the mice were injected through intraperitoneal route. Dilution of chemicals were so made that the volume of each injection was maintained to 1ml/100g body weight of mice. Mice from each group were sacrificed from 5th to 8th weeks of post-treatment. Both liver and testes were dissected out, free from other accessory tissues.

Procedure

Assay of Lipid Peroxidation

Mice from each group were sacrificed from 5th to 8th weeks post treatment: liver and testes were dissected out, free from other accessory tissues. Both tissues were processed for the determination of lipid peroxidation potential (LPP) following the simplified thiobarbituric acid (TBA) of Stroev and Makarova (1989). Amount of TBA reactive substances (TBA-Rs) produced in ì mol/g of wet tissue were calculated.

Assay Protein

Estimation of protein was done by following the standard method of Lowry et al. (1951).

Assay of Ascorbic Acid

Ascorbic acid was extracted by homogenizing and centrifuging the tissue with 5 per cent cold trichloroacetic acid. The supernatant was used to estimate the ascorbic acid concentration following the method of Roe (1954) with minimum modification as suggested by Tewary and Pandey (1957).

Assay of Enzymes

For enzyme estimation tissues were processed by mincing in ice-cold saline (0.85% (w/v) NaCl) and homogenized gently in phosphate buffer, pH 7.4 at 0-4°C using a glass-potter type homogenizer at 500-800rpm in ice. The homogenates were filtered through a muslin cloth and were centrifuged at 10,000 rpm for 30 min at 4°C to obtain supernatants of tissue homogenates.

The resultant supernatants were immediately processed for measuring levels of enzyme activity of peroxidase (PD) and catalase (CT).

Assay of PD Activity

PD activity was determined following the method of Maehly and Chance (1967). The concentration of purpurogallin formed was determined using a spectrophotometer (Systronics 106) at 430nm. The enzyme activity was expressed in U/mg of tissue protein.

Assay of CT Activity

Catalase activity was estimated following the method of Mittal and Dubey (1995). Optical density (OD) was recorded in the digital spectrophotometer (Systronics 106) at 570nm. The enzyme activity was expressed in U/mg of tissue protein.

Stastical Analysis

Data generated from different tissues were calculated and comparison of data was done between control and experimental tissue following Students't' test. Data generated at the level of 0.05 were considered significant.

Results

Results of the present study indicated a sharp and significant increase in LPP in both liver and testes tissues in lead-exposed mice compared to controls (Pd≤0.001) over the post-treatment phase. In lead-treated mice group supplemented with vitamins, LPP level declined significantly (Pd≤0.05 and Pd≤0.01) over the post-treatment weeks; but it could not approach to the control level. Significant decline of LPP in both the tissues have been observed in Pb-treated mice supplemented with vitamin E than the lead-treated mice groups over the post-treatment phase. Supplementation of both vitamins (C+E) to lead-treated mice, however, could significantly decline the LPP (Graph 5.1).

Protein content of both liver and testes significantly declined throughout the 5th - 8th week (Pd≤0.001) post-treatment phase. Treatment with vitamins could enhance the protein content (Pd≤0.001 and Pd≤0.01) to some extent (Graph 5.2).

Ascorbic acid content of both liver and testes significantly declined (Pd≤0.001) throughout the post-treatment phase. Treatment with vitamins could enhance vitamin C content (Pd≤0.01, Pd≤0.001, P d≤0.02) to some extent (Graph 5.3).

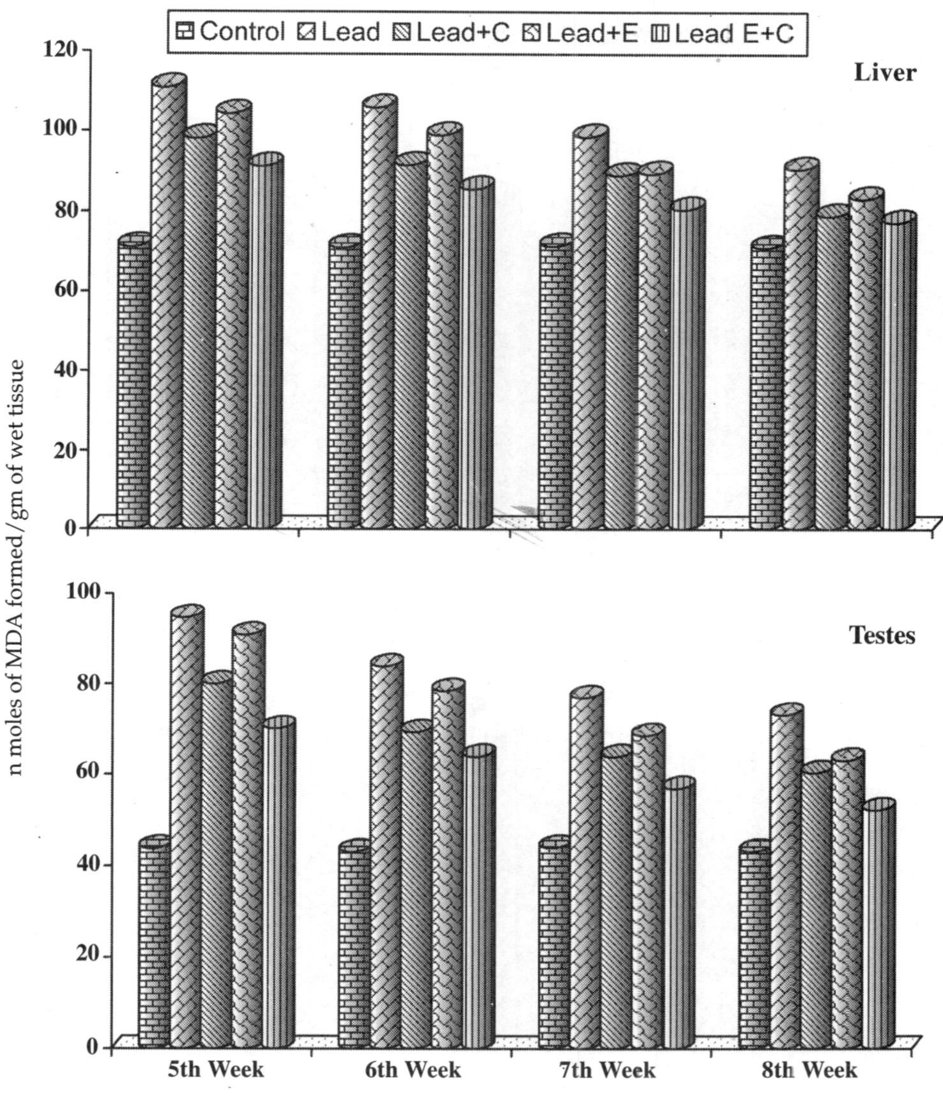

Graph 5.1: Effect of single intraperitoneal injection of lead acetate (5mg/kg b.w.) on lipid perixodation malonicdialdehyde (m moles/gm of wet. tissue) in tissues of Swiss mice

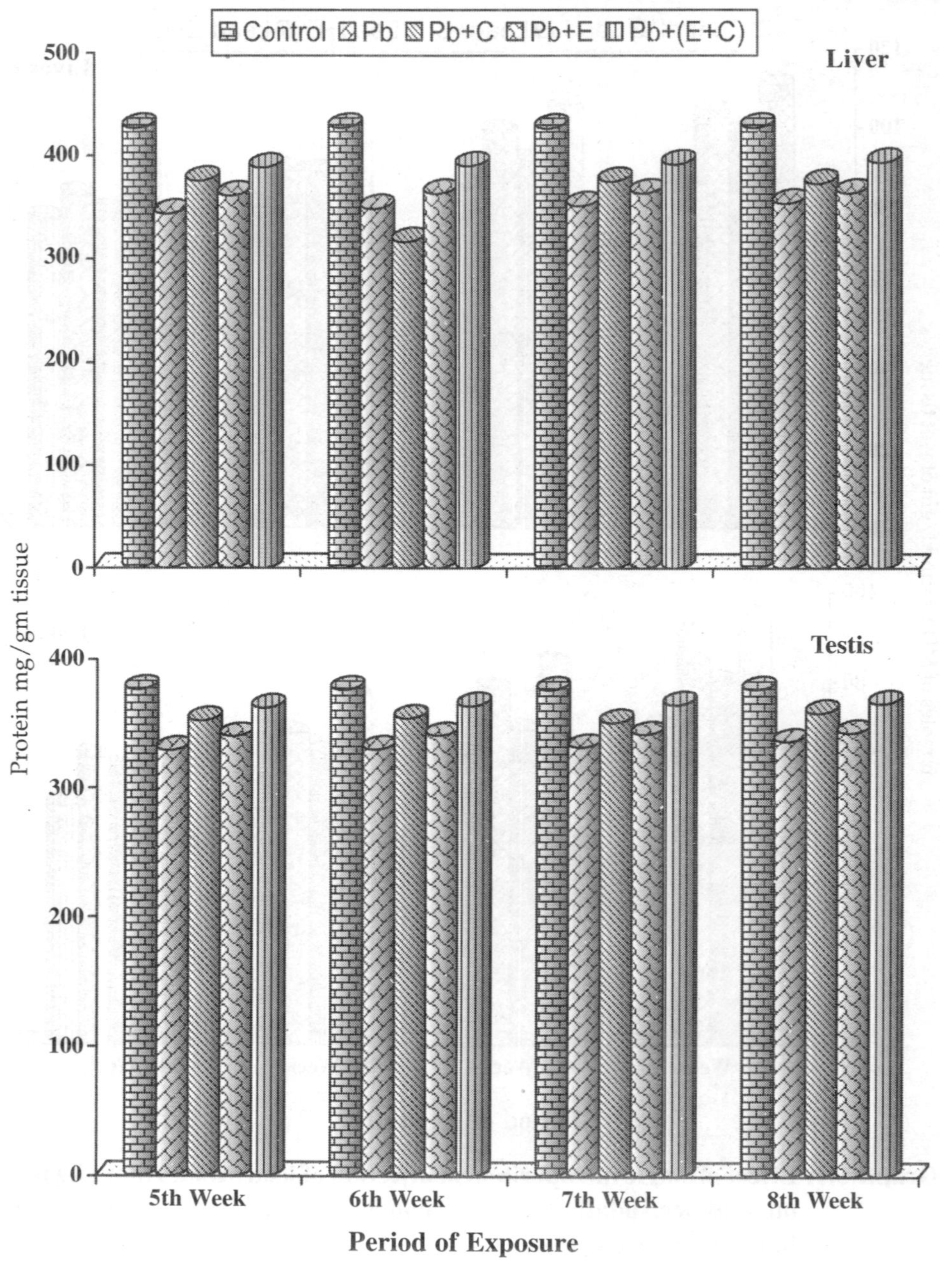

Graph 5.2: Effect of single intraperitoneal injection of lead acetate (5mg/kg b.w.) on protein (mg/gm tissue) in liver and testis of Swiss mice

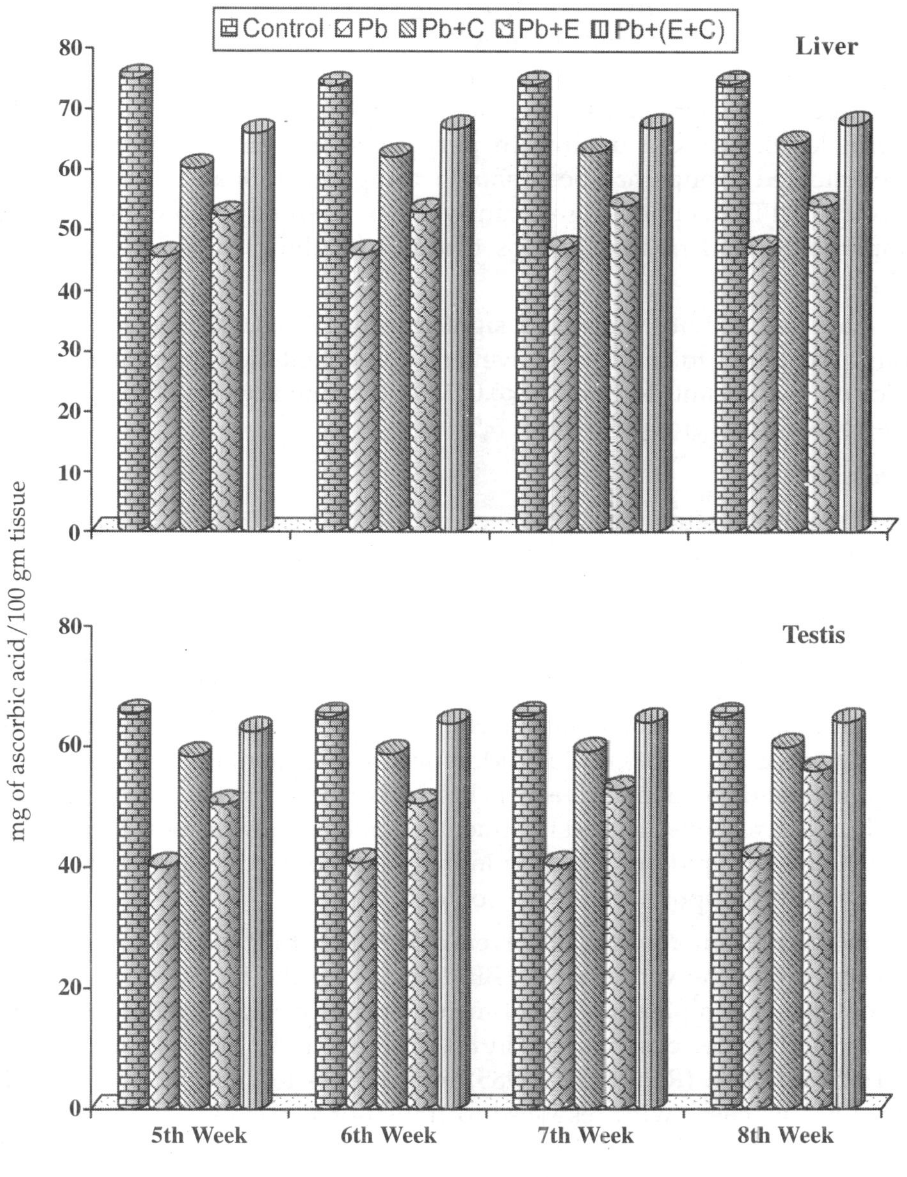

Graph 5.3: Effect of single intraperitoneal injection of lead acetate (5mg/kg b.w.) on mg of ascorbic acid/100gm tissue in liver and testis of Swiss mice

Peroxidase activity increased (Pd≤0.001) in all the weeks of post-treatment in lead-treated mice with respect to controls. Vitamin C supplementation also indicated a marked decline in the activity of PD, compared to lead-treated mice group, but, it did not come down to the control level. Marked decline in peroxidase enzyme activity in vit E supplemented groups has been shown compared to lead-treated groups. Activity of PD declined significantly in vit C+E supplemented groups compared to lead-treated groups throughout the post-treatment phase (Graph 5.4).

Catalase activity increased significantly (Pd≤0.001) in lead-treated groups compared to controls. However, supplementation of vitamins could indicate a significant decline (Pd≤0.001) in enzyme activity with respect to lead-treated mice groups. (Graph 5.5)

Discussion

The present study describes increased lipid per-oxidation in both liver and testes after a single intraperitoneal injection of lead acetate (5mg/kg b.w.). LPP is considered as an index of oxidative stress. A number of studies demonstrate that lead like all other transitional metals is able to react with H_2O_2, superoxide and hydroxyl ions of the cell (which are generated during the metabolism of oxygen) and generate ROS (Riborva and Ludmil, 1981; Quinlan et al., 1988; Stohs and Bagchi, 1995; Ercal et al., 2001; Patro et al., 2001; Acharya et al., 2003, 2004). Moreover, experimental evidence reveals dose and time-dependent increases in lipid peroxidation in hepatic microsomal membrane in response to lead treatment in animals (Lowton and Donaldson, 1991). Increased lipid peroxidation in the tissues of lead-treated mice, in the present study, supports the above contention.

In the present context, however, differential LPP for both tissues has been observed. The variation of LPP depends on the metabolic status and the contents of complex profiles of membrane fatty acids (Devlin, 1986; Das et al., 1987). Earlier observations in rat (Oshino et al., 1975), lizard (Jena et al., 1995) and fish (Radi et al., 1985) indicate tissue differences in LPP. In liver, LPP increases with response to transitional metals, xenobiotics and pesticides (Stohs and Bagchi, 1995; Chainy et al., 1997; Jena and Patnaik 1998; Meng and Zhang, 2003, Acharya et al., 2004). Our results relating to the enhanced LPP in lead treated mice liver is in agreement with the previous findings. On the other hand, lipid-rich membranes of the testes, accompanied with large number of mitochondria and microsomes, make it more vulnerable towards oxidative stress (Dobrestov et al., 1977; Hall, 1995). Furthermore, mammalian spermatozoa generate substantially higher hydrogen peroxide and ROS to further promote testicular oxidative stress (Alvarez et al., 1987;

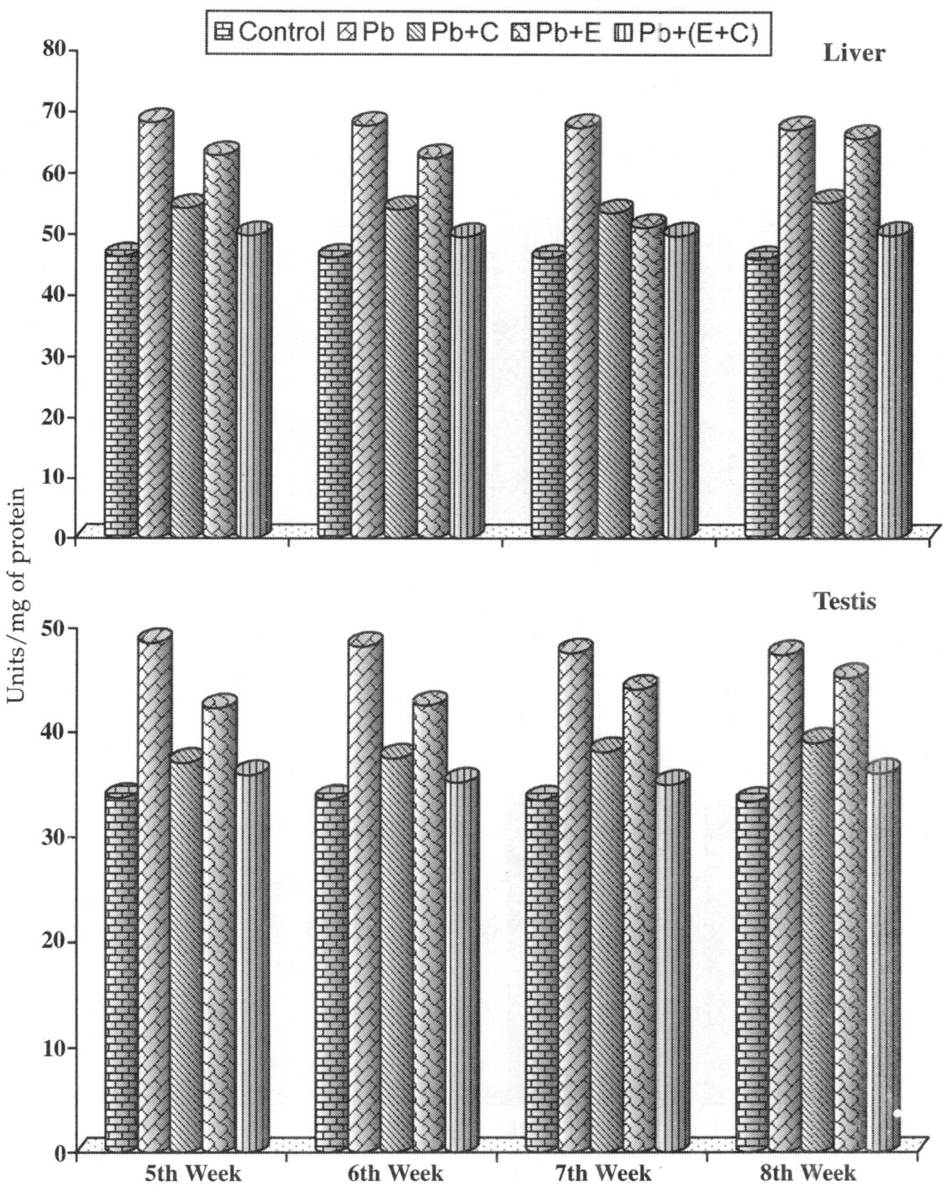

Graph 5.4: Effect of single intraperitoneal injection of lead acetate (5mg/kg b.w.) on peroxidase in Units/mg of protein in liver and testis of Swiss mice

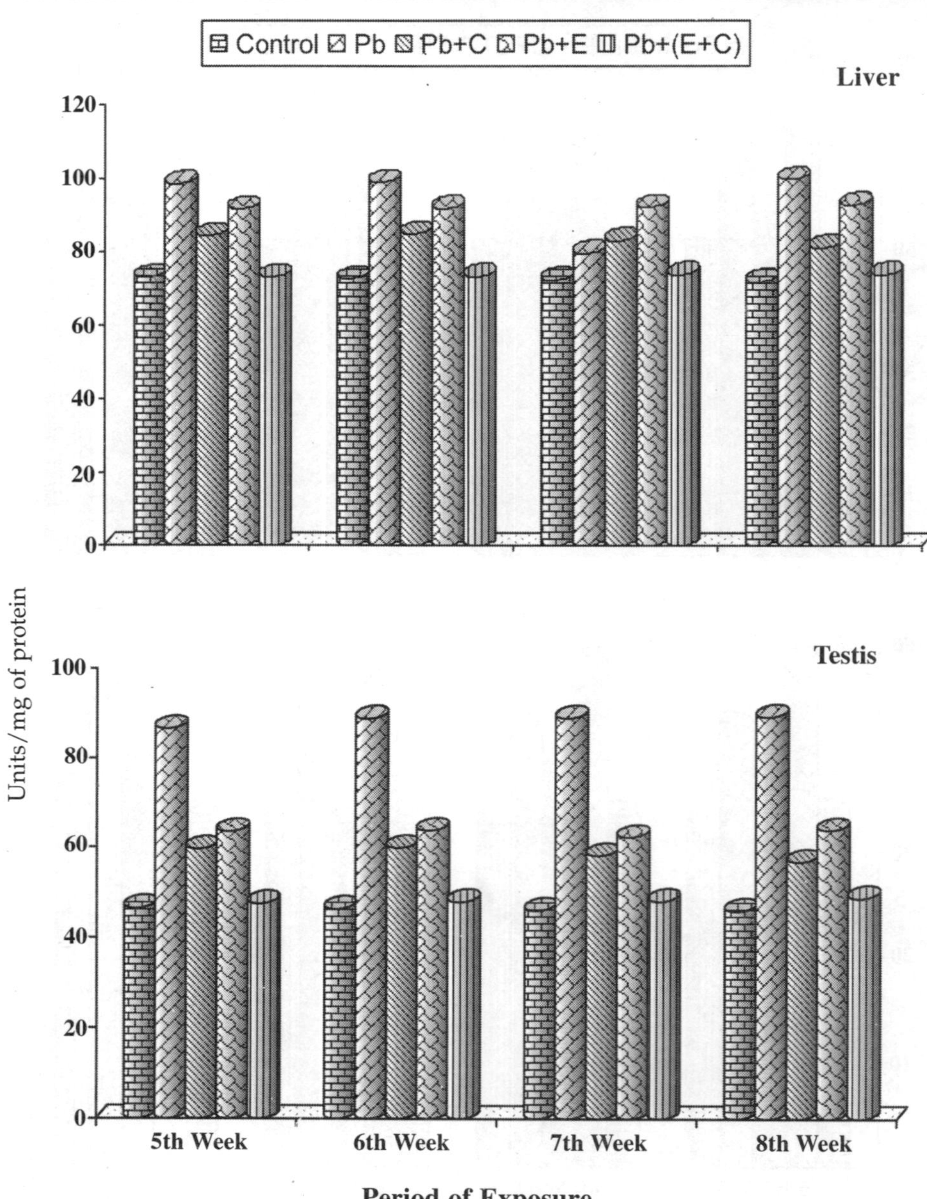

Graph 5.5: Effect of single intraperitoneal injection of lead acetate (5mg/kg b.w.) on catalase in Units/mg of protein in liver and testis of Swiss mice.

Atiken et al., 1992). Testicular oxidative stress is correlated with sperm dysfunction through various mechanisms, including lipid peroxidation of the spermatocytes plasma membrane and impairment of sperm metabolism, motility and capacitation (Miesel et al., 1993). Higher frequencies of single and double-stranded DNA breaks (Saleh et al., 2003) of sperm chromatin are often associated with oxidative stress. Oxidative stress was reported to be the mechanism of lead toxicity through its induced generation of ROS and through depletion of the cells' anti-oxidant defense system (Gurer and Ercal, 2000). Moreover, spermatozoa are particularly susceptible to oxidative damage because their cell membrane contains large quantities of polyunsaturated fatty acids and their cytoplasm contains low concentration of scavenging enzymes (Hsu et al., 1998; Fisher et al., 2003). Besides, emerging data suggest that some of the effects of lead on testes may be due to production of ROS with increased lipid per-oxidation (Hsu et al., 1998; Mariola et al., 2004; Pace et al., 2005; Wang et al., 2006). In our study, male mice were exposed to lead for 35 days with a view that all the cells would be exposed simultaneously to the metal, and in due course, lead-induced ROS may impair sperm structure and function causing decline in sperm count and generating structurally abnormal sperm population during spermatogenesis (Cooke and Saunders, 2002). Increased lipid peroxidation in the lead-exposed testes, in the present study is in agreement with the previous findings.

Effect of lead on protein content, including soluble and insoluble parts, of both liver and testes was studied. The protein content of liver, recorded a significant decline when mice injected with 5mg/kg b.w. of lead acetate were compared with the control. Vitamin C supplemented groups of mice indicated significant increase in protein content in this tissue when compared with lead-treated groups. Similar results were obtained following with vit E treatment in all the weeks of post-treatment except after 8 weeks.

Enzymatic antioxidant defense system comprising of peroxidase and catalase of the testes and liver in lead-treated mice, in the present study, is significantly increased compared to controls indicating an adaptive response to safeguard the tissues against metal-catalyzed oxygen toxicity. Our previous studies, however, indicated a declined enzymatic activity in the testes and liver in chromium treated mice (Acharya et al., 2004, 2006) which could have been corroborated with the high amount of ROS generated that imposed an inhibitory effect on the enzymes. In the present study, increased enzymatic activity in both the tissues, possibly correspond to the adaptive response. In essence, antioxidant enzymes show either increased or declined activity depending on the amount of ROS generation, or through their modification in gene expression, decreased uptake or when cells are overloaded with oxidants (Vuillaume, 1987; Sies, 1991; Barber and Harris, 1994). However, reactive oxygen radicals, posses the ability to sufficiently modify a protein, leading to altered enzyme activity (White et al., 1976; Bellamo et al., 1983).

Co-administration of ascorbic acid to lead-treated mice groups somehow declined lipid peroxidation. Mechanistically, ascorbic acid acts as a chelating agent in treatment of lead toxicity, and has been reported to be protecting the cells from oxidative stress (Ramanathan et al., 2002; Patro and Swarup, 2004). It is also believed that vitC, as an antioxidant, might prevent the production of mutagenic electrophilic metabolites (Goncharova and Kuzhir, 1989), and stimulate 7-α-hydroxylation of lipids and cholesterol nuclei, thus enhancing their degradation to bile acids, which could be excreted from the body (Rees and Salton, 1987). In fact, ascorbic acid is considered as the most important antioxidant of plasma and also acts as an anti-stress factor (Frei et al., 1989). Even in small amounts, ascorbic acid can protect important bio-molecules, such as proteins, carbohydrates, lipids and nucleic acids from oxidative damage by scavenging the ROS (Car and Frie, 1999). Two major properties of ascorbic acid make it an ideal antioxidant. The first one being the low one-electron reduction potential of ascorbate and its one-electron oxidation product, the ascorbyl radical. In fact, these low reduction potentials enable ascorbate and the ascorbyl radical to react with and reduce basically all physiologically relevant radicals and oxidants. The second major antioxidant property of vitamin C is the stability and low reactivity of ascorbyl radical formed when ascorbate scavenges a reactive oxygen or nitrogen species (Tsao, 1997). Experimental evidences demonstrate that ascorbic acid can scavenge the free radicals in different tissues generated due to metal intoxication in animals. (Fraga et al., 1991; Hsu et al., 1998; Pavolvic et al., 2001; Acharya et al., 2003, 2004; Pari and Murugavel, 2005; Wang et al., 2006). Higher dose of ascorbic acid is demonstrated to act as a proxidant alleviating lipid peroxidation. Since in the present study ascorbic acid equivalent to human therapeutic dose has been given to mice, and, hence the possibility of prooxidant nature is customarily ruled out.

Vitamin E supplementation of lead-treated mice, in the present study, has remarkably lowered the activity of antioxidant enzymes and lowered the LPP with an increase in endogenous ascorbic acid content in both the tissues. α-tochopherol is lipophilic in nature and thus play a crucial role in terminating the irreversible lipid peroxidation chain and thereby ameliorates lead-induced oxidative stress to some extent (Burton et al., 1982). Besides, vitE is a known androgenic stimulant (Ghosh et al., 2002), which can protect spermatogonial cells from being degraded by the damaging radicals. Earlier studies (Terao and Matsushita, 1986; Dmitriev et al., 1995) however, suggest that vitE can carry out superoxide radical reduction when in association with GSH-dependent enzyme and in this way happens to be efficient in reducing lipid peroxidation potential of tissues. In the present study, significantly increased GSH-peroxidase in both the tissues might be a possible reason for vitE, induced inclination of LPP.

Supplementation of both vitamins could efficiently reduce LPP of both the tissues concomitantly by reducing the status of antioxidant enzymes to the maximum limit. This result explicitly emphasizes the synergistic action of both vitamins (Packer et al., 1979). In fact, vitC is widely known to restore and recycle the anti-oxidative properties of vitE, when attacked by pro-oxidants (Leung et al., 1981). Such synergistic action of vitC and vitE has been found under various experimental conditions (Mirvish, 1986; Mishra and Acharya, 2004; Krajcovicova et al., 2004).

Results of the present study demonstrate the detrimental activity of lead acetate on two tissues: liver and testes where the impact of oxidative stress could be realized after 35 days of post-treatment. An increase in antioxidant enzymes in the two tissues emphasizes an adaptive response of the tissues to get rid of from lipid peroxides and other singlet oxygen molecules. Supplementation of individual vitamins like vitC and vitE to lead-treated mice groups could ameliorate the cytotoxic effects to certain extent. Among the two vitamins, vitE seems to be more reliable than vitC. However, the combination therapy of vitamins was more effective in reducing lead-induced oxidative stress.

REFERENCES

Acharya, S., Acharya, U.R., 1997. In vivo Lipid Peroxidation Responses of Tissues in Lead-induced Swiss mice. Ind. Health 35, 542-544.

Acharya, U.R., Mishra, M., Mishra, I., 2004. Status of Antioxidant Defense System in Chromium-induced Swiss Mice Tissues. Environ. Toxicol. Pharmacol. 17, 117-123.

Acharya, U.R., Mishra, M., Tripathy, R. R., Mishra, I., 2006. Testicular Dysfunction and Antioxidative Defense System of Swiss Mice After Chromic Acid Exposure. Reprod. Toxicol. 22, 87-91.

Acharya, U.R., Mishra, N., Acharya, S., 1997. Effect of Lead Acetate on Male Germinal Cells of Swiss Mice. Cytologia 62, 231-236.

Acharya, U.R., Rathore, R.M., Mishra, M., 2003. Role of Vitamin C on Lead Acetate-induced Spermatogenesis in Swiss Mice. Environ. Toxicol. Pharmacol.13, 9-14.

Adonyalo, V.N., Oteiza, I., 1999. Lead Intoxication: Antioxidant Defenses and Oxidative Damage in Rat Brain. Toxicology 135, 77-85.

Alphen, M.V., 1999. Lead Poisioning Prevention and Treatment. In: George Abraham M. (ed.), Proceedings of the International Conference on Lead Poisoning, Prevention and Treatment. Feb. 8-10, p. 265.

Alvarez, J.G., Touchstone, J.C., Blasco, L., Storey, B. T., 1987. Spontaneous Lipid Peroxidation and Production of Hydrogen Peroxide and Superoxide in Human Spermatozoa. Superoxide Dismutase As Major Enzyme Protectent Against Oxygen Toxicity. J. Androl. 8, 338-348.

Atiken, R.J., Buckingham, D., West, K., Wu, F.C., Zikopoulos, K., Richardson, D.W., 1992. Differential Contribution of Leucocytes and Spermatozoa to the Generation of Reactive Oxygen Species in the Ejaculates of Oligospermic Patients and Fertile Donors. J. Reprod. Fertile. 94, 451-462.

Barber, D.A., Harris, S.R., 1994. Oxygen Free Radicals and Antioxidants: A Review. Am. Pharma. 34, 26-35.

Bellamo, G., Mirabelli, F., Richelmi, P., Orrenius, S., 1983. Critical Role of Sulphahydryl Group (s) in the ATP-dependent Ca^{2+} Sequestration by the Plasma Membrane Fraction from Rat Liver. FEBS Lett. 163, 136-139.

Burton, G.W., Joyce, A., Ingold, K.U., 1982. First Proof that Vitamin E is Major Lipid-soluble, Chain-breaking Antioxidant in Human Blood Plasma. Lancet 2, 327.

Carr, A.C., Frei, B., 1999. Does Vitamin C Act as Pro-oxidant Under Physiological Conditions? The Federation of American Societies for Experimental Biology. The FASEB Journal. 13, 1007-1024.

Chainy, G.B. N., Samanta, L., Rout, N. B., 1997. Effect of Aluminium on Superoxide Dismutase, Catalase and Lipid Peroxidation of Rat Liver. Res. Commun. Mol. Pathol. Pharmacol. 94, 217-222.

Cooke, H.J., Saunders, P. T., 2002. Mouse Model of Male Infertility. Nat. Rev. Gen. 3, 790-801.

Das, D.K., Engelman, R.M., Flansas, D., Otani, H., Rousou, J., Breyer, R. H., 1987. Developmental Profiles of Protective Mechanisms Against Peroxidative Injury. Basic Res. Cardiol. 82, 36-50.

Devlin, T.M., 1986. Biological Membranes: Structure and Membrane Transport. In: Devlin, T. M., (Ed.), Text Book of Biochemistry. John Wiley and Sons. New York, pp. 177-210.

Ding, Y., Gonik, H.C., Vaziri, N. D.2001. Lead Promotes Hydroxyl Radical Generation and Lipid Peroxidation in Cultured Endothelial Cells. Am. J. Hypertens.13, 525-55.

Dmitriev, L.F., Ivanova, M.V., Lebdev, A.V., 1995. Effect of pH and Glutathione on Lipid Peroxidation in Tochopherol-enriched Liposomes. Phrmacol. Toxicol. 120, 908-910.

Dobrestov, G.F., Brochevskaya, T.A., Vadimirov, Y.A., 1977. The Increase in Phospholipids Bilayer Rigidity Afterlipid Peroxidation. FEBS Lett. 84, 125-128.

Ercal, N., Gurer-Orhan, H., Aykin-Burns, N., 2001. Toxic Metals and Oxidative Stress. Part I. Mechanisms Involved in Metal-induced Oxidative Damage. Curr. Top. Med. Chem. 1, 529-539.

Fisher, M. A., Willis, J., Zini, A., 2003. Human Sperm DNA Integrity: Correlation with Sperm Cytoplasmic Droplets. Urology 61, 207-211.

Fraga, C.G., Motchnik, P.A., Shigenega, M.K., Helbock, H.J., Jacob, R.A., Ames, B.N., 1991. Ascorbic Acid Protects Against Endogenous Oxidative DNA Damage in Human Sperm. Proc. Natl. Acad. Sci. 88, 11003-11006.

Frie, B., Stocker, R., England, L., Ames, B. N., 1990. Ascorbate, the most Effective Antioxidant in Human Blood Plasma. Adv. Exp. Med. Biol. 264, 155-163.

Ghosh, D., Das, U.B., Misro, M., 2002. Protective role of α- Tochopherol -succinate (provitamin-E) in Cyclophosphamide Induced Testicular Gametogenesis and Steroidogenesis Disorders: A Correlative Approach to Oxidative Stress. Free Rad. Res. 36, 1209-1218.

Goncharova, R.I., Kuzhir, T.D., 1989. A Comparative Study of the Antimutagenic Effects of Antioxidants on Chemical Mutagenesis in Drosophila Melanogaster. Mutat. Res. 214, 33-36.

Gurer, H., Ercal, N, 2000. Can Antioxidant be Beneficial in the Treatment of Lead Poisioning? Free Rad. Biol. 29(10), 927-995.

Hall, P. F., 1995. Testicular Steroid Synthesis: Organisation and Regulation. Physiol. Rep. 1, 1335-13362.

Halliwel, B., Gutteridge J.M.C., 1992: Free Radicals in Biology and Medicine 2nd Edn. New York: Oxford University Press. pp. 201.

Heffner, J.E., and Repine, J.E., 1989. Pulmonary Statergies of Antioxidant Defense. Am. Rev. Restr. Dis.140, 531-554.

Hernández-Ochoa, I., Sánchez-Gutiérrez, M., Solís-Heredia, M. J., Quintanilla-Vega, B., 2006. Spermatozoa Nucleus takes up Lead during the Epididymal Maturation Altering Chromatin Condensation. Rep. Toxicol. 21 (2), 171-178.

Hsu, P.C., Liu, Y., Hsu, C.C., Chen, L. Y., Guo, L. Y., 1998. Effects of Vitamin E and C on Reactive Oxygen Species-related Lead Toxicity in the Rat Sperm. Toxicology 128(3), 169-179.

Jena, B.S., Das, S., Patnaik, B. K., 1995. Effect of Age on Lipid Peroxidation in a Short-lived Species of Reptile, *calotes verscicolar.* Arch. Gerentol. Geriatr. 20, 263-272.

Jena, B.S., Patnaik, B.K., 1998. Asprin Reduces Aluminium-induced Increase in Lipid Peroxidation in Liver and Kidneys of Swiss Mice. Rev. Int. Contam. Ambient. 14, 55-58.

Kappus, H. (1985): Lipid Peroxidation Mechanisms, Analysis, Enzymology and Biological Relevance. Oxidative Stress. Academic Press, London pp. 273-310.

Krajcovicova-Kudlackova, M., Paucova, V., Bacekova, M., Dusinska, M., 2004. Lipid Peroxidation in Relation to Vitamin C and Vitamin E Levels. Cent. Euro. J. Publ. Health. 12 (1), 46-48.

Landrigan, P.J., Boffeta, P., Apostoli, P., 2000. The Reproductive Toxicity and Carcinogenicity of Lead: A Critical Review. Am. J. Ind. Med. 38, 231-243.

Lawton, L.J., Donaldson, W.E., 1991. Lead-induced Tissue Fatty Acid Alterations and Lipid Peroxidation . Biol. Trace Elem. Res. 28, 83-97.

Leung, H.W., Vang, M.J., Mavis, R.D. 1981. The Cooperative Interaction Between Vitamin E and Vitamin C in Suppression of Peroxidation of Membrane Phospholipids. Biochim. Biophys Acta. 664, 266-272.

Lowry, O.H., Rosenburgh, N.J., Farr, A.L., Randall, R.J., 1951. Protein Measurement with Folin-phenol Reagent. J. Biol. Chem. 193, 265-275.

Maehly, A.C., Chance, B., 1967. The Assay of Catalase and Peroxidases. In: Glick, D. (Ed.), Methods of Biochemical Analysis. Interscience Publishers, New York, pp. 357-427.

Mariola, M., Teresa, M., Barbara, W., 2004. Detection of Lead-induced Oxidative Stress in the Rat Epididymis by Chemiluminiscence. Chemosphere. 57, 1553-1562.

Meng, Z., Zhang, B., 2003. Oxidative Damage of Sulfur Dioxide Inhalation on Brains Livers of Mice. Environ. Toxicol. Pharmacol. 13, 1-8.

Miesel, R., Drzejczak, P.J.E., Kurpisz, M., 1993. Oxidative Stress during the Interaction of Gamets. Biol. Reprod. 49, 918-923.

Mirvish, S.S., 1986. Effects of Vitamin E and Vitamin C on N-nitroso Compound Formation, Carcinogenesis, and Cancer. Cancer. 58, 1842-1850.

Mishra, M., Acharya, U. R., 2004. Protective Action of Vitamins on the Spermatogenesis in Lead-treated Swiss Mice. J. Trace Elem. Med. Biol. 18(2), 173-178.

Mittal, R., Dubey, R.S., 1995. Influence of Sodium Chloride Salinity on Polyphenol Oxidase, Indole 3-acetic Oxidase and Catalase Activities in Rice Seedling Differing in Salt Tolerance. Trop. Sci. 35, 141-149.

Oshino, N., Jamieason, D., Sugano, T., Chance, B., 1975. Optical Measurement of the Catalase-hydrogen Peroxide Intermediate (Compound 1) in the Liver of Anesthetized Rats and its Implication by Hydrogen Peroxide Formation *in situ*. Biochem. J. 146, 67-77.

Pace, B.M., Lawrence, D.A., Behr, M.J., Parsons, P.J., Dias, J.A., 2005. Neonatal Lead Exposure Changes Quality of Sperm and Number of Macrophages in Testes of BALB/c Mice. Toxicology 210, 247-256.

Packer, J.E., Slater, T.F., Willson, R.L.1979. Direct Observation of a Free Radical Interaction Between Vitamin E and Vitamin C. Nature 278, 737-738.

Pari, L., Murugavel, P., 2005. Role of Diallyl Tetrasulfide in Ameliorating the Cadmium-induced Biochemical Changes in Rats. Environ. Toxicol. Pharmacol. 20, 493-500.

Patra, R.C., Swarup, D., Dwedi, S. K., 2001. Antioxidant Effect of Alpha-tochopherol, Ascorbic Acid and L-methionine on Lead-induced Oxidative Stress to the Liver, Kidney and Brain in Rats. Toxicology 162 (2), 81-88.

Patra, R., Swarup, D. 2004. Effect of Antioxidant Ascorbic Acid, L-metionine on Tocopherol Alone or Along with Chelator on Cardiac Tissue of Lead-treated Rats. Veterinarski Arch.74, 235-244.

Quinlan, G.J., Halliwell, B., Moorhouse, C.P., Gutteridge, I.M.C. 1988. Action of Lead (ii) and Aluminium (ii) Ions on Iron Stimulated Lipid Peroxidation in Liposomes, Erythrocytes and Rat Liver Microsomal Fractions. Biochim. Biophys. Acta. 296, 196-200.

Radi, A.A., Hay, D.Q., Gabrileck, T., Maktovics, B., 1985. Comparative Antioxidative Enzyme Study in Fresh Water Fishes, 1. Distribution of Superoxide Dismutase, Peroxide Decomposing Enzymes and Lipid Peroxidation in Herbivorous Fishes. Acta. Biol. Acad. Sci. Hung. 36, 169-174.

Ramnathan, K., Balkumar, B., Paneerselvam, C. 2002. Effects of Ascorbic Acid and Alpha Tocopherol on Arsenic Induced Oxidative Stress. Hum Exp. Toxicol. 21, 675-680.

Rees, S., Salten, T. F., 1987. Ascorbic Acid and Lipid Peroxidation: The cross-over Effect. Acta. Biochm. Biophys. Hung. 22, 241-252.

Riborva, S.R., Ludmil, C. Benow 1981. Relationship Between the Hemolytic Action of Heavy Metals and Lipid Peroxidation. Biochem. Biophys. Acta. 640, 721-726.

Roe, J.H., 1954. In.: Glick, D. (Ed.), Methods in Biochemical Analysis, Vol. 1. Inter Science, New York, pp. 115-139.

Saleh, R.A., Agarwal, A., Nada, E.A., El-Tonsy, M.H., Sharma, R.K., Meyer, A., Nelson, A.R., Thomas, A.J., 2003. Negative Effects of Increased Sperm DNA Damage in Relation to Seminal Oxidative Stress in Men with Idiopathic and Male Factor Infertility. Fert. Steril. 79, 1597-1560.

Sies, H. 1991. Oxidative Stress: Introduction. In: Sies. H. (Ed.), Oxidative Stress: Oxidants and Antioxidants, pp.15-22.

Soldin, O.P, Hanak B, Soldin, S.J., 2003. Blood Lead Concentrations in Children: New Ranges. Clinica Chimica Acta 327, 109-113

Stohs, S.J., Bagchi, D., 1995. Oxidative Mechanisms in the Toxicity of Metal Ions. Free Radic. Biol. Med. 18, 321-336.

Stroev, E.A., Makarova, V. G., 1989. Metabolism of Xenobiotics in Laboratory Manual. In: Biochemistry. Mir Publishers, Moscow, pp.173.

Tewary, C.P., Pandey, V. C., 1957. Further Studies on the 2, 4- DNPH Method of Roe Kuether for the Estimation of Ascorbic Acid, DHA and DKA. Indian J. Biochem. 1, 171.

Tsao, C.S., 1997. An Overview of Ascorbic Acid Chemistry and Biochemistry. In: Packer, L. Fuchs J. (Eds.), Vitamin C in health and disease. Marcel Dekker Inc., New York, pp. 25-58.

Vuillaume, M., 1987. Reduced Oxygen Species, Mutation, Induction and Cancer Initiation. Mutat. Res. 186, 43-72.

Wang, C., Zhang, Y., Liang, J., Shan, G., Wang, Y., Shi, Q., 2006. Impacts of Ascorbic Acid and Thiamine Supplementation at Different Concentrations on Lead Toxicity in Testis. Clinica Chemica Acta. 370, 82-86.

White, A.A., Crawford, K.M., Patt, C.S., Lad, P.J., 1976. Activation of Soluble Guanylate Cyclase from Rat Lung by Incubation or by Hydrogen Peroxide. J. Boil. Chem. 251, 7304-7312.

CHAPTER

6

Keratinolytic Proteases
A New Tool to Tackle Industrial Pollution

Amit Verma, *India*; **Hukum Singh,** *India*

Introduction

Enzymes are well known biocatalysts that perform a multitude of chemical reactions and are commercially exploited in the detergent, food, pharmaceutical, diagnostics, and fine chemical industries. More than 3000 different enzymes described to date the majority have been isolated from mesophilic organisms. These enzymes mainly function in a narrow range of pH, temperature, and ionic strength. Moreover, the technological application of enzymes under demanding industrial conditions makes the currently known enzymes unrecommendable. Thus, the search for new microbial sources is a continual exercise, where one must respect microbial diversity.

The microorganisms from diverse and exotic environments called as extremophiles, are an important source of enzymes, whose specific properties are expected to result in novel process applications (Kumar & Takagi, 1999). The role of enzymes in many processes has been known for a long time. Their existence was associated with the history of ancient Greece where they were using enzymes from microorganisms in baking, brewing, alcohol production, cheese making etc. With better knowledge and purification of enzymes the number of applications has increased manifold, and with the availability of engineered enzymes a number of new possibilities for industrial processes have emerged (Brandelli, 2008).

The current estimated value of the worldwide sales of industrial enzymes is $1 billion. However, proteases represent one of the three largest groups of industrial enzymes and account for about 60 per cent of total worldwide enzyme sales. This dominance of proteases in the industrial market is expected to increase further (Rao et. al., 1998). Microbial proteases are among the most important hydrolytic enzymes and have been studied extensively since the advent of enzymology. They are essential constituents of all forms of life on earth, including prokaryotes, fungi, plants and animals. They can be cultured in large quantities in relatively short time by established fermentation methods and produce an abundant, regular supply of the desired product. In recent years there has been a phenomenal increase in the use of alkaline protease as industrial catalysts.

Alkaline proteases (EC.3.4.21-24, 99) are defined as those proteases which are active in a neutral to alkaline pH range. They either have a serine center (serine protease) or are of metallo-type (metalloprotease). The alkaline serine proteases are the most important group of enzymes so far exploited (Gupta et. al., 2002). These enzymes offer advantages over the use of conventional chemical catalysts for numerous reasons viz. they exhibit high catalytic activity, a high degree of substrate specificity can be produced in large amounts and are economically viable.

Microbial alkaline proteases dominate the worldwide enzyme market, accounting for two-third of the share of the detergent industry. Although production is inherent property of all organisms, only those microbes that produce a substantial amount of extracellular protease have been exploited commercially. Alkaline proteases of bacterial origin possess considerable industrial potential due to their biochemical diversity and wide applications in tannery and food industries, medicinal formulations, detergents and processes like waste treatment, silver recovery and resolution of amino acid mixtures (Anbu et. al., 2008).

Keratinase is a protease capable of digesting keratins in chicken feathers as well as animal wool and hair. Proteases are by and large classified into two major groups based on their cleavage habits. First group is called "*Endopeptidases*" which cleaves non-terminal peptide bonds inside polypeptide chains. Second group so-called "*Exoproteases*" breaks down peptide bond at the amino termini (aminopeptidases) or at the carboxy termini (carboxypeptidases) of their substrates (Bressollier et. al., 1999). Proteases are further categorized based on functional groups of their active sites. Four major groups are: serine proteases, cysteine proteases, aspartic proteases, and metallo-proteases. Keratinases are mostly known to be endopeptidase which is a member of serine protease family.

Keratins are less likely to be digested by enzyme such as trypsin, pepsin, and papain (Cleveland C.J., 2006). Because the stiff packing of the protein chain in α-helix and β-sheet structures resists and mechanically stabilizes the keratin to microbial degradation. However, keratin can be degraded by a number of species of saprophytic and parasitic fungi, a few actinomyces and *Bacillus* species (Radha & Gunasekharan, 2008). Keratin proteolysis like the other proteins is effectively directed by proteases having keratinolytic property. Nevertheless, keratinases are known to have an effect on their hydrolysis (Cleveland C.J., 2006). Keratinases have already been purified from several microorganisms such as fungi, a few bacteria, and some *Streptomyces* species (Radha & Gunasekharan, 2008).

Keratinase belongs to a group of proteinase enzymes that have high level of activity on insoluble keratin, playing a crucial role in hydrolyzing feather, hair, wool, collagen and casein in removing barriers in waste water treatment systems. Not only have these enzymes been applied in sewage systems but have also recently emerged in many applications including food, textile, medicine, and cosmetics industries (Gupta & Ramnani, 2006). In fact, use of keratinases in skin medications to get rid of acne and psoriasis as well as removing of human callus in medical applications is well known. It is also utilized for the erection of a vaccine for dermatophytosis therapy (Cleveland C.J., 2006; Radha & Gunasekharan, 2008). More interestingly, keratinases are well identified in leather industry to have been employed in dehairing process of animal skins instead of treating them with sodium sulfide, which is one of the causes of water pollution due to leather industries.

Ever since the discovery of water solubility and proteolytic ability of keratinase, many keratinase application have been emerged. A newly invented application to handle poultry waste is to turn feathers into biogas. These huge amounts of keratins are required to break down by keratinase before the feathers can be turned into biogas. Keratin-consisting materials have always been plentiful in the nature but restricted in practical usages, mainly because of their insolubility and non-degradability by the ordinary proteolytic enzymes. Thus, solving the solid waste problem created by keratinous wastes.

New developments of keratinase production have attracted many attentions to apply keratinase in poultry industry. Feathers waste in poultry industries present a high-quality supply of keratins. This valuable source of keratin could be used either as a source of fertilizer glues and films, or many selected amino acids, and proteins which are applied in animal feed industry (Bressollier et. al., 1999). Obviously, large amounts of keratinase for industrial scale processes are essentially needed which is not cheap. Many researchers show bacteria able to produce keratinase. However, best host cell for overproduction of keratinase will remain unknown. Several efforts have been done to overproduce keratinase as demands increasing.

Keratinolytic Microorganisms: Diversity

Keratinases one of very widespread enzyme in microbes which can be identified from microorganisms of the three domains: Eucarya, Bacteria, and Archaea. The sources of keratinase have been isolated from the most distinct sites i.e. from Antarctic soils to hot springs, including aerobic and anaerobic environments. Therefore, microbial keratinases present a great diversity in their biochemical and biophysical properties (Brandelli et. al., 2009).

The most keratinolytic group among fungi belongs to fungi imperfectii including the following genera: *Aspergillus, Alternaria, Chrysosporium, Curvularia, Cladosporium, Fusarium, Geomyces, Gleomastis, Monodictys, Myrothecium, Paecilomyces, Stachybotrys, Trichurus, Urocladium, Scopulariopsis, Sepedonium, Penicillium, Doratomyces* (Gupta & Ramnani, 2006). Among nondermatophytic fungi, keratinases showing attractive biochemical properties were reported to be produced by *Aspergillus* (Santos et. al., 1996; Farag & Hassan, 2004), *Trichoderma* (Cao et. al., 2008), *Doratomyces* (Gradisar et. al., 2000), *Myrothecium* (Moreira-Gasparin et. al., 2009), *Paecilomyces* (Gradisar et. al., 2005), *Scopulariopsis* (Anbu et. al., 2005), and also *Acremonium, Alternaria, Beauveria, Curvularia, and Penicillium* (Marcondes et. al., 2008). Besides the biotechnological interest, these investigations may help in understanding the role of fungi in the degradation of complex keratinous substrates in the nature (Marcondes et. al., 2008).

Several keratinolytic bacteria have been isolated from soils and poultry wastes. Although these isolates are mostly confined to the genera Streptomyces and Bacillus, some studies indicate that the diversity of feather-degrading bacteria is significantly greater (Lucas et. al., 2003). Diverse strains of *Bacillus licheniformis* and *Bacillus subtilis* are described as keratinolytic (Lin et. al., 1999; Suh & Lee, 2001; Manczinger et. al., 2003; Balaji et. al., 2008; Cai et. al., 2008; Zhang et. al., 2009), but other species such as *Bacillus pumilus* and *Bacillus cereus* also produce keratinases (Kim et. al., 2001; Werlang & Brandelli, 2005; Kumar et. al., 2008; Ghosh et. al., 2008). Some thermophilic and alkaliphilic strains of Bacillus have also been described to show keratin-degrading activity, such as *Bacillus halodurans* AH-101 (Takami et. al., 1992, 1999), *Bacillis pseudofirmus* AL-89 (Gessesse et. al., 2003), and *B. pseudofirmus* FA30-01 (Kojima et. al., 2006). Besides, microorganisms belonging to the same genus can produce different keratinases. In this regard, the exploitation of microbial diversity might provide keratinases with suitable properties for biotechnological uses. For instance recently the keratinolytic potential and keratinolytic enzymes from novel mesophilic Bacillus species isolated from the Amazon basin have been characterized, presenting interesting features for diverse potential applications (Giongo et. al., 2007; Correa et. al., 2009; Daroit et. al., 2009).

Among bacteria, degradation is mostly confined to gram-positives, including Bacillus, Lysobacter, Nesternokia, Kocuria and Microbacterium. However, feather degrading strains of gram-negative bacteria, viz. Vibrio, Xanthomonas, Stenotrophomonas and Chryseobacterium (Sangali & Brandelli, 2000; De Toni et. al., 2002; Yamamura et. al., 2002; Lucas et. al., 2003), have also been reported. In addition, a few thermophiles and extremophiles belonging to the genera Fervidobacterium, Thermoanaerobacter, Bacillus and Nesternokia have also been described (Friedrich & Antranikian, 1996; Rissen & Antranikian, 2001; Nam et. al., 2002; Gassesse et. al., 2003). Besides these, actinomycetes from the Streptomyces group, viz. *S. fradiae* (Novel & Nickerson, 1959), *S. sp.* A11 (Mukhopadhyay & Chandra, 1990), *S. pactum* (Bockle et. al., 1995), *S. albidoflavus* (Letourneau et. al., 1998), *S. thermoviolaceus* SD8 (Chitte et. al., 1999) and *S. graminofaciens* (Szabo et. al., 2000), and the Thermoactinomyces group, viz. *T. candidus* (Ignatova et. al., 1999) and another *Thermoactinomyces sp.* (Gousterova et. al., 2005), is commonly described as keratin degraders with an ability to act on a wide variety of keratin substrates including hair, wool and feather.

Thus the property of keratinolysis is widespread in the microbial world. However, only a few have reached commercial exploitation. Keratinases from Bacillus sp. particularly *B. licheniformis* and *B. subtilis* have been extensively studied due to their effectiveness in terms of feather degradation (Manczinger et. al., 2003; Thys et. al., 2004). *B. licheniformis* PWD1—a source of the Versazyme—the first commercial keratinase developed by Shih and coworkers at Bio Resource International (North Carolina), not only guarantees to turn chick feathers into dollars through feather meal generation but also promises to treat the dreaded mad cow's disease and turn feather protein into biodegradable plastic (Gregg, 2002).

Keratinases: Low Cost Production

The utility of keratinolytic proteases requires the production to be carried out in sufficient amounts at a low cost, so that utilized in commercial purposes. Keratinase production is usually induced by keratin (Chao et. al., 2007; Anbu et al. 2008; Cai et al. 2008; Ghosh et al. 2009) and, thus, a keratinous substrate (chicken feathers, feather meal, hair) is often added to the cultivation medium. These keratinous materials are produced in huge amounts by agroindustrial activities and usually discarded as a waste which creates a solid waste problem. Therefore, this microbial technology connects the production of valuable products (keratinases, microbial biomass, protein hydrolysates) from low-cost substrates with an alternative and efficient way of waste management (Gessesse et al. 2003; Brandelli 2008; Tatineni et al. 2008; Daroit et al. 2009).

Supplementation of keratin-containing media with different carbon and/ or nitrogen sources might result in higher levels of keratinase production. For instance, the addition of glucose (Ramnani and Gupta 2004; Anbu et al. 2008; Son et al. 2008), sucrose (Cai and Zheng 2009), starch (Kojima et al. 2006; Syed et al. 2009), molasses (Cheng et al. 1995), and bagasses (Gioppo et al. 2009); and additional nitrogen sources, such as urea, peptone, tryptone, yeast extract, ammonium chloride, and sodium nitrate are reported to enhance enzyme yields (Ramnani and Gupta 2004; Bernal et al. 2006; Ionata et al. 2008; Cai and Zheng 2009; Khardenavis et al. 2009).

Conversely, the addition of supplementary substrates (carbohydrates; inorganic and/or organic nitrogen sources) often decrease enzyme production by some microorganisms, mainly due to catabolite repression mechanisms (Brandelli and Riffel 2005; Mabrouk 2008; Son et al. 2008; Gioppo et al. 2009). Therefore, the effect of different growth substrates on keratinase production is highly variable and depends on the microorganism, the substrate and the carbon and nitrogen concentration in the media etc (Cai and Zheng 2009).

Besides the composition of the culture medium factors like incubation temperature, pH, aeration etc are among the other variables which should be keeped in mind in view to obtain high keratinase yields. Maximum keratinase activities are usually achieved in the late exponential or stationary growth phases (Thys et al. 2004; Gupta and Ramnani 2006; Kojima et al. 2006; Zhang et al. 2009). In this sense, keratinase production was observed to be growth-associated in B. licheniformis FK 14 (Suntornsuk et al. 2005); similar results were observed with Chryseobacterium sp. kr6 (Brandelli and Riffel 2005) and Streptomyces gulbargensis DAS 131 (Syed et al. 2009). Nevertheless, Serratia sp. HPC 1383 showed the highest proteolytic activity in the initial phase of growth (24 h) on feather meal medium, whereas maximum biomass was achieved after 96 h (Khardenavis et al. 2009).

Development of mutant and recombinant microbial strains was also investigated, representing useful techniques to enhance keratinase production and keratin degradation (Radha and Gunasekaran 2007, 2008; Wang et al. 2007; Cai et al. 2008; Haddar et al. 2009). In the specific case of the opportunistic pathogen P. aeruginosa, cloning and heterologous expression of its keratinase gene also represents a viable alternative to ensure safety (Lin et al. 2009). The gene *kerA*, which encodes a B. licheniformis keratinase, is expressed specifically for feather hydrolysis (Lin et al. 1995); therefore, the presence of feather keratin as the sole carbon and nitrogen source in the culture medium may result in preferential expression of the keratinolytic protease. This gene has been cloned and expressed in heterologous microorganisms such as Escherichia coli and B. subtilis, but the keratinase yields are lower than the wild strain (Wang and Shih 1999; Wang et al. 2003).

However, increased keratinase yield was achieved by chromosomal integration of multiple copies of the kerA gene in B. licheniformis and B. subtilis (Wang et al. 2004).

Keratinases: Biochemical Properties

The biochemical characteristics of keratinases from several microorganisms have been studied and reviewed extensively (Gupta & Ramnani, 2006; Brandelli et. al., 2010). The important properties include pH and temperature optima, pI, molecular weight and substrate specificity, which are covered in the following sections as below:

pH and Temperature Kinetics

Microbial keratinases are mostly alkaline or neutral proteases showing optima pH ranging 7.5–9.0. However, some enzymes are optimally active outside this range, even at extreme alkalophilic pH (Takami et al. 1999; Mitsuiki et al. 2004) or at slightly acidic pH (Tsuboi et al. 1989; Qin et al. 1992; Balaji et al. 2008). A feature showed by several keratinases is the stability over a wide pH range (Gupta and Ramnani, 2006). This property is remarkable for the keratinase of Nocardiopsis TOA-1, which is stable over a pH range of 1.5 to 12.0 for 24 h at 30°C (Mitsuiki et al. 2002). Increased stability has been recently achieved by recombinant keratinases, such as the B. licheniformis MKU3 keratinase expressed in Pichia pastoris X33 (Radha and Gunasekaran 2009).

The temperature optima of keratinases may also be very variable, often depending on the source and origin of the isolate (Table pH & temp. opt.). The enzyme of the thermophilic F. pennavorans has optimum temperature at 80°C (Friedrich and Antranikian, 1996) while the mesophilic Stenotrophomonas maltophila DHHJ showed maximum activity at 40°C (Cao et al. 2009). In some exceptional cases, as for F. islandicum AW-1, the optimum of 100°C has been reported (Nam et al. 2002).

Applications

Keratinases from microorganisms have attracted a great deal of attention in the recent decade, particularly due to their multitude of industrial applications such as in the feed, fertilizer, detergent, leather and pharmaceutical industries. Currently, the most promising application of keratinases/keratinolytic microorganisms is the production of nutritious, cost-effective, environmentally benign feather meal for poultry. Other applications of keratinases have yet to be thoroughly explored before commercialization. The following section will discuss some of the prospective applications of keratinases that are rapidly gaining importance.

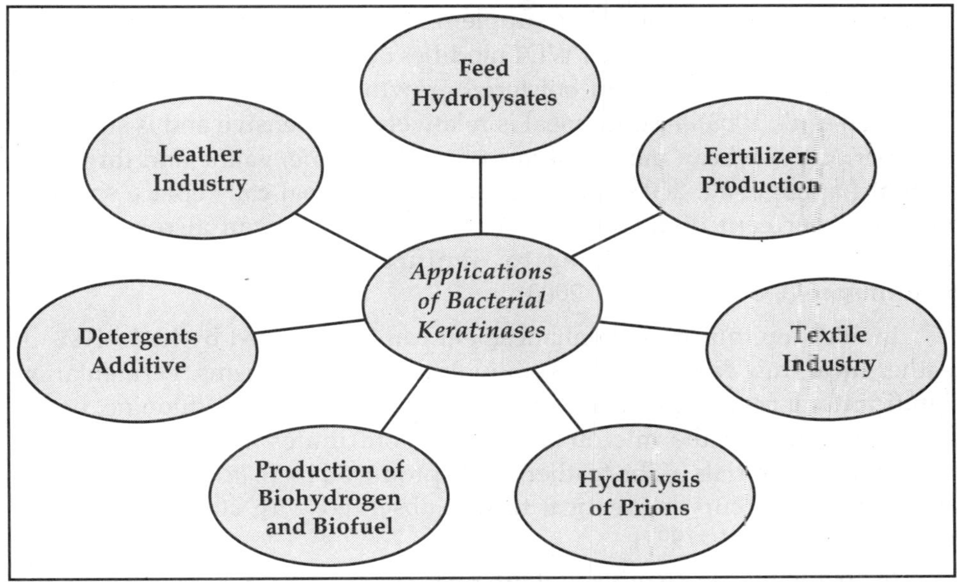

Fig. 6.1: Processing of Keratin Residues

Feather Meal As Feed

Feathers represent over 90 per cent protein, the major component being β-keratin, a fibrous and insoluble structural protein extensively cross-linked by disulfide, hydrogen and hydrophobic bonds. Owing to their insoluble nature, feathers are resistant to degradation by common microbial proteases, viz. trypsin, pepsin and papain. Thus, the several million tons of feathers generated annually by the livestock industry leads to troublesome environmental pollution and wastage of a protein-rich reserve (Onifade *et al.*, 1998; Gousterova *et al.*, 2005).

Until recent years, feathers were baked at high temperature and pressure and used as animal feed supplement in the form of feather meal. The hydrothermal treatment, in addition to being expensive, resulted in the destruction of certain essential amino acids, viz. methionine, lysine and tryptophan, yielding a product with poor digestibility and variable nutrient quality (Wang and Parsons, 1997). The drawbacks of the high-temperature treatment impel the use of microbial keratinases that serve as attractive alternatives to hydrolyze feather into nutritionally rich animal feed (Onifade *et al.*, 1998).

The application of keratinases/keratinolytic microbes for improvement of feather as poultry feed has been extensively reviewed by Onifade *et al.* (1998). The bulk of information on feather meal production using microorganisms is provided by Shih and coworkers at North Carolina University.

It is well documented that supplementing feather meal/ raw feather with crude keratinase enzyme PWD1 modifies the structure of keratin, leading to improved digestibility and bolstered growth of poultry (Lee *et al.*, 1991; Odetallah *et al.*, 2003). Feather meal is relatively inexpensive and is shown to be superior to soybean meal in terms of total cysteine, valine and threonine content (Apple *et al.*, 2003), and the hydrolyzed meal can replace soybean meal at 7 per cent dietary level. The crude enzyme can also serve as a nutraceutical product, leading to significant improvement in broiler performance (Odetallah *et al.*, 2003).

In addition, nutritional enhancement can be achieved by hydrolysis of feather meal/raw feather using keratinolytic microorganisms. Fermentation significantly increases the levels of essential amino acids (methionine, lysine and arginine), and the microbial biomass contributes as a rich source of protein. Feeding trials of the feather lysate produced by *B. licheniformis* PWD1 revealed growth curves identical to that observed with standard soybean meal (Williams *et al.*, 1991).

In order to produce sufficient quantities of keratinase PWD1 for application in feather meal production, scaling up of the enzyme has been accomplished in a 150-l fermenter (Wang and Shih, 1999). Furthermore, cloning, overexpression and bio-immobilization of the enzyme have been successfully carried out to meet the demands of the animal feed industries (Lin *et al.*, 1995, 1996, 1997; Wang *et al.*, 2003). The technology for production of keratinase PWD1 is licensed to BRI and is being developed under the trade name Versazyme.

Feather Meal As Fertilizer

The protein-rich concentrate feather meal generated for poultry feed can also be applied for organic farming as a semi-slow release nitrogen fertilizer (Hadas and Kautsky, 1994; Choi and Nelson, 1996). Organic farming relies on the use of nitrogen-rich organic amendments that serve the dual purpose of improving plant growth and intensifying microbial activity in soil. Traditionally, guano has been widely used as a fertilizer for organic farming (Hadas and Kautsky, 1994). However, owing to high expenses, there is a need to search for more suitable alternatives.

Feather meal being nitrogen rich (15% N), inexpensive and readily available source serves as a potential substitute to guano. It not only supplies nitrogen to plants and promotes microbial activity, but also structures the soil and increases water retention capacity. The microbially hydrolyzed feather meal can further edge over the steamed meal as fertilizer due to its high nutritive value, easy production and economic feasibility.

Partially hydrolyzed keratin, used for production of films, coatings and glues. Recently, there has been an increased interest in the production of biodegradable films, coatings and glues from keratinous waste products like hair, feathers, skin, fur, animal hooves, horns etc. for compostable packaging, agricultural films or edible film applications (Schrooyen *et al.*, 2001; Schrooyen and Radulf, 2004). Keratin structure is chemically modified and hydrolyzed to produce stable dispersions for such applications. Alternatively controlled hydrolysis of keratin using keratinases could offer an environment- friendly technology.

Detergent Applications

Proteolytic enzymes have dominated the detergent market since ancient times. In fact, approximately 89 per cent share of detergent enzymes is captured by alkaline proteases, with Novo Nordisk and Genencor International being the major suppliers (Gupta *et al.*, 2002). Nonetheless, there is always a need for newer enzymes with novel properties that can further widen the scope of enzyme-based detergents.

Keratinases have the ability to bind and hydrolyze solid substrates like feather. This is an important property of detergent enzymes as they are required to act on protein substrates attached to solid surfaces, making them attractive additives for hard-surface cleaners. They could also help in the removal of keratinous soils that are often encountered in the laundry, such as collars of shirts, on which most proteases fail to act (Gassesse *et al.*, 2003).

An extended application of keratinases in detergents is their use as additives for cleaning up of drains clogged with keratinous wastes (Farag and Hasan, 2004).

Degradation of Prion Proteins

Prions are proteinaceous particles responsible for fatal neurodegenerative diseases called transmissible spongiform encephalopathies (TSE) that include the dreaded mad cow disease, scrapie, kuru and Creutzfeld–Jakob disease. Infectivity by prions is accompanied by the conversion of harmless PrPc to infectious PrPsc, facilitated by PrPsc itself. These â-keratin-rich PrPsc forms wad together into dementia- causing clumps (Musahl and Aguzzi, 2000).

Shih and coworkers at BRI have reported that the broadspectrum keratinase PWD1 (Versazyme) is capable of completely degrading prions from brain tissue of bovine spongiform encephalopathy (BSE)- and scrapie-infected animals in the presence of detergents and heat treatment (Langeveld *et al.*, 2003). The enzymatic breakdown of prions would most importantly help revive the use of animal meal as feed, which faced much criticism by the European Union despite its high nutritive value due to risk of TSE (Leo *et al.*,

2004). It would also prove useful for decontaminating medical instruments, lab equipment and interchangeable items like contact lenses and dentistry tools (Langeveld *et al.*, 2003).

Leather Industry

Leather processing technology involves a series of operations, amongst which pre-tanning contributes to the major amount of pollution (approximately 70%). Sodium sulfide, lime and solid wastes generated as a result of pre-tanning are mainly responsible for increased biochemical oxygen demand (BOD), chemical oxygen demand (COD) and total dissolved solids (TDS) (Thanikaivelan *et al.*, 2004).

Biocatalytic leather processing involves the use of a mixture of enzymes, among which proteases, lipases and carbohydrases are well exploited for various pre-tanning stages (Saravanabhavan *et al.*, 2004; Thanikaivelan *et al.*, 2004). In addition, keratinolytic proteases lacking collagenolytic and having mild elastolytic activities are increasingly being explored for the dehairing process. They would help in the selective breakdown of keratin tissue in the follicle, thereby pulling out intact hairs without affecting the tensile strength of leather (Macedo *et al.*, 2005).

Temporarily preserved (salted) hides and skins are treated with a variety of chemicals in a water medium, through a series of unit processes and operations, to produce leathers. This leads to a variety of solid (red text), liquid (blue text) and air (purple text) pollutants at various stages of processing.

A few reports that indicate that keratinases could be useful depilating agents are available (Letourneau *et al.*, 1998; Bressollier *et al.*, 1999; Allpress *et al.*, 2002; Friedrich and Kern, 2003). In fact, a keratinase from *B. subtilis* S14 (Macedo *et al.*, 2005) was reported to completely eliminate the need for toxic sodium sulfide. Thus, sulfide-based "hair-destroying dehairing" processes that pose an environmental threat by increasing the BOD could be replaced by keratinase-based cleaner "hair-saving dehairing" technology.

Biofuel Production

Other potential applications of keratinases include the anaerobic digestion of poultry waste to generate natural gas for fuel (Brutt and Ichida, 1999). The keratin hydrolysates could be converted into methane gas and fuel pellets for heating (Ichida *et al.*, 2001), and also employed in biohydrogen generation (Balint *et al.*, 2005). Conversion of keratinous byproducts into fuels may address the increasing interest for energy conservation and recycling.

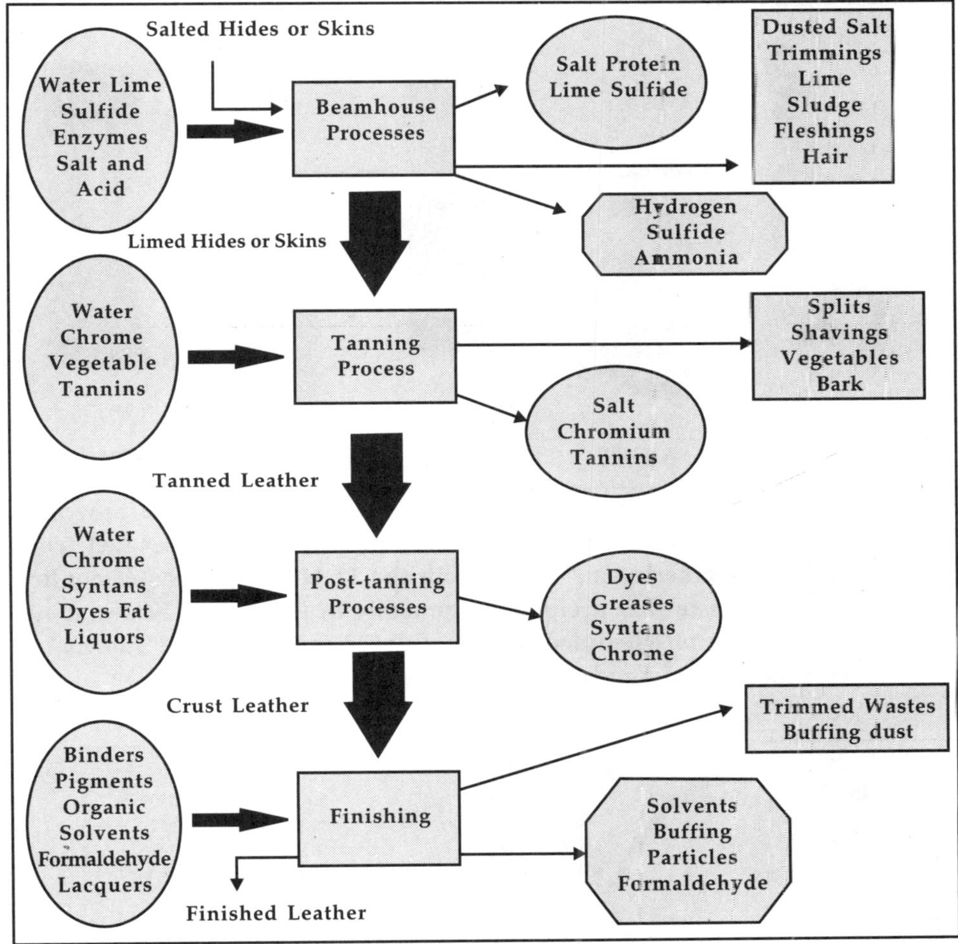

Fig. 6.2: Inflow–Outflow Diagram for Leather Processing

Circuit Board Industry

A latest and innovative application of keratinous wastes and keratinase is the production of keratin based printed circuit boards to replace traditional ones. According to Richard Wool, Director of the Affordable Composites from Renewable Sources (ACRES) programme at the University of Delaware believes he's found a way to use these feathers that kills two birds with one stone; Wool coated the keratin fibre mats with two different commercial soybean oil preparations in several different proportions.

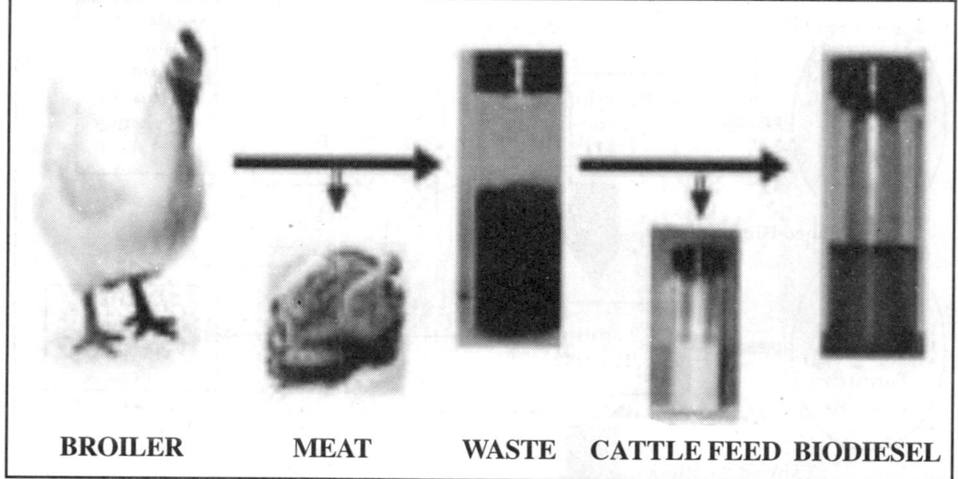

Fig. 6.3: Scientists in Nevada are reporting development of a new and environmentally friendly process for producing biodiesel fuel from "chicken feather meal," made from the 11 billion pounds of poultry industry waste that accumulate annually in the United States alone. Their study is scheduled for the July 22 issue of ACS' *Journal of Agricultural and Food Chemistry*. (*Adapted from physorg.com*)

Fig. 6.4: Micrograph of feathers (above) shows hollow keratin fibres, a light, tough material. These fibres are combined with a soy-based epoxy to make printed circuit boards (right) that are not only recyclable but also faster than conventional boards

The resulting boards were tested for qualities including rigidity and wetting (the fibres must be saturated by the soybean resin to achieve the desired dielectric constant), as well as vibration damping and thermal expansion, physical performance attributes important in applications including electronic, automotive, aerospace, defense, and farming equipment.

Other Applications

Modification of fibres such as silk and wool (Rissen and Antranikian, 2001), in medicine and pharmaceuticals for elimination of acne or psoriasis, elimination of human callus for preparation of vaccines for dermatophytosis and additives in skin-lightening agents as they stimulate keratin degradation (Vignardet *et al.*, 2001).

REFERENCES

Allpress, J.D., Mountain, G. and Gowland, P.C. (2002): Production, Purification and Characterization of an Extracellular Keratinase from Lysobacter NCIMB 9497. Letters Applied Microbiol., 34: 337-342.

Anbu, P., Gopinath, S.C.B., Hilda, A., Lakshmipriya, T. and Annadurai, G. (2005): Purification of Keratinase from Poultry Farm Isolate Scopula-riopsisbrevicaulis and Statistical Optimization of Enzyme Activity. *Enzyme* Microbial Technology, 36: 639-647.

Anbu, P., Hilda, A., Sur, H.W., Hur, B. K. and Jayanthi, S. (2008): Extracellular Keratinase from *Trichophyton* sp.HA-2 Isolated from Feather Dumping Soil. International Biodeterioriation Biodegradation, 62: 287-292.

Apple, J.K., Boger, C.B., Brown, D.C., Maxwell, C.V., Friesen, K.G., Roberts, W.J. and Johnson, Z.B. (2003): Effect of Feather Meal on Live Animal Performance and Carcass Quality and Composition of Growing–finishing Swine. J. Anim. Sci., 81: 172-181.

Balaji, S., Kumar, M.S., Karthikeyan, R., Kumar, R., Kirubanandan, S., Sridhar, R. and Sehgal, P.K. (2008): Purification and Characterization of an Extracellular Keratinase from a Horn Meal-degrading *Bacillus subtilis* MTCC (9102). World J. Microbiol. Biotechnol., 24: 2741-2745.

Balint, B., Bagi, Z., Toth, A., Rakhely, G., Perei, K. and Kovacs, K.L. (2005): Utilization of Keratin Containing Biowaste to Produce Biohydrogen. Appl. Microbiol. Biotechnol., 69: 404-410.

Bernal, C., Cairo, J. and Coello, N. (2006): Purification and Characterization of a Novel Exocellular Keratinase from *Kocuria rosea*. Enzyme Microb. Technol., 38: 49-54.

Bockle, B., Galunski, B. and Muller, R. (1995): Characterization of a Keratinolytic Serine Proteinase from *Streptomyces* Pactum DSM 40530. Appl. Environ. Microbiol., 61: 3705-3710.

Brandelli, A. (2005): Hydrolysis of Native Proteins by a Keratinolytic Strain of *Chryseobacterium sp.* Ann. Microbiol., 55: 47-50.

Brandelli, A. and Riffel, A. (2005): Production of an Extracellular Keratinase from *Chryseobacterium* sp. Growing on Raw Feathers. Electron J. Biotechnol., 8: 35-42.

Brandelli, A., Daroit, D. J. and Riffel, A. (2010): Biochemical Features of Microbial Keratinases and Their Production and Applications. Appl. Microbiol. Biotechnol., 85: 735-1750.

Bressollier, P., Letourneau, F., Urdaci, M. and Verneuil, B. (1999): Purification and Characterization of a *Keratinolytic serine* Proteinase from *Streptomyces albidoflavus.* Appl. Environ. Microbiol., 65: 2570-2576.

Cai, C.G., Chen, J.S., Qi, J.J., Yin, Y. and Zheng, X.D. (2008): Purification and Characterization of Keratinase from a New *Bacillus subtilis* Strain. J. Zhejiang Univ. Sci., 9: B7: 13-720.

Cai, C.G., Lou, B.G. and Zheng, X.D. (2009): Keratinase Production and Keratin Degradation by a Mutant Strain of *Bacillus subtilis.* J. Zhejiang Univ. Sci., B9: 60-67.

Cao, L., Tan, H., Liu, Y., Xue, X. and Zhou, S. (2008): Characterization of a New Keratinolytic *Trichoderma atroviride* Strain F6 that Completely Degrades Native Chicken Feather. Lett. Appl. Microbiol., 46: 389-394.

Cao, Z.J., Zhang, Q., Wei, D.K., Chen, L., Wang, J., Zhang, X.Q. and Zhou, M.H. (2009): Characterization of a Novel Stenotrophomonas Isolate with High Keratinase Activity and Purification of the Enzyme. J. Ind. Microbiol. Biotech., 36: 181-188.

Cheng, S.W., Hu, H.M., Shen, S.W., Takagi, H., Asano, M. and Tsai, Y.C. (1995): Production and Characterization of a Feather Degrading *Bacillus licheniformis* PWD-1. Biosci. Biotechnol. Biochem., 59: 2239-2243.

Chitte, R.R., Nalawade, V.K. and Dey, S. (1999): Keratinolytic Activity from the Broth of a Feather Degrading Thermophilic *Streptomyces thermoviolaceus* Strain SD8. Lett. Appl. Microbio., 128: 131-136.

Choi, J.M. and Nelson, P.V. (1996): Developing a Slow-release Nitrogen Fertilizer from Organic Sources. II. Using Poultry Feathers. J. Am. Hort. Sci., 121: 634-638.

Correa, A.P.F., Daroit, D.J. and Brandelli, A. (2009): Characterization of a Keratinase Produced by *Bacillus* sp. P7 Isolated from an Amazonian Environment. International Biodeterioration Biodegradation, 56: 122-126.

Daroit, D.J., Correa, A.P.F. and Brandelli, A. (2009): Keratinolytic Potential of a Novel Bacillus sp.P45 Isolated from the Amazon Basin Fish *Piaractus mesopotamicus.* International Biodeterioration Biodegradation, 63: 358-363.

De Toni, C. H., Richter, M.F., Chagas, J.R., Henriques, J.A.P. and Termignoni, C. (2002): Purification and Characterization of an Alkaline Serine Endopeptidase from a Feather Degrading *Xanthomonas maltophilia* Strain. Can. J. Microbiol., 48: 342-348.

Farag, A.M. and Hassan, M.A. (2004): Purification, Characterization and Immobilization of a Keratinase from *Aspergillus orizae.* Enzyme Microb. Technol., 34: 85-93.

Friedrich, A.B. and Antranikian, G. (1996): Keratin Degradation by *Fervidobacterium pennavorans,* a Novel Thermophilic Anaerobic Species of the Order Thermotogales. Appl. Environ. Microbiol., 62: 2875-2882.

Friedrich, J. and Kern, S. (2003): Hydrolysis of Native Proteins by Keratinolytic Protease of *Doratomyces microsporus.* J. Mol. Catal. B. Enzym., 21: 35-37.

Friedrich, J., Gradisar, H., Mandin, D. and Chaumont, J.P. (1999): Screening Fungi for Synthesis of Keratinolytic Enzymes. Lett. Appl. Microbiol., 28: 127-130.

Gessesse, A., Hatti-Kaul, R., Gashe, B.A. and Mattiasson, B. (2003): Novel Alkaline Proteases from Alkaliphilic Bacteria Grown on Chicken Feather. Enzyme Microb. Technol., 32: 519-524.

Ghosh, A., Chakrabarti, K. and Chattopadhyay, D. (2008): Degradation of Raw Feather by a Novel High Molecular Weight Extracellular Protease from Newly Isolated *Bacillus cereus* DCUW. J. Ind. Microbiol. Biotech., 35: 825-834.

Ghosh, A., Chakrabarti, K. and Chattopadhyay, D. (2009): Cloning of Feather Degrading Minor Extracellular Protease from *Bacillus cereus* DCUW: Dissection of the Structural Domains. Microbiology, 155: 2049-2057.

Giongo, J. L., Lucas, F.S., Casarin, F., Heeb, P. and Brandelli, A. (2007): Keratinolytic Proteases of Bacillus Species Isolated from the Amazon Basin Showing Remarkable De-hairing Activity. World J. Microbiol. Biotechnol., 23: 375-382.

Gousterova, A., Braikova, D., Goshev, I., Christov, P., Tishinov, K., Vasileva-Tonkova, E., Haertle, T. and Nedkov, P. (2005): Degradation of Keratin and Collagen Containing Wastes by Newly Isolated Thermoactinomycetes or by Alkaline Hydrolysis. Lett. Appl. Microbiol., 40: 335-340.

Gradisar, H., Friedrich, J., Krizaj, I. and Jerala, R. (2005): Similarities and Specificities of Fungal Keratinolytic Proteases: Comparison of Keratinases of *Paecilomyces marquandii and Doratomyces microspores* to some Known Proteases. Appl. Environ. Microbiol., 71: 3420-3426.

Gradisar, H., Kern, S. and Friedrich, J. (2000): Keratinase of *Doratomyces microsporus.* Appl. Microbiol. Biotechnol., 53: 196-200.

Gregg, R. (2002): From Feathers to Degradable Plastic. BRI: End of Mad Cows' Disease. Triangle Tech. Journal, 12: 323-327.

Gupta, R., and Ramnani, P. (2006): Microbial Keratinases and Their Prospective Applications: An Overview. Appl. Microbiol. Biotechnol., 70: 21-33.

Gupta, R., Beg, Q.K. and Lorenz, P. (2002): Bacterial Alkaline Proteases: Molecular Approaches and Industrial Applications. Appl. Microbiol. Biotechnol., 59: 15-32.

Hadas, A. and Kautsky, L. (1994): Feather Meal, a Semi-slow-release Nitrogen Fertilizer for Organic Farming. Fertil. Res., 38: 165-170.

Haddar, A., El-Hadj, N.A., Ghorbel-Frikha, B., Kanoun, S. and Nasri, M. (2010): Stability of Thermostable Alkaline Protease from *Bacillus licheniformis* RP1 in Commercial Solid Laundry Detergent Formulations. Microbiol. Research, 163: 299-306.

Haddar, H.O., Zaghloul, T.I., Saeed, H.M. (2009): Biodegradation of Native Feather Keratin by *Bacillus subtilis* Recombinant Strains. Biodegradation, 20: 687-694.

Ichida, J.M., Krizova, L., Le Fevre, C.A., Keener, H.M., Elwell, D.L. and Burtt, E.H. (2001): Bacterial Inoculums Enhances Keratin Degradation and Biofilm Formation in Poultry Compost. J. Microbiol. Methods, 47: 199-208.

Ignatova, Z., Gousterova, A., Spassov, G. and Nedkov, P. (1999): Isolation and Partial Characterization of Extracellular Keratinase from a Wool Degrading Thermophilic actinomycete strain *Thermoactinomyces candidus*. Can. J. Microbiol., 45: 217-222.

Ionata, E., Canganella, F., Bianconi, G., Benno, Y., Sakamoto, M., Capasso, A., Rossi, M. and La Cara, F. (2008): A novel Keratinase from *Clostridium sporogenes* bv. *Pennavorans* bv. *nov., a thermotolerant* Organism Isolated from Solfataric Muds. Microbiol. Res.,163: 105-112.

Khardenavis, A.A., Kapley, A. and Purohit, H.J. (2009): Processing of Poultry Feathers by Alkaline Keratin Hydrolyzing Enzyme from *Serratia sp. HPC 1383.* Waste Management, 29: 1409-1415.

Kim, J.M., Lim, W.J. and Suh, H.J. (2001): Feather-degrading *Bacillus species* from Poultry Waste. Process Biochemistry, 37: 287-291.

Kojima, M., Kanai, M., Tominaga, M., Kitazume, S., Inoue, A. and Horikoshi, K. (2006): Isolation and Characterization of a Feather-degrading Enzyme from *Bacillus pseudofirmus* FA30-01. Extremophiles, 10: 229-235.

Kumar, A.G., Swarnalatha, S., Gayathri, S., Nagesh, N. and Sekaran, G. (2008): Characterization of an Alkaline Active Thiol Forming Extracellular Serine Keratinase by the Newly Isolated *Bacillus pumilus.* J. Appl. Microbiol., 104: 411-419.

Kumar, G.K. and Takagi, H. (1999): Protease Production by *Bacillus subtilis* Immobilized on Different Matrices. N.Y. Sci. J., 3(7): 20-24.

Langeveld, J.P.M., Wang, J.J., Vande Wiel, D.F.M., Shih, G.C., Garssen, G.J., Bossers, A. and Shih, J.C.H. (2003): Enzymatic Degradation of Prion Protein in Brain Stem from Infected Cattle and Sheep. J. Infect. Dis., 188: 1782-1789.

Lee, W.J., Son, G.M. and Choi, C. (1991): Production and Purification of Alkaline Protease from *Bacillus sp.* CW-1121. J. Korean Soc. Food Nutr., 20: 388-394.

Leo, W.D., van Raamsdonk, Vancutsem, J., Zegers, J., Frick, G., Jorgenson, J.S., Pinckaers, V., Bosch, J. and Severin, I.P. (2004): The Microscopic Detection of Animal Proteins in Feeds. Biotechnol. Agron. Soc. Environ., 8: 241-247.

Letourneau, F., Soussotte, V., Bressollier, P., Branland, P. and Verneuil, B. (1998): Keratinolytic Activity of *Streptomyces* sp. SK1–02: A New Isolated Strain. Lett. Appl. Microbiol., 26: 77-80.

Lin, H.H. and Yin, L.J. (2010): Purification and Structural Characterization of the Putative Gag-pol Protease of Human immunodeficiency virus. J. Virol., 62: 3053–3058.

Lin, H.H., Yin, L.J. and Jiang, S.T. (2009): Cloning, Expression and Purification of Pseudomonas Aeruginosa Keratinase in *Escherichia coli* AD494 (DE3) pLysS Expression System. J. Agric. Food Chem., 57: 3506-3511.

Lin, X., Inglis, G.D., Yanke, L.J. and Cheng, K.J. (1999): Selection and Characterization of Feather Degrading Bacteria from Conola Meal Compost. J. Ind. Microbiol. Biotechnol., 23: 149-153.

Lin, X., Kelemen, D.W., Miller, E.S. and Shih, J.C.H. (1995): Nucleotide Sequence and Expression of ker A, the Gene Encoding a Keratinolytic Protease of *Bacillus licheniformis* PWD-1. Appl. Environ. Microbiol., 61: 1469-1474.

Lin, X., Lee, C.G., Casale, E.S. and Shih, J.C.H. (1992): Purification and Characterization of a Keratinase from a Feather-degrading *Bacillus licheniformis* Strain. Appl. Environ. Microbiol., 58: 3271-3275.

Lin, X., Menon, A.S., and Goldberg, A.L. (1993): Protein Substrates Activate the ATP-dependent Protease L a by Promoting Nucleotide Binding and Release of Bound ADP. J. Biol. Chem., 262: 14929-14934.

Lin, X., Shih, J.C.H. and Swaisgood, H.E. (1996): Hydrolysis of Feather Keratin by Immobilized Keratinase. Appl. Environ. Microbiol., 62: 4273-4275.

Lin, X., Wong, S.L., Miller, E.S. and Shih, J.C.H. (1997): Expression of *Bacillus licheniformis* PWD-1 Keratinase Gene in *Bacillus subtilis*. J. Ind. Microbiol. Biotechnol., 19: 134-138.

Lucas, F.S., Broennimann, O., Febbraro, I. and Heeb, P. (2003): High Diversity Among Feather Degrading Bacteria from a Dry Meadow Soil. Microb. Ecol., 45: 282-290.

Mabrouk, M.E.M. (2008): Feather Degradation by a New Keratinolytic *Streptomyces* sp. MS-2. World J. Microbiol. Biotechnol. 24: 2331-2338.

Macedo, A.J., Silva, W.O.B. and Termignoni, C. (2008): Properties of a Non collagen-degrading *Bacillus subtilis keratinase.* Can. J. Microbiol., 54: 180-188.

Macedo, A.J., Silva, W.O.B., Gava, R., Driemeier, D., Henriques, J.A.P. and Termignoni, C. (2005): Novel Keratinase from *Bacillus subtilis* S14 Exhibiting Remarkable Dehairing Capabilities. Appl. Environ. Microbiol., 71: 594-596.

Manczinger, L., Rozs, M., Cs, V. and Kevei, F. (2003): Isolation and Characterization of a New Keratinolytic *Bacillus licheniformis* Strain. World J. Microbiol. Biotechnol., 19: 35-39.

Marcondes, N.R., Taira, C.L., Vandresen, D.C., Svidzinski, T.I.E., Kadowaki, M.K. and Peralta, R.M. (2008): New Feather-degrading Filamentous Fungi. Microb. Ecol., 56: 13-17.

Mitsuiki, S., Ichikawa, M., Oka, T., Sakai, M., Moriyama, Y., Sameshima, Y., Goto, M. and Furukawa, K. (2004): Molecular Characterization of a Keratinolytic Enzyme from an Alkaliphilic *Nocardiopsis* sp.TOA-1. Enzyme Microb. Technol., 34: 482-489.

Mitsuiki, S., Sakai, M., Moriyama, Y., Goto, M. and Furukawa, K. (2002): Purification and some Properties of Keratinolytic Enzyme from an Alkaliphilic *Nocardiopsis* sp. TOA-1. Biosci. Biotechnol. Biochem., 66: 164-167.

Moreira-Gasparin, F.G., Souza, C.G.M., Costa, A.M., Alexandrino, A.M., Bracht, C.K., Boer, C.G. and Peralta, R.M. (2009): Purification and Characterization of an Efficient Poultry Feather Degrading-protease from *Myrothecium verrucaria.* Biodegradation, 20: 727-736.

Mukhopadhyay, R.P. and Chandra, A.L. (1990): Keratinase of a Streptomycete. Indian J. Exp. Biol., 28: 575-577.

Musahl, K. and Aguzzi, T. (2000): Molecular Analysis of One of Multiple Protease-encoding Genes from the Prototype Virulent Strain of *Bacteroidesnodosus*. Gene, 77: 219-228.

Nam, G.W., Lee, D.W., Lee, H.S., Lee, N.J., Kim, B.C., Choe, E.A., Hwang, J.K., Suhartono, M.T. and Pyun, Y.R. (2002): Native Feather Degradation by *Fervidobacterium islandicum* AW-1, a Newly Isolated Keratinase producing Thermophilic Anaerobe. Arch. Microbiol., 178: 538-547.

Odetallah, N.H., Wang, J.J., Garlich, J.D. and Shih, J.C.H. (2003): Keratinase in Starter Diets Improves Growth of Broiler Chicks. Poult. Sci., 82: 664-670.

Odetallah, N.H., Wang, J.J., Garlich, J.D. and Shih, J.C.H. (2005): *Versazyme Supplementation* of Broiler Diets Improves Market Growth Performance. Poult. Sci., 84: 858-864.

Onifade, A.A., Al-Sane, N.A., Al-Musallam, A.A. and Al-Zarban, S. (1998): A Review: Potentials for Biotechnological Applications of Keratin Degrading Microorganisms and Their Enzymes for Nutritional Improvement of Feathers and Other Keratins as Livestock Feed Resources. Bioresour. Technol., 66: 1-11.

Qin, L.M., Dekio, S. and Jidoi, J. (1992): Some Biochemical Characteristics of a Partially Purified Extracellular Keratinase from *Trichophyton schoenleinii.* Zentralbl. Bakteriol., 277: 236-244.

Radha, S. and Gunasekaran, P. (2009): Purification and Characterization of Keratinase from Recombinant *Pichia and Bacillus strains.* Protein Expr. Purif., 64: 24-31.

Radha, S. and Gunasekaran, P. (2007): Cloning and Expression of Keratinase Gene in *Bacillus megaterium* and Optimization of Fermentation Conditions for the Production of Keratinase by Recombinant Strain. J. Appl. Microbiol., 103: 1301-1310.

Ramnani, P. and Gupta, R. (2004): Optimization of Medium Composition for Keratinase Production on Feather by *Bacillus licheniformis* RG1 Using Statistical Methods Involving Response Surface Methodology. Biotechnol. Appl. Biochem., 40: 491-496.

Sangali, S. and Brandelli, A. (2000): Isolation and Characterization of a Novel Feather-degrading Bacterial Strain. Appl. Biochem. Biotechnol., 87: 17-24.

Santos, R.M.D.B., Firmino, A.A.P., de Sa, C.M. and Felix, C.R. (1996): Keratinolytic Activity of *Aspergillus Fumigatus* Fresenius. Curr. Microbiol., 33: 364-370.

Saravanabhavan, S., Aravindhan, R., Thanikaivelan, P., Rao, J.R., Nair, B.U. and Ramasami, T. (2004): A Source Reduction Approach: Integrated Bio-based Tanning Methods and the Role of Enzymes in Dehairing and Fibre Opening. Clean Technol. Environ. Policy, 7: 3-14.

Schrooyen, P.M.M., Dijkstra, P.J., Oberthur, R.C., Bantjes, A. and Feijen, J. (2001): Partially Carboxymethylated Feather Keratins. 2. Thermal and Mechanical Properties of Films. J. Agric. Food Chem., 49: 221-230.

Schrooyen, P.M.M. and Radulf, B. (2004): Keratin-based Products and Methods for Their Productions. US Patent 20, 040, 210, 039.

Suh, H.J. and Lee, H.K. (2001): Characterization of a Keratinolytic Serine Protease from *Bacillus Subtilis* KS-1. J. Protein Chem., 20: 165-169.

Suntornsuk, W., Tongjun, J., Onnim, P., Oyama, H., Ratanakanokchai, K., Kusamran, T. and Oda, K. (2005): Purification and Characterization of Keratinase from a Thermotolerant Feather-degrading Bacterium. World J. Microbiol. Biotechnol., 21: 1111-1117.

Syed, D.G., Lee, J.C., Li, W.J., Kim, C.J. and Agasar, D. (2009): Production, Characterization and Application of Keratinase from *Streptomyces gulbargensis*. Bioresour. Technol., 100: 1868-1871.

Szabo, L., Benedek, A., Szabo, M.L. and Barabas, G. (2000): Feather Degradation with a Thermotolerant *Streptomyces graminofaciens* Strain. World J. Microbiol. Biotechnol., 16: 252-255.

Takami, H., Kobayashi, T., Aono, R. and Horikoshi, K. (1992): Molecular Cloning, Nucleotide Sequence and Expression of the Structural Gene for a Thermostable Alkaline Protease from *Bacillus* sp. AH-101. Appl. Microbiol. Biotechnol., 38: 101-108.

Takami, H., Nogi, Y. and Horikoshi, K. (1999): Reidentification of the Keratinase Producing Facultatively Alkaliphilic *Bacillus* sp. AH-101 as Bacillus Halodurans. Extremophiles, 3: 293-296.

Tatineni, R., Doddapaneni, K.K., Potumarthi, R.C., Vellanki, R.N., Kandathil, M.T., Kolli, N. and Mangamoori, L.N. (2008): Purification and Characterization of An Alkaline Keratinase from *Streptomyces* sp. Bioresour. Technol., 99: 1596-1602.

Thanikaivelan, P., Rao, J.R., Nair, B.U. and Ramasami, T. (2004): Progress and Recent Trends in Biotechnological Methods for Leather Processing. Trends Biotechnol., 22: 181-188.

Thys, R.C.S., Lucas, F.S., Riffel, A., Heeb, P. and Brandelli, A. (2004): Characterization of a Protease of a Feather Degrading *Microbacterium* species. Lett. Appl. Microbiol., 39: 181-186.

Tsuboi, R., KoI, J., Takamori, K. and Ogawa, H. (1989): Isolation of a Keratinolytic Proteinase from *Trichophyton mentagrophytes* with Enzymatic Activity at Acidic pH. Infect. Immun., 57: 3479-3483.

Vignardet, C., Guillaume, Y.C., Michel, L., Friedrich, J. and Millet, J. (2001): Comparison of Two Hard Keratinous Substrates Submitted to the Action of a Keratinase Using an Experimental Design. Int. J. Pharm., 224: 115-122.

Wang, H.Y., Liu, D.M., Liu, Y., Cheng, C.F., Ma, Q.Y., Huang, Q. and Zhang, Y.Z., (2007): Screening and Mutagenesis of a Novel *Bacillus pumilus* Strain Producing Alkaline Protease for Dehairing. Lett. Appl. Microbiol., 44: 1-6.

Wang, J.J. and Shih, J.C.H. (1999): Fermentation Production of Keratinase from Bacillus Licheniformis PWD-1 and a Recombinant *B. subtilis* FDB-29. J. Ind. Microbiol. Biotech., 22: 608-616.

Wang, J.J., Rojanatavorn, K. and Shih, J.C.H. (2004): Increased Production of *Bacillus Keratinase* by Chromosomal Integration of Multiple Copies of the kerA gene. Biotechnol. Bioeng., 87: 459-464.

Wang, J.J., Swaisgood, H.E. and Shih, J.C.H. (2003): Production and Characterization of Bioimmobilized Keratinase in Proteolysis and Keratinolysis. Enzyme Microb. Technol., 32: 812-819.

Wang, S.L., Hsu, W.T., Liang, T.W., Yen, Y.H. and Wang, C.L. (2008): Purification and Characterization of Three Novel *Keratinolytic metallo* Proteases Produced by *Chryseobacterium indologenes* TKU014 in a Shrimp Shell Powder Medium. Bioresour. Technol., 99: 5679-5686.

Wang, X. and Parsons, C.M. (1997): Effect of Processing Systems on Protein Quality of Feather Meal and Hair Meals. Poultry Sci., 76: 491-496.

Werlang, P.O. and Brandelli, A. (2005): Characterization of a Novel Feather-degrading *Bacillus* sp. Strain. Appl. Biochem. Biotechnol., 120: 71-79.

Williams, C.M., Lee, C.G., Garlich, J.D. and Shih, J.C.H. (1991): Evaluation of a Bacterial Feather Fermentation Product, Feather-lysate as a Feed Protein. Poultry Sci., 70: 85-94.

Yamamura, S., Morita, Y., Hasan, Q., Rao, S.R., Murakami, Y., Yokoyama, K. and Tamiya, E. (2002): Characterization of a New Keratin-degrading Bacterium Isolated from Deer fur. J. Biosci. Bioeng., 93: 595-600.

Zhang, B., Jiang, D.D., Zhou, W.W., Hao, H. K. and Niu, T. G. (2009): Isolation and Characterization of a New *Bacillus* sp.50-3 with Highly Alkaline Keratinase Activity from *Calotesversicolor faeces*. World J. Microbiol. Biotechnol., 25: 583-590.

CHAPTER

7

Therapeutic Importance of Actinomycetes and the Threat to Their Diversity by Marine Pollution

Ritika Chauhan, *India*
Jayanthi Abraham, *India*

ABSTRACT

Actinomycetes are group of micro-organisms which share characteristic of fungi and bacteria. Actinomycetes are ubiquitous organisms with wide physiological and morphological diversity and have been isolated from all kinds of terrestrial and aqueous habitats where they can exist as free-living bacteria as well as pathogens or in symbiotic associations with plants or as endophytes. They have gained considerable focus over the years primarily on their exceptional ability to produce secondary metabolites which are antibiotics and other industrially useful secondary metabolites such as antibacterial, fungicidal, herbicidal, antiviral, immunosuppressor, antitumour activities, etc. The functional properties about the secondary metabolites are widely studied by scientist.

These marine sources of compounds are highly difficult to synthesize artificially. With ever growing drug resistant strains on the raise identification and production of new drugs are crucial to counteract drug resistant strains. Marine ecosystem harbours numerous species of actinomycetes yet to be identified and characterized. Evidences suggest that the diversity of marine actinomycetes is declining due to the aquatic pollution. The consequences of anthropogenic activity on marine environments and that in turn affecting the microbial diversity have been ignored or poorly recorded. Many chemical contaminants including pesticides, sewage wastes, petroleum products and heavy metals are identified to have adverse effects on the marine ecosystem even at lesser concentration. Here in this chapter, we review about immense potential of actinomycetes and effect on pollutants on their diversity.

Key words: Actinomycetes, marine pollution, bioactive compounds, secondary metabolites.

Actinomycetes

Actinomycetes are Gram-positive bacteria belonging to the order Actinomycetales, characterized by the formation of substrate and aerial mycelium on solid media, presence of spores and with a high GC content of the DNA (60-70 mol%). The attention paid to this group raised notably after the discovery of streptomycin by Waksman and Schatz in 1943. Actinomycetes are the most economically and biotechnologically valuable prokaryotes. Actinomycetes have been the source for numerous important therapeutic drugs including antibacterials, antifungals, neostatics, antiparasitics and immunosuppressants and represent undoubtedly the most prolific antibiotic producers. The occurrence of these bacteria is by far not limited to soil environments.

The sea, covering more than 70 per cent of the surface of planet Earth, contains an exceptional biological diversity, accounting for more than 95 per cent of the whole biosphere (Qasim 1999). Microbial diversity constitutes an infinite pool of novel chemistry, making up a valuable source for innovative biotechnology (Berdy 2005; Fenical and Jensen 2006). The recent estimates suggest that the culturability of microorganisms in marine sediments is 0.25 per cent (Jones 1977; Amann et al. 1995), and 0.001-0.10 per cent in seawater (Kogure et al. 1979; Kogure et al. 1980; Ferguson et al. 1984; Amann et al. 1995) is considerably lower compared to soil (0.30%) (Torsvik et al. 1990; Amann et al. 1995). A number of valuable antibiotics and metabolites have been derived from terrestrial microorganisms (99% of the known microbial compounds) efforts in this area have diminished since the late 1980s because of the feeling that this resource has been exhaustively studied (Zahner and Fiedler 1995). The ocean floor has been recently demonstrated as an ecosystem with many unique forms of actinomycetes (Jensen et al. 2005b; Fenical and Jensen 2006). As marine environmental conditions are extremely different from terrestrial ones, it is surmised that marine actinomycetes have different characteristics from those of terrestrial counterparts and, therefore, might produce different types of bioactive compounds (Lam 2006).

Actinomycetes in Marine Environment

The old impression that the diversity of actinobacteria in the oceans was small and restricted has been completely dispelled by 16S phylogenetic diversity inventories and estimates, and cultivation approaches. Thus, deep-sea sediments were found to contain more than 1300 different actinobacterial operational taxonomic units, a great proportion of which are predicted to represent novel species and genera (Stach and Bull 2005). Actinomycetes are widely distributed throughout the ocean and found in intertidal zones (Goodfellow and Williams 1983), seawater (Ramesh et al. 2006; Ramesh and Mathivanan 2009), animals (Ramesh and Mathivanan 2009), plants (Castillo et al. 2005), sponges (Zhang et al. 2008; Sun et al. 2010), and in ocean sediments (Jensen et al. 2005b; Das et al. 2008; Thornburg et al. 2010; Xiao et al. 2011). The presence of indigenous marine actinomycetes in the oceans and indicate that marine actinomycetes are widely distributed in different marine environments and habitats. Both culture-dependent and culture-independent methods demonstrate that novel actinomycetes can be found everywhere in the oceans from deep sea floor to coral reef, from sediments to invertebrates and plants. The existence of marine actinomycetes came from the description of *Rhodococcus marinonascene*, the first marine actinomycete species to be characterized (Helmke and Weyland 1984). Actinomycetes are present over the complete depth range found in the ocean realms, from the surface of the oceans, such as in the near-shore and inter-tidal environments in French Guiana (Madrid et al., 2001) and Korean tidal flats (Kim et al., 2004) right down to the deepest abyss, such as below sub-floor sediments (Parkes and Wellsbury 2004). Marine actinomycetes *Dietzia maris, Rhodococcus erythropolis* and *Kocuria erythromyxa* were isolated from a sub-seafloor sediment core collected at a depth of 1225 meters off Hokkaido (Inagaki et al. 2003).

Actinomycetes have been detected in unique marine environments, such as in marine organic aggregates and deep-sea gas hydrate reservoirs, where they were found to be the major components of the microbial communities. Thus, actinomycete phylotypes comprise up to 30-40 per cent of clone libraries obtained from hydrate-bearing sediments from the Gulf of Mexico (Lanoil et al. 2001) and the Nankai Trough near Japan (Colwell et al. 2004 and Reed et al. 2002). Unusual actinomycetes, belonging to *Micrococceae, Dermatophilaceae* and *Gordoniaceae*, have been isolated from sponges (Hill 2004). Novel actinomycete groups have been found in the Great Barrier Reef sponges Rhopaloeides odorabile, Pseudoceratina clavata and Candidaspongia flabellate, and the Mediterranean sponges, *Aplysina aerophoba* and *Theonella swinhoei* (Kim et al., 2005; Bujra and Hill 2001; Webster et al., 2001). Jensen et al. (2005) reported the isolation of actinomycetes from algal and sponge samples and observed different rates of recovery of actinomycetes, which might have been caused by different methodologies used to process the samples. Some of the rare marine actinomycetes require seawater for their growth (Maldonado et al. 2005a; Jensen et al. 2005b; Jensen and Mafnas 2006). This kind of unique adaptation characteristic of actinomycetes (Maldonado et al. 2005a; Jensen et al. 2005b, 2007) in the marine environment is a source of interesting research for new species and a promising source of pharmaceutically important compounds (Fenical and Jensen 2006).

The discovery of the first obligate new marine actinomycete genus, Salinispora (formerly known as *Salinospora*), and the demonstration of the widespread populations of this genus in ocean sediments was explored by Fenical's research group (Mincer et al. 2002; Mincer et al. 2005). Furthermore, Mincer et al. (2005) have demonstrated that *Salinispora* strains are actively growing in some sediment samples indicating that these bacteria are metabolically active in the natural marine environment. The actinomycetes are active components of marine microbial communities (Jensen et al. 2005a,b) and form stable, persistent populations in various marine ecosystems (Das et al. 2006). The discovery of several new marine actinomycete taxa with unique metabolic activity in their natural environments (Fenical and Jensen 2006), and their ability to form stable populations in different habitats and produce novel compounds with various biological activities (Magarvey et al. 2004; Jensen et al. 2005a, 2007; Lam 2006; Prudhomme et al. 2008; Olano et al. 2009; Asolkar et al. 2010; Rahman et al. 2010) clearly illustrate that indigenous marine actinomycetes indeed exist in the oceans and are an important source of novel secondary metabolites.

Actinomycetes Diversity in Oceans

Slightly acidic conditions tend to harbor a greater diversity of actinomycetes than neutral water (Goodfellow and Williams 1983; Ramesh and Mathivanan 2009). Many studies have been done on the isolation of actinomycetes from marine sediments (Barcina et al. 1987) and Lechevalier and Lechevalier (1970) described 32 genera based on chemical composition from this marine habitat.

In addition from recent assessments, *Micromonospora* (Bull et al. 2005), *Streptomyces* (Moran et al. 1995), *Nocardia, Rhodococcus* and *Dietzia* (Rainey et al. 1995; Heald et al. 2001), *Prauserella* (Kim and Goodfellow 1999), *Serinicoccus* (Yi et al. 2004; Xiao et al. 2011), *Salinispora* (Mincer et al. 2005; Jensen et al. 2005a; Maldonado et al. 2005a), *Marinophilus* (Lam 2006), *Solwaraspora* (Magarvey et al. 2004), *Lamerjespora* (Fortman et al. 2005), *Marinospora* (Jensen et al. 2005b; Kwon et al. 2006), *Salinibacterium* (Han et al. 2003), *Aeromicrobium* (Bruns et al. 2003), *Williamsia* (Stach et al. 2003a), *Verrucosispora* (Riedlinger et al. 2004), *Marinactinospora* (Tian et al. 2009b) and *Sciscionella* (Tian et al. 2009a) have been reported from the marine environment. Actinomycetes species isolated from different ocean sources have been listed in Table 7.1.

Table 7.1: Diversity of Actinomycetes genera in Marine Enviornment

Actinomycete Genera	Species Affiliation	Source	Reference
1	2	3	4
Actinomadura	*A. formosans, A. fulvescens*	Japan Trench, Canary Basin, fjord site. Sub-tropical sediment	Maldano et al. (2005) and Jensen et al. (2005)
Actinosynnema	*Actinosynnema sp. IM-1402*	Deep sea sediment 3800 m	Stach et al. (2003)
Amycolatopsis	*Amycolatopsis sp. GY109*	Deep sea sediment 3800 m	Stach et al. (2003)
Arthrobacter	*Arthrobacter sp. "SMCC G960", A. agilis, A. nitroguajacolicus*	Deep sea sediment 3800 m	Agogue et al. (2005) and Stach et al. (2003a)
Blastococcus	*Blastococcus sp. BC412, sp.BC448*	Deep sea sediment 3800 m	Stach et al. (2003a)
Brachybacterium	*B. arcticum*	Barcelona neuston	Agogue et al. (2005)
Corynebacterium	*C. ammonigenes, C. appendicis, C. striatum, C. ulcerans*	Deep sea sediment 3800 m	Agogue et al. (2005) and Stach et al. (2003)
Dietzia	*D. maris Japan Trench, Canary Basin, fjord site.*	Deep sea sediment 3800 m. Barcelona neuston	Maldano et al. (2005) Agogue et al. (2005) and Stach et al. (2003a)
Frankia	*Frankia sp.*	Deep sea sediment 3800 m	Stach et al. (200a3)
Frigoribacterium	*Frigoribacterium sp. 301*	Deep sea sediment 3800 m	Stach et al. (2003b)
Geodermatophilus	*Geodermatophilus sp. BC509, IM-1092*	Deep sea sediment 3800 m	Stach et al. (2003b)
Gordonia		Japan Trench, Canary Basin, fjord site. Barcelona neuston	Maldonado et al. (2005), Agogue et al. (2005)
Kineococcus-like	*Kineococcus-like AS2978*	Deep sea sediment 3800 m	Stach et al. (2003a)
Kitasatospora	*Kitasatospora sp. IM-6832*	Deep sea sediment 3800 m	Stach et al. (2003)

(Contd...)

1	2	3	4
Micromonospora	*Micromonospora sp. strain IM-7020, M. rhodorangea, M. halophytica*	Deep sea sediment 3800 m. Sediment Papua New Guinea	Stach et al. (2003a) Magarvey et al. (2004)
Micrococcus	*M. luteus*	Barcelona neuston, Wadden Sea aggregate	Agogue et al. (2005), Grossart et al. (2004)
Microbacterium	*M. kitamiense, M. esteraromaticum*	Japan Trench, Canary Basin, fjord site. Barcelona neuston. Wadden Sea aggregate	Maldonado et al. (2005), Agogue et al. (2005), Grossart et al. (2004)
Mycobacterium	*M. manitobense, STR-11, STR-21*	Japan Trench, Canary Basin, fjord site. Deep sea sediment 3800 m	Stach et al. (2003b) Maldonado et al. (2005)
Nocardioides	*Nocardioides sp. V4.BO.15, N. jensenii*	Deep sea sediment 3800 m. Barcelonaneuston	Agogue et al. (2005), Stach et al. (2003)
Nocardiopsis i	*N. dassonville*	Ovaries of Pufferfish, Bohai Sea of China	Maldonado et al. (2005, Wu et al. (2005)
Nonomurea		Japan Trench, Canary Basin, fjord site	Maldonado et al. (2005)
Pseudonocardia	*P. alaniniphila, P. aurantiaca, P. alnii*	Deep sea sediment 3800 m	Maldonado et al. (2005), Stach et al. (2003b)
Rhodococcus	*R. fascians, R. koreensis, R. opacus, R. ruber, R. tsukamurensis, R. zopfii*	Deep sea sediment 3800 m, Pelagic clay	Stach et al. (2003a)
Saccharopolyspora		Japan Trench, Canary Basin and fjord site	Maldonado et al. (2005)
Salinispora	*S. arenicola, S. tropica*	Sub-tropical sediment	Jensen et al. (1991), Maldonado et al. (2005)
Serinicoccus	*S. marinus*	Sea water East Sea, Korea	Yi et al. (2004)

(Contd...)

1	2	3	4
Streptomyces	*S. capensis, S. giseus (MAR4), 'S. maritimus', S. pallidus, S. somaliensis, S. thermocarboxydovorans*	Deep sea sediment 3800 m	Moore et al. (2005), Jensen et al. (2005), and Stach et al. (2003)
Streptosporangium		Japan Trench, Canary Basin and fjord site	Maldonado et al. (2005)
Tsukamurella	*T. inchonensis*	Deep sea sediment 3800 m	Stach et al. (2003a)
Turicella	*T. otitidis*	Deep sea sediment 3800 m	Stach et al. (2003b)
Verrucosispora	*Verrucosispora sp. AB-18-032, IM-6907*	Japan Trench, Canary Basin and fjord site	Maldonado et al. (2005)
Williamsia	*W. maris, W. marianensis*	Japan Trench, Canary Basin and fjord site	Maldonado et al. (2005)

Role of Actinomycetes in Marine Environment and Their Beneficial Aspects

Actinomycetes have a profound role in the marine environment apart from antibiotic production (Das et al. 2006). The degradation and turnover of various materials are a continuous process mediated by the action of a variety of microorganisms (Jensen et al. 2005a; Lam 2006). There is a speculation that the increase or decrease of a particular enzyme-producing microorganism may indicate the concentration of natural substrate and conditions of the environment (Ramesh and Mathivanan 2009). The cellulolytic activity of marine actinomycetes was described by Chandramohan et al. (1972), chitinolytic actinomycetes were reported by Pisano et al. (1992) and various industrially important enzyme producing actinomycetes have been reported (Ramesh and Mathivanan 2009). Actinomycetes are also reported to contribute to the break-down and recycling of organic compounds (Goodfellow and Haynes 1984). In addition, they play a significant role in mineralization of organic matter, immobilization of mineral nutrients, fixation of nitrogen, improvement of physical parameters and environmental protection (Goodfellow and Williams 1983).

Actinomycetes play a major role in producing antibiotics and other metabolites such as extracellular enzymes, pigments, growth-promoting factors and various therapeutic agents. Marine actinomycetes have furnished new and unique antibiotics. The marine microorganisms especially bacteria and actinomycetes are virtually unlimited sources of novel compounds with many therapeutic applications. Actinomycetes are the most economically and biotechnologically priceless prokaryotes which hold a prominent position due to their diversity and proven ability to produce novel bioactive compounds (Adinarayana et al. 2007). About 70-80 per cent of relevant secondary metabolites account under *Streptomyces*, with small contributions from other genera, such as *Saccharopolyspora, Amycolatopsis, Micromonospora* and *Actinoplanes* (Renu et al. 2008).

Marine Pollution

The oceans are one of the most important natural resources on the planet. Contaminating the oceans will damage every living thing in one way or another. Deadly chemicals and radioactive materials get into the oceans and cause serious damages. One of the most deadly of all the toxins that enter the ocean is oil. Specific threats include sewage pollution, fertilizer run-off, litter, construction, and quarrying. Point sources of pollutants include cesspits and injection boreholes, Due to the lack of a central septic system, domestic waste is deposited. Ocean acidification has been recognized as one of the major threat to a diverse range of marine organisms. The acidification may have a deleterious effect on the physiology of marine organisms. Marine litter has been characterized as an environmental, economic, human health and aesthetic problem, posing a complex and multidimensional challenge with significant implications for the marine environment and human activities all over the world (UNEP 2009). These impacts are both cultural and multisectoral, rooted primarily in poor practices of solid waste management, a lack of infrastructure, various human activities, an inadequate understanding on the part of the public of the potential consequences of their actions, the lack of adequate legal and enforcement systems and a lack of financial resources. Marine litter is found in all the oceans of the world, not only in densely populated regions, but also in remote areas far from obvious sources and human contact. Every year marine litter takes an enormous social and economic toll on people and communities around the world. In the oceans, the threat to marine life comes in various forms, such as over exploitation and harvesting, dumping of waste, pollution, alien species, land reclamation, dredging and global climate change (Beatley, 1991; National Research Council, 1995; Irish and Norse, 1996; Ormond et al. 1997; Tickel, 1997; Snelgrove, 1999). In the marine environment, typically 40-80 per cent of the larger categories of marine debris items are plastic. Much of this is packaging, carrier bags, footwear, cigarette lighters and other domestic items and much originates from land, as a recent study in Central and South America showed (Ivar and Costa 2007). Many plastics are buoyant, and plastic items are commonly found at the sea surface or washed up on the shoreline (Barnes et al. 1998). Higher quantities are found in the mid-latitudes and tropics, with particular concentrations associated with shipping lanes, fishing areas, and ocean convergence zones.

About 2000 items of anthropogenic debris are found on north Atlantic shores per linear km per year and 500 per linear km per year on south Atlantic shores. More than half of this debris is plastic. By comparison, more than six times as much plastic has been reported washing ashore annually in the Mediterranean Sea. Observed global trends include a sustained and considerable increase over time and an increase in the associations of macroplastics with some wildlife (e.g., in bird nests and stomachs, and entangling seals) (Barnes et al. 1998). A study done on 1033 birds collected off the coast of North Carolina in the USA found that individuals from 55 per cent of the species recorded had plastic particles in their guts (Moser and Lee, 1992). There are many incidents indicating the plastic ingestion and plastic entanglement which is a major threat to marine biota. From plastic bags to pesticides - most of the waste we produce on land eventually reaches the oceans, either through deliberate dumping or from run-off through drains and rivers. It has been estimated that over 80 per cent of marine pollution comes from land based activities.

Industrial Waste

Since the Industrial Revolution, mankind has been engaged in the discovery, use and exploitation of the earth's mineral resources, thus creating extensive demands on the environment. Incidents of the inappropriate treatment of the environment have increased in number and extensiveness, and raised serious environmental concerns. It appears that the environment's state seems to be deteriorating persistently as a result of man's so called progress.

Industrial wastes primarily enter coastal waters from terrestrial (land-based) activities. Industries, like municipalities and other entities that generate wastes, dispose of many liquid wastes through wastewater systems (and ultimately to water bodies), whereas they dispose of their solid wastes in landfills. Industrial waste frequently goes down the same sewers as domestic and commercial nonindustrial waste, sewage often contains high levels of industrial chemicals and heavy metals (e.g., lead, mercury, cadmium, and arsenic) causing major threat to marine life.

Fertilizers used on golf courses, gardens and residential lawns are a non-point source form of pollution that increases the nutrient input to the near shore waters and creates an additional environmental threat. Water contaminated with fertilizers percolates through the topsoil, seeping into subterranean water, or is transferred by surface run-off to the inshore waters. If this nutrient enriched water seeps into a cave, contaminants could be transported to inshore waters.

Pesticide Pollution

Chlorinated organic compounds (or organochlorines) are organic (carbon based) chemicals which contain bound chlorine. A majority of these compounds are artificial and enter the environment through human activities, although it is now recognised that marine algae and invertebrates, and natural processes such as forest fires also contribute large and variable quantities of organochlorines (and other halogenated organics) to the environment (Leach et al. 1985; Enell and Wennberg 1991; Gribble 1994). Chlorinated organic compounds have a wide range of industrial and agricultural applications. They include pesticides such as DDT (dichloro-diphenyl-trichloroethane) and lindane (HCH or gamma-hexachlorocyclohexane) and polychlorinated biphenyls (PCBs) which were, and are still used in a range of industrial applications including dielectrics in electrical transformers. The few studies of the impact of organochlorine compounds carried out on Australian freshwater and marine environments indicate that environmental contamination by organochlorine substances has occurred at relatively low concentrations in Australia, and that highest concentrations have been associated with centres of urbanisation (Richardson 1995).

Metal Pollution

Metals are also strongly associated with particulates and enter the marine environment in a similar fashion to organochlorine compounds. The major routes of environmental entry include atmospheric transport of dust and sediment movement in overland flows and in waterways (Bryan 1971). Additional quantities of metals are also added to the environment via the discharge of effluent and urban storm water. Particulate metals in suspension and in bottom sediments are not generally directly available to aquatic organisms. The exception to this is sediment bound metals which can be accumulated following solubilisation in the acidic juices of a sediment-feeders gut. The rates at which metals are solubilised from particulates are dependent on environmental factors including dissolved oxygen concentrations, pH, salinity and temperature (Waldichuk 1985).

Following industrialisation, unnatural quantities of metals such as arsenic (As), cadmium (Cd), copper (Cu), mercury (Hg), lead (Pb), nickel (Ni)and zinc (Zn) have been released, and continue to be released into the aquatic environment through storm water and wastewater discharges. As, Cd, Cu, Hg and Zn are the five metals with most potential impact that are added to the environment in elevated concentrations as a consequence of agricultural activity. Zn and Cu are used in small amounts as fertilisers in some soils deficient in these elements, and As, Cd and Hg are constituents of some fungicides (Hunter 1992). Cu is also used as an algicide and Cd and Zn occur as contaminants of phosphatic fertilisers (Rayment et al. 1989). As a consequence, potential impacts from heavy metals are generally restricted to locations adjacent to major cities or industrialised areas on the coastal fringe and to sites draining areas of intensive agriculture. Results of Australian studies of marine environmental metal contamination indicate that surficial sediments adjacent to most urbanised and industrialised estuaries are contaminated with metals, particularly Pb and Zn (Batley 1995).

Inorganic phosphorus is often found in lower concentrations in the marine environment than nitrogen, limiting algae and plant growth. Dissolution of minerals in soil and decomposition of organic matter are the primary natural sources of phosphorus to aquatic. Anthropogenic sources of the nutrient include sewage, cesspit seepage, fertilizer runoff, soil erosion, and animal waste (Slomp and Van Cappellen 2004). Phosphorus has a natural affinity to calcium carbonate, thus it is readily binds to limestone through the formation of calcium-carbonate-phosphate minerals (e.g. apatite) (Simmons and Lyons 1994). Plants, algae, and bacteria can rapidly uptake dissolved inorganic phosphate (PO4), also called soluble reactive phosphate (SRP). Under aerobic conditions, decomposition of organic material on the bottom of the ocean releases usable phosphorus, which becomes converted to a less usable form, soluble nonreactive phosphorus (SNP) (Thompson and Karl 1998).

As limestone dissolves, caused by an decrease in pH or natural erosion, phosphate is rereleased into the marine environment allowing the uptake by autotrophic organisms that pass it on to heterotrophs when consumed (Pomeroy et al. 1963). Some sources of nitrogen into the marine environment include atmospheric deposition, wastewater seepage, commercial fertilizers, and the natural contributions from soil organic matter (Slomp and Van Cappellen 2004).

Sewage Pollution

Sewage discharge generates increasing loads of fecal wastes in natural waters. One of the most important factors of water pollution is the microbial contamination; especially with pathogenic microorganisms. Enteric pathogens are typically responsible for waterborne sickness (Karaboze et al., 2003). Contamination of water is a serious environmental problem as it adversely affects the human health and the biodiversity in the aquatic ecosystem. In many cases, the extent of pollution causes increases in numbers of fecal bacteria and may contain pathogenic microorganisms in high numbers beyond the assimilation capacity of the receiving water bodies (Mato 2002). The receiving water therefore becomes unfit for various purposes such as recreation in the case of seawater (Jagals et al. 2000). It is well known that enteric pathogens do not die quickly once exposed to the seawater as they tend to survive with survival rates varying from a few minutes to many days depending upon the marine environmental conditions e.g. nutrient availability, sedimentation, predation (by copepods and protozoa), parasitism, inactivation by sunlight, temperature, osmotic stress, or toxic chemicals and therefore pose several health risks to humans (Henrickson et al. 2001). While most reported recreational water-related illnesses are the result of ingestion during swimming, non-swimmers are also at risk of exposure to waterborne pathogens. Poor microbiological quality of beach water is not only a public health threat, but is also of economic concern.

While the global discharge of sewage from ships is relatively low when compared to both treated and untreated sewage from land based sources. Ship sewage consists of waterborne human waste, and of waste water generated in preparing food, washing dishes, in laundries, lavoratories and by medical facility. Human sewage contains pathogens, enteric bacteria, viruses, and eggs of the intestinal parasites which may pose considerable public health risk (USEPA 2007; Clarke 2001). Sewage has been known to lead to deterioration of water quality, after faunal and floral assemblages near large ocean outfalls and has been responsible for disease outbreaks attributed to fecal coliforms (Clarke 2001). A major concern has been the spread of disease micro-organism in coliform bacteria which are capable of entering a dormant phase and therefore survive in seawater for long periods. The major health risk is contamination of seafood particularly shellfish. In addition, detergents and chemicals found in cleaning solutions and toilet disinfectants can be toxic to marine life and humans.

Pollution by Oil Spills

With the rapid development of industrial economy, a large amount of anthropogenic chemicals has been released into the environment (Lewis et al. 1999). As one of the primary energy sources applied widely, petroleum products are becoming the most prevalent contaminants in the environment, especially in China (Wang et al. 2007). The main sources of petroleum contamination include storage leaking, transport loss, land disposal of petroleum waste, and accidental or intentional spills (Gerhardt et al. 2009; White et al. 2006). Petroleum products are believed to be common soil contaminants which may contain many toxic compounds (Euliss et al. 2008). Petroleum hydrocarbons are major pollutants of marine environments as a result of terrestrial and freshwater runoff, refuse from coastal oil refineries, offshore oil production, shipping activities and accidental spills (Alejandro et al. 2006).

Oil spills occur during generation, transport and consumption of fuel resulting in origin of major environmental problem. Oil is carried at sea in bulk and is used by vessels as fuel and lubricant. These are the principle sources of oil to the open ocean. Oil spills from the ships in the open ocean are generally attributed to the structural or mechanical failure, often in storms that cause the ship to break up and sink or to leakages from cargo and fuel compartments. Oil can also occur due to collision and allusions (hitting a stationery object), these accidents are less likely to occur in open-ocean waters than near shore, except in heavily travelled shipping lanes with limited visibility. International spills also occur such as when petroleum cargo is jettisoned for safety reasons in an emergency or as a result of terrorist and military attack (e.g. the 1991 Gulf War Spillage).

A ship that sinks may contain large volume of oil in the form of cargo (for oil tankers) and fuel, bunkers and oils in the machinery space unless the vessel has released all its oil during breakup. Sunken vessels can then become potential seeps, discharging oil at varying rates over long period of time. Occasionally, a sunken vessel may suddenly release a large volume of oil if its integrity is compromised due to rusting or other physical change. Oil spills are huge damage to marine environment as oil penetrates into the structure of the plumage of birds and the fur of mammals, reducing its insulating ability, and making them more vulnerable to temperature fluctuations and much less buoyant in the water.

PAHs are aromatic hydrocarbons with two or more fused benzene rings with natural as well as anthropogenic sources. They are widely distributed environmental contaminants that have detrimental biological effects, toxicity, mutagenecity and carcinogenicity. Anthropogenic sources of PAH include burning of fossil fuel, coal tar, wood, garbage, refuse, used lubricating oil and oil filters (Kaushik and Haritash 2006) municipal solid waste incineration and petroleum spills and discharge. They are ubiquitously present contaminants which are toxic, mutagenic and carcinogenic (IARC 1983). PAHs were, perhaps, the first recognized environmental carcinogens. They do not degrade easily under natural conditions. Persistence increases with increase in the molecular weight. They have gathered significant concern because of their presence in all components of environment, resistance towards biodegradation, potential to bio-accumulate and carcinogenic activity.

Pollution by Chemicals and Toxins

Chemicals are another addition to marine environment pollution. Almost every marine organism, from the tiniest plankton to whales and polar bears, is contaminated with man-made chemicals, such as pesticides and chemicals used in common consumer products. Some of these chemicals enter the sea through deliberate dumping. For centuries, the oceans have been a convenient dumping ground for waste generated on land. This continued until the 1970s, with dumping at sea the accepted practice for disposal of nearly everything, including toxic material such as pesticides, chemical weapons, and radioactive waste. Dumping of the most toxic materials was banned by the London Dumping Convention in 1972, and an amended treaty in 1996 (the London

Convention) further restricted what could be dumped at sea. However, there are still the problems of already-dumped toxic material, and even the disposal of permitted substances at sea can be a substantial environmental hazard.

Chemicals also enter the sea from land-based activities. Chemicals can escape into water, soil, and air during their manufacture, use, or disposal, as well as from accidental leaks or fires in products containing these chemicals. People once assumed that the ocean was so large that all pollutants would be diluted and dispersed to safe levels. But in reality, they have not disappeared and some toxic man-made chemicals have even become more concentrated as they have entered the food chain. Tiny animals at the bottom of the food chain, such as plankton in the oceans, absorb the chemicals as they feed. Because they do not break down easily, the chemicals accumulate in these organisms, becoming much more concentrated in their bodies than in the surrounding water or soil. These organisms are eaten by small animals, and the concentration rises again. These animals are in turn eaten by larger animals, which can travel large distances with their even further increased chemical load. Animals higher up the food chain, such as seals, can have contamination levels millions of times higher than the water in which they live. And polar bears, which feed on seals, can have contamination levels up to 3 billion times higher than their environment. People become contaminated either directly from household products or by eating contaminated seafood and animal fats. Evidence is mounting that a number of man-made chemicals can cause serious health problems including cancer, damage to the immune system, behavioral problems, and reduced fertility.

Other factors responsible for marine pollution include hurricanes, tsunami, volcanic eruptions and landslides. Hurricanes have significant effect on the marine life, and life of the inhabitants on the coastal areas. Hurricane stirs about 100 m of ocean surface, and mix oxygen from the atmosphere and mix nutrients in the water. This affects the plankton and micro life in the water that is basic food chain for many animals. However, hurricanes destroy coral reefs and sea bed that is close beneath ocean surface. Tsunami causes a lot of damage to coral reefs, which are complex groups of diverse animals and are usually very sensitive to turbidity like the mud stirred up from the currents of a tsunami. As anthropogenic activities and natural calamities affect marine biodiversity at the same time it affects microbial marine diversity. Ocean acidification, toxification are the major adverse events affecting marine microbial colonization. Marine microbial natural products are rich sources of antibiotics and bioactive potential compounds, among these marine actinomycetes are one of the leading producers of secondary metabolites. A wide variety of synthetic organic compounds contaminate the environment from chemical and industrial processes resulting in acidification of sea water.

Table 7.2: Bioactive Potential Compounds from Actinomycetes

Compound	Source	Activity	Reference
1	2	3	4
1-hydroxy-1-norresistomycin	*Streptomyces chinaensis*	Antibacterial, anticancer	Gorajana et al. (2005) Kock et al. (2005)
3,6-disubstituted indoles	*Streptomyces sp.*	Anticancer	Sanchez et al. (2003)
Abyssomicins.	*Verrucosispora sp*	Antibacterial	Riedlinger et al. (2004)
Arenimycin	*Salinispora arenicola*	Antibacterial, anticancer	Asolkar et al. (2010)
Aureoverticillactam	*Streptomyces aureoverticillatus*	Anticancer	Mitchell et al. (2004)
Bonactin	*Streptomyces sp.*	Antibacterial, antifungal	Schumacher et al. (2003)
Caprolactones	*Streptomyces sp.*	Anticancer	Stritzke et al. (2004)
Chandrananimycins	*Actinomadura sp. Antialagl;*	Antibacterial, anticancer, antifungal	Maskey et al. (2003)
Chinikomycins	*Streptomyces sp.*	Anticancer	Li et al. (2005)
Chloro-dihydroquinones	*Novel actinomycete*	Antibacterial, anticancer	Soria et al. (2005)
Diazepinomicin (ECO-4601)	*Micromonosproa sp*	Antibacterial, anticancer, anti-inflammatory	Charan et al. (2004)
Frigocyclinone	*Streptomyces griseus*	Antibacterial	Brutner et al. (2005)
Glaciapyrroles	*Streptomyces sp.*	Antibacteria l	Macherla et al. (2005)
Gutingimycin	*Streptomyces sp.*	Antibacterial	Maskey et al. (2004)
Helquinoline	*Janibacter limosus*	Antibacterial	Asolkar et al. (2004)
Himalomycins	*Streptomyces sp.*	Antibacterial	Maskey et al. (2003)
IB-00208	*Actinomadura sp.*	Anticancer	Rodriguez et al. (2003)
Komodoquinone A	*Streptomyces sp.*	Neuritogenic activity	Itoh et al. (2003)
Lajollamycin	*Streptomyces nodosus*	Antibacterial	Manam et al. (2005)
Lodopyridone	*Saccharomonospora sp.*	Anticancer	Maloney et al. (2009)
Marinomycins'	*Marinispora'*	Antibacterial, anticancer	Kwon et al. (2006)
Marinomycins A-D	*Marinispora*	Antimicrobial, anticancer	Kwon et al. (2006)

(Contd...)

1	2	3	4
Mechercharmycins	*Thermoactinomyces sp.*	Anticancer	Kanoh et al. (2005)
MKN-349A]	*Nocardiopsis sp.*	Unknown biological activity	Shin et al. (2003)
Saliniketal	*Salinispora arenicola*	Cancer chemoprevention	Jensen et al. (2007)
Salinipyrones A & B	*Salinispora pacifica*	Mild cytotoxicity	Oh et al. (2008)
Salinosporamide A (NPI-0052)	*Salinispora tropica*	Anticancer	Feling et al. (2003)
Sporolides	*Salinispora tropica*	Unknown biological activity	Buchanan et al. (2005)
Trioxacarcins	*Streptomyces sp.*	Antibacterial, anticancer; antimalarial	Maskey et al. (2004)
Resistoflavin methyl ether	*Streptomyces sp.*	Antibacterial, anti-oxidative	Kock et al. (2005)
1,8-Dihydroxy-2-ethyl-3 methylanthraquinone	*Streptomyces sp.*	Antitumor	Huang et al. (2006)
Daryamides	*Streptomyces sp.*	Antifungal, anticancer	Asolkar et al. (2006)
Bisanthraquinone	*Streptomyces sp.*	Antibacterial	Socha et al. (2006)
Proximicins	*Verrucosispora sp.*	Antibacterial, anticancer	Fiedler et al. (2008)
2-Allyloxyphenol	*Streptomyces sp.*	Antimicrobial, food preservative; oral disinfectant	Arumugam et al. (2009)
Butenolides	*Streptoverticillium*	luteoverticillatum Antitumor	Li et al. (2006)
ZHD-0501	*Actinomadura sp.*	Anticancer	Han et al. (2005)
Tirandamycins	*Streptomyces sp.*	Antibacterial	Carlson et al. (2009)
Pyridinium	*Amycolatopsis alba var. nov. DVR D4*	Antimicrobial Cytotoxicity	Dasari et al. (2012)

Conclusion

Life in our planet is sustained in a fragile biological balance of microorganisms which play an important role on nutritional chains. Adapting several abilities, microorganisms have become an important influence on the ecological systems, making them necessary for superior organisms life in this planet. Actinomycetes are diverse group of microorganisms sharing properties with bacteria and fungi. They are the major producers of antibiotics and other industrially useful secondary metabolites. Much progress has been made in search of newer sources of bioactive materials from microbes marine organisms like coral reefs and sponges. The marine microbial organisms are main promising sources of the bioactive molecules. It is a very unfortunate that many of the secondary metabolites which have promising therapeutic value are vanishing without being identified. On the other hand marine pollution is of major concern as marine environment harbours innumerable forms of life and the diversity is immense. The only safe and environmental safe way of removing or reducing the pollution is through bioremediation. Bioremediation is the tool to transform the compounds to less hazardous or convert them into non-hazardous forms with less input of chemicals, energy, and time. It is an approach to degrade or remove pollutants in an eco-friendly manner. The bioremediation of a pollutant and the rate at which it is achieved depends on the environmental conditions, number and type of the microorganisms, nature sand chemical structure of the chemical compound being degraded. Thus, to devise a bioremediation system, several factors are responsible which need to be addressed and explored. There are a number of bacterial species isolated from different environments and capable of degrading PAHs. Acclimatization of these species can serve as a key for enhanced degradation. The induction of degradation capacity by exposing the microbes to higher levels of pollutants may, at times, result in genetic adaptability/changes responsible for higher rate of removal. Monitoring and regulation of the environmental factors in specific areas can help the plants/ microorganisms sustain even in adverse environments. Control at the source can significantly reduce harmful levels in environment and the strategies involved in mitigation and remediation.

REFERENCES

Adinarayana, K., Prabhakar, T., Srinivasulu, V., Anitha, R.M., Jhansi, L.P., Elliah, P. (2003): Optimization of Process Parametres for Cephalosporin C Production Under Solid State Fermentation from *Acremonium chrysogenum*. In Process. Biochem, 39:171-177.

Agogue H., Casamayor E.O., Bourrain M., Obernosterer I., Joux F., Herndl G.J., Lebaron P. (2005): A Survey on Bacteria Inhabiting the Sea Surface Microlayer of Coastal Ecosystems. FEMS Microbiol Ecol,54: 269-280.

Alejandro R., Gentilia, Marýa A., Cubittoa, Ferrerob, Rodriguezc. (2006): Bioremediation of Crude Oil Polluted Seawater by a Hydrocarbondegrading Bacterial Strain Immobilized on Chitin and Chitosan Flakes International Biodeterioration & Biodegradation, 57: 222-228.

Amann R.I., Kuhl M. (1998): *In situ* Methods for Assessment of Microorganisms and Their Activities. Curr Opin Microbiol, 1:352-358.

Asolkar R.N., Kirkland T.N., Jensen P.R., Fenical W. (2010): Arenimycin, an Antibiotic Effective Against Rifampin and Methicillin-resistant *Staphylococcus aureus* from the Marine Actinomycete *Salinispora arenicola*. J Antibiot (Tokyo), 63: 37-39.

Asolkar R.N., Schroder D., Heckmann R., Lang S., WagneDobler I., Laatsch H. (2004): Helquinoline, A New Tetrahydroquinoline Antibiotic from *Janibacter limosus* Hel 1. J Antibiot (Tokyo), 57:17-23.

Barcina I., Iriberri J., Egea L. (1987): Enumeration, Isolation and some Physiological Properties of Actinomycetes from Sea Water and Sediment. Syst Appl Microbiol, 10:85-91.

Barnes D.K.A., Galgani F., Thompson R.C., and Barlaz M. (2009): Accumulation and Fragmentation of Plastic Debris in Global Environments. Philosophical Transactions of the Royal Society B., 364: 1985-1998.

Batley, G.E. (1995): Technical Annex: 2, Eds. Heavy Metals and Tributyltin in Australian Coastal and Estuarine Waters. In the State of the Marine Environment Report for Australia.

Beatley, T. (1991): Protecting Biodiversity in Coastal Environments: Introduction and Overview. Coastal Management 19: 1-19.

Berdy J. (2005): Bioactive Microbial Metabolites. J Antibiot (Tokyo), 58: 1-26.

Bruns A., Philipp H., Cypionka H., Brinkhoff T. (2003): *Aeromicrobium marinum* sp. nov., An Abundant Pelagic Bacterium Isolated from the German Wadden Sea. Antonie Van Leeuwenhoek, 53: 1917-23.

Bruntner C., Binder T., Pathomaree W., Goodfellow M., Bull A.T., Potterat O., Puder C., Horer S., Schmid A., Bolek. (2005): Frigocyclinone, a Novel Angucyclinone Antibiotic Produced by a *Streptomyces griseus* Strain from Antarctica. J Antibiot (Tokyo), 58: 346-349.

Bryan, G.W. (1971): Proceedings of the Ecological Society of London. The Effects of Heavy Metals (Other Than Mercury) on Marine and Estuarine Organisms. 177, 389-410.

Buchanan G.O., Williams P.G., Feling R.H., Kauffman C.A., Jensen P.R., Fenical W. (2005): Sporolides A and B: Structurally Unprecedented Halogenated Macrolides from the Marine Actinomycete *Salinispora tropica*. Org Lett, 7: 2731-2734.

Bull A.T., Stach J.E.M., Ward A.C., Goodfellow M. (2005): Marine Actinobacteria: Perspectives, Challenges, Future Directions. Antonie Van Leeuwenhoek, 87: 65-79.

Burja A.M., Hill R.T. (2001): Microbial Symbionts of the Australian Great Barrier Reef Sponge *Candidaspongia flabellate*. Hydrobiologia, 461: 41-47.

Castillo U., Myera S., Brown L., Strobel G., Hess W.M., Hanks. (2005): Scanning Electron Microscopy of some Endophytic *Streptomycetes* in Snake Vine *Kennedia nigricans*. Scanning, 27: 305-11.

Charan R.D., Schlingmann G., Janso J., Bernan V., Feng X., Carter G.T. (2004): Diazepinomicin, a New Antimicrobial Alkaloid from Marine *Micromonospora* sp. J Nat Prod, 67: 1431-1433.

Colwell F., Matsumoto R., Reed D. (2004): A Review of Gas Hydrates, Geology, and Biology of Nankai Trough. Chem Geol, 205: 391-404.

Das S., Lyla P.S., Ajmal Khan S. (2008): Distribution and Generic Composition of Culturable Marine Actinomycetes from the Sediments of Indian Continental Slope of Bay of Bengal. Chin J Oceanol Limnol, 26: 166-77.

Das S., Lyla P.S., Khan S.A. (2006): Marine Microbial Diversity and Ecology: Importance and Future Perspectives. Curr Sci 90: 1325-35.

Euliss K., Ho C.H., Schwab A.P., Rock S., Banks M.K. (2008): Greenhouse and Field Assessment of Phytoremediation for Petroleum Contaminants in a Riparian Zone. Bioresour Technol, 99: 1961-1971.

Feling R.H., Buchanan G.O., Mincer T.J., Kauffman C.A., Jensen P.R., Fenical W. (2003): Salinosporamide A: A Highly Cytotoxic Proteasome Inhibitor from a Novel Microbial Source, A Marine Bacterium of the New Genus *Salinospora*. Angew Chem Int Ed Engl, 42: 355-357.

Fenical W., Jensen P.R. (2006): Developing a New Resource for Drug Discovery: Marine Actinomycete Bacteria. Nat Chem Biol, 2: 666-73.

Ferguson R.L., Buckley E.N., Palumbo A.V. (1984): Response of Marine Bacterioplankton to Differential Filtration and Confinement. Appl Environ Microbiol, 47: 49-55.

Fortman J.L., Magarvey N.A., Sherman D.H. (2005): Something Old, Something New; Ongoing Studies of Marine Actinomycetes. Proc SIM, Abstract S86.

Gerhardt K.E., Huang X.D., Glick B.R., Greenberg B.M. (2009): Phytoremediation and Rhizoremediation of Organic Soil Contaminants: Potential and Challenges. Plant Sci, 176: 20-30.

Goodfellow M, Williams S.T. (1983): Ecology of Actinomycetes. Annu Rev Microbiol, 37: 189-216.

Goodfellow M., Haynes J.A. (1984): Actinomycetes in Marine Sediments. In Biological, Biochemical and Biomedical Aspects of Actinomycetes. Edited by Ortiz-Ortiz L., Bojalil L.F., Yakoleff V. New York: Academic Press, 453-472.

Gorajana A., Kurada B.V., Peela S., Jangam P., Vinjamuri S., Poluri E. (2005): 1-Hydroxy- 1-norresistomycin, a New Cytotoxic Compound from a Marine Actinomycete, *Streptomyces chibaensis* AUBN1/7. J Antibiot, 58: 526-9.

Grossart H.P., Schlingoff A., Bernhard M., Simon M., Brinkhoff T. (2004): Antagonistic Activity of Bacteria Isolated from Organic Aggregates of the German Wadden Sea. FEMS Microbiol Ecol, 47: 387-396.

Han S.K., Nadashkovskaya O.I., Mikhailov V.V., Kim S.B., Bae K.S. (2003): *Salinibacterium amurskyense* gen. nov., a Novel Genus of the Family Microbacteriaceae from the Marine Environment. Int J Syst Evol Microbiol, 53: 2061-6.

Heald S.C., Brandao P.F.B., Hardicre R., Bull A.T. (2001): Physiology, Biochemistry and Taxonomy of Deep Sea Nitrile Metabolizing *Rhodococcus* Strains. Antonie Van Leeuwenhoek, 80: 169-83.

Helmke E. and Weyland H. (1984): *Rhodococcus marinonascens* sp. Nov., an actinomycete from the Sea. Int J Syst Bacteriol, 34: 127-138.

Henrickson S., Wong T., Allen P., Ford T. and Epstein P. (2001): Marine Swimming Related Illness: Implications for Monitoring and Environmental Policy. Environ. Health Persp, 109: 245- 250.

Hill R.T. (2004): Microbes from Marine Sponges: A Trove of Biodiversity of Natural Products Discovery. In Microbial Diversity and Bioprospecting. Edited by Bull AT. ASM Press, 177-190.

Hunter, H.M. (1992): Agricultural Contaminants in Aquatic Environments: A Review. Department of Primary Industry, Brisbane.

Inagaki F., Suzuki M., Takai K., Oida H., Sakamoo T., Aoki K., Nealson K.H, Horikoshi K. (2003): Microbial Communities Associated with Geological Horizons in Coastal Sub-seafloor Sediments from the Sea of Okhotsk. Appl Environ Microbiol, 69: 7224-7235.

International Agency for Research on Cancer (IARC) Benzopyrene, Polynuclear Aromatic Compounds, Part 1, Chemical, Environmental and Experimental Data, Vol. 32, Monographs on the Evaluation of the Carcinogenic Risk of Chemicals to Humans, 1983, pp. 211-224.

Irish, K.E. and Norse, E.A. (1996): Scant Emphasis on Marine Biodiversity. Conservation Biology, 10, 680.

Itoh T., Kinoshita M., Aoki S., Kobayashi M. (2003): Komodoquinone A, a Novel Neutritogenic Anthracycline, from Marine *Streptomyces* sp. KS3. J Nat Prod, 66: 1373-1377.

Ivar J. A. and Costa M. F. (2007): Marine Debris Review for Latin America and the Wider Caribbean Region: from the 1970s Until Now, and where do we go from here? Marine Pollution Bulletin, 54: 1087-1104.

Jagals P., Grabow W., Griesel M and Jagals C. (2000): Valuation of Selected Membrane Filtration and most Probable Number Methods for the Enumeration of Fecal Coliforms, *Escherichia coli* and *Enterococci* in Environmental Waters. Quantitative Microbiology, 2: 129-140.

Jensen P.R, Dwight R, Fenical W. (1991): Distribution of Actinomycetes in Near-shore Tropical Marine Sediments. Appl Environ. Microbiol, 57: 1102-1108.

Jensen P.R, Gontang E., Mafnas C., Mincer T.J., Fenical W. (2005b): Culturable Marine Actinomycetes Diversity from Tropical Pacific Ocean sediments. Environ. Microbiol, 7: 1039-48.

Jensen P.R., Mafnas C. (2006): Biogeography of the Marine Actinomycetes *Salinispora*. Environ Microbiol, 8: 1881-8.

Jensen P.R., Mincer T.J., Williams P.G., Fenical W. (2005a). Marine Actinomycete Diversity and Natural Product Discovery. Antonie van Leeuwenhoek, 87: 43-48.

Jones J.G. (1977): The Effect of Environmental Factors on Estimated Viable and Total Populations of Planktonic Bacteria in Lakes and Experimental Enclosures. Freshw Biol, 7: 67-91.

Kaeberlein T., Lewis K., Epstein S.S. (2002): Isolating 'Uncultivable' Microorganisms in Pure Culture in a Simulated Natural Environment. Science, 296: 1127-1129.

Kanoh K., Matsuo Y., Adachi K., Imagawa H., Nishizawa M., Shizuri Y. (2005) Mechercharmycins A and B, Cytotoxic Substances from Marine-derived *Thermoactinomyces* sp. YM3-251. J Antibiot (Tokyo), 58: 289-292.

Karaboze I., Ucar F., Eltem R., Ozdmir G. and Ates M. (2003): Determination of Existence and Count of Pathogenic Microorganisms in Izmir Bay. JES 26: 1-18.

Kaushik C.P. and Haritash A.K. (2006): Polycyclic Aromatic Hydrocarbons (PAHs) and Environmental Health, Our Earth, 33: 1-7.

Kim B.S., Oh H.M., Kang H., Park S.S, Chun J. (2004): Remarkable Bacterial Diversity in the Tidal Flat Sediment as Revealed by 16S rRNA Analysis. J Microbiol Biotechnol, 14: 205-211.

Kim S.B., Goodfellow M. (1999): Reclassification of *Amycolatopsis rugosa*. Int J Syst Bacteriol, 49: 507-512.

Kim T.K., Garson M.J., Fuerst J.A. (2005): Marine Actinomycetes Related to the *'Salinospora'* Group from the Great Barrier Reef Sponge *Pseudoceratina clavata*. Environ Microbiol, 7: 509-518.

Kock I, Maskey R.P., Biabani M.A., Helmke E., Laatsch H. (2005): 1-Hydroxy-1-norresistomycin and Resistoflavin Methyl Ether: New Antibiotics from Marine-derived *Streptomycetes*. J Antibiot, 58: 530-4.

Kogure K., Simidu U., Taga N. (1979). A Tentative Direct Microscopic Method for Counting Living Marine Bacteria. Can J Microbiol, 25: 415-20.

Kogure K., Simidu U., Taga N. (1980): Distribution of Viable Marine Bacteria in Neritic Seawater Around Japan. Can J Microbiol, 26: 318-23.

Kwon H.C., Kauffman C.A., Jensen P.R., Fenical W. (2006): Marinomycins A-D, Antitumor Antibiotics of a New Structure Class from a Marine Actinomycete of the Recently Discovered Genus *Marinispora*. J Am Chem Soc, 128: 1622-32.

Lam K.S. Discovery of Novel Metabolites from Marine Actinomycetes. Curr Opin Microbiol. 2006; 9: 245-51.

Lanoil B.D., Sassen R., La Duc M.T., Sweet S.T., Nealson K.H. (2001): Bacteria and Archaea Physically Associated with Gulf of Mexico Gas Hydrates. Appl Environ. Microbiol, 67: 5143-5153.

Lechevalier M.P., Lechevalier H. (1970): Chemical Composition as a Criterion in the Classification of Aerobic Actinomycetes. Int J Syst Bacteriol, 20: 435-43.

Li F., Maskey R.P., Qin S., Sattler I., Fiebig H.H., Maier A., Zeeck A., Laatsch H.(2005): Chinikomycins A and B: Isolation, Structure Elucidation, and Biological Activity of Novel Antibiotics from a Marine *Streptomyces* sp. Isolate M045. J Nat Prod, 68: 349-353.

Macherla V.R., Liu J., Bellows C., Teisan S., Lam K.S., Potts B.C.M. (2005): Glaciapyrroles A, B and C, Pyrrolosesquiterpenes from a *Streptomyces* sp. Isolated from an Alaskan Marine Sediment. J Nat Prod, 68: 780-783.

Madrid V.M., Aller J.Y., Aller R.C. and Chistoserdov A.Y. (2001): High Prokaryote Diversity and Analysis of Community Structure in Mobile Mud Off French Guiana: Identification of Two New Bacterial Candidate Divisions. FEMS Microbiol Ecol, 37: 197-209.

Magarvey N.A., Keller J.M., Bernan V., Dworkin M., Sherman D.H. (2004): Isolation and Characterization of Novel Marine-derived Actinomycete Taxa Rich in Bioactive Metabolites. Appl Environ. Microbiol, 70: 7520-9.

Maldonado L.A., Fenical W., Jensen P.R., Kauffman C.A., Mincer T.J., Bull A.T., Ward A.C., Goodfellow M. (2005a): *Salinispora arenicola* gen. nov., sp nov and *Salinispora tropica* sp nov., Obligate Marine Actinomcyetes Belonging to the Family *Micromonosporaceae*. Int J Syst Evol Microbiol, 55: 1759-1766.

Maldonado L.A., Stach J.E.M., Pathomaree W., Ward A.C., Bull A.T., Goodfellow M. (2005b): Diversity of Cultivable Actinobacteria in Geographically Widespread Marine Sediments. Antonie Van Leeuwenhoek, 87: 11-18.

Manam R.R., Teisan S., White D.J., Nicholson B., Grodberg J., Neuteboom S.T.C., Lam K.S., Mosca D.A., Lloyd G.K., Potts B.C.M. (2005): Lajollamycin, a Nitrotetraene spiro-β-lactone-γ-lactam Antibiotic from the Marine Actinomycete *Streptomyces nodosus*. J Nat Prod, 68: 240-243.

Maskey R.P., Helmke E., Kayser O., Fiebig H.H., Maier A., Busche A., Laatsch H. (2004): Anticancer and Antibacterial Trioxacarcins with High Anti-malaria Activity from a Marine *Streptomycete* and Their Absolute Stereochemistry. J Antibiot (Tokyo), 57: 771-779.

Maskey R.P., Helmke E., Laatsch H. (2003): Himalomycin A and B: Isolation and Structure Elucidation of New Fridamycin Type Antibiotics from a Marine *Streptomyces* Isolate. J Antibiot (Tokyo) 2003, 56: 942-949.

Maskey R.P., Li F. C., Qin S., Fiebig H.H, Laatsch H. (2003): Chandrananimycins A, C: Production of Novel Anticancer Antibiotics from a Marine *Actinomadura* sp. isolate M048 by Variation of Medium Composition and Growth Conditions. J Antibiot (Tokyo), 56: 622-629.

Maskey R.P., Sevvana M., Uson I., Helmke E., Laatsch H. (2004): Gutingimycin: a Highly Complex Metabolite from a Marine *Streptomycete*. Angew Chem Int Ed Engl, 43: 1281-1283.

Mato R. (2002): Groundwater Pollution in Urban Dar as Salaam, Tanzania. Assessing Vulnerability and Protection Priorities. Ph.D. Thesis, Eindhoven Technische Universitie.

Mincer T.J., Fenical W., Jensen P.R. (2005): Culture-dependent and Culture-independent Diversity within the Obligate Marine Actinomycete Genus *Salinispora*. Appl Environ Microbiol, 71: 7019-7028.

Mitchell S.S., Nicholson B., Teisan S., Lam K.S., Potts B.C.M. (2004): Aureoverticillactam, a novel 22-atom Macrocyclic Lactam from the Marine Actinomycete *Streptomyces aureoverticillatus*. J Nat Prod, 67:1400-1402.

Moore B.S., Kalaitzis J.A., Xiang L. (2005): Exploiting Marine Actinomycete Biosynthetic Pathways for Drug Discovery. Antonie van Leeuwenhoek, 87: 49-57.

Moran M.A., Rutherfford L.T., Hodson R.E. (1995): Evidence for Indigenous *Streptomyces* Populations in a Marine Environment Determined with a 16S rRNA Probe. Appl Environ Microbiol, 61: 3695-700.

Moser, M.L., Lee, D.S. (1992): A Fourteen-year Survey of Plastic Ingestion by Western North Atlantic seabirds. Colonial Waterbirds, 15: 83-94.

Olano C., Mendez C., Salas J.A. (2009): Antitumor Compounds from Actinomycetes: from Gene Clusters to New Derivatives by Combinatorial Biosynthesis. Nat Prod Rep, 26: 628-60.

Ormond, R.F.G., Gage, J.D., Angel, M.V. (1997): Marine Biodiversity: Patterns and Processes. Cambridge University Press, Cambridge.

Parkes R.J., Wellsbury P. (2004): Deep biospheres. In Microbial Diversity and Bioprospecting. Edited by Bull A.T. ASM Press, 120-129.

Pisano M.A., Sommer M.J., Taras L. (1992): Bioactivity of Chitinolytic Actinomycetes of Marine Origin. Appl Microbiol Biotechnol, 36: 553-5.

Pomeroy L.R., Mathews H.M., Min H.S. (1963): Excretion of Phosphate and Soluble Organic Phosphorus Compounds by Zooplankton. Limnol Oceanogr, 8: 50-55.

Prudhomme J., McDaniel E., Ponts N., Bertani S., Fenical W., Jensen P., et al. (2008): Marine Actinomycetes: A New Source of Compounds Against the Human Malaria Parasite. PLoS One, 3: 2335.

Qasim S.Z. (1999): The Indian Ocean: Images and Realities, Oxford and IBH, New Delhi, p. 57-90.

Rahman H., Austin B., Mitchell W.J., Morris P.C., Jamieson D.J., and Adams D.R., et al. (2010): Novel Anti-infective Compounds from Marine Bacteria. Mar Drugs, 8: 498-518.

Rainey F.A., Burghardt J., Kroppenstedt R.M., Klatte S., Stackebrandt E. (1995): Phylogenetic Analysis of the Genera *Rhodococcus* and *Nocardia* and Evidence for the Evolutionary Origin of the Genus Nocardia from within the Radiation of *Rhodococcus* Species. Microbiology (UK), 141: 523-528.

Ramesh S., Jayaprakashvel M., Mathivanan N. (2006): Microbial Status in Seawater and Coastal Sediments during Pre- and Post-tsunami Periods in the Bay of Bengal, India. Mar Ecol, 27: 198-203.

Ramesh S., Mathivanan N. (2009): Screening of Marine Actinomycetes Isolated from the Bay of Bengal, India for Antimicrobial Activity and Industrial Enzymes. World J Microbiol Biotechnol, 25: 2103-2111.

Rayment, G.E., Best, E.K., and Hamilton, D.J. (1989): Cadmium in Fertilizers and Soil Amendments. 10th Australian Symposium for Analytical Chemistry.

Reed D.W., Fujita Y., Delwiche M.E., Blackwelder D.B., Sheridian P.P., Uchida T., Colwell F.S. (2002): Microbial Communities from Methane Hydrate-bearing Deep Marine Sediments in a Forearc Basin. Appl Environ Microbiol, 68: 3759-3770.

Richardson, B.J. (2005): The Problem of Chlorinated Compounds in Australia's Marine Environment. In The State of the Marine Environment Report for Australia, Technical Annex: 2. Eds. L. P. Zann and D. C. Sutton. Great Barrier Reef Marine Park Authority, Townsville. pp. 53-61.

Riedlinger J., Reicke A., Zahner H., Krismer B., Bull A.T., Maldonado L.A., Ward A.C., Goodfellow M., Bister B., Bischoff D. et al. (2004): Abyssomicins, Inhibitors of the Paraaminobenzoic Acid Pathway Produced by the Marine *Verrucosispora* Strain AB-18- 032. J Antibiot (Tokyo), 57: 271-279.

Rodriguez J.C., Fernandez Puentes J.L., Perez Baz J., Canedo L.M. (2003): IB-00208, a New Cytotoxic Polycyclic Xanthone Produced by a Marine-derived *Actinomadura*. II. Isolation, Physicochemical Properties and Structure Determination. J Antibiot (Tokyo), 56: 318-321.

Sanchez Lopez J.M., Martinez Insua M., Perez Baz J., Fernandez Puentes J.L., Canedo Hernandez L.M. (2003): New Cytotoxic Indolic Metabolites from a Marine *Streptomyces*. J Nat Prod, 66: 863-864.

Schumacher R.W., Talmage S.C., Miller S.A., Sarris K.E., Davidson B.S., Goldberg A. (2003): Isolation and Structure Determination of an Antimicrobial Ester from a Marine-derived Bacterium. J Nat Prod, 66: 1291-1293.

Shin J., Seo Y., Lee H.S., Rho J.R., Mo S.J. (2003): A New Cyclic Peptide from a Marine Derived Bacterium of the Genus *Nocardiopsis*. J Nat Prod, 66: 883-884.

Simmons J.A.K., Lyons W.B. (1994): The Groundwater Flux of Nitrogen and Phosphorus to Bermuda's Coastal Waters. Water Resour Bull, 30: 983-991.

Slomp C.P., Van Cappellen P. (2004): Nutrient Inputs to the Coastal Ocean Through Submarine Groundwater Discharge: Controls and Potential Impact. J Hydrol, 295: 64-86.

Snelgrove, P.V.R. (1999): Getting to the Bottom of Marine Biodiversity: Sedimentary Habitats. BioScience, 49: 129-138.

Soria Mercado I.E., Prieto-Davo A., Jensen P.R., Fenical W. (2005): Antibiotic Terpenoid Chlorodihydroquinones from a New Marine Actinomycete. J Nat Prod, 68: 904-910.

Stach J.E.M., Maldonado L.A., Masson D.G., Ward A.C., Goodfellow M., Bull A.T. (2003a): Statistical Approaches to Estimating Bacterial Diversity in Marine Sediments. Appl Environ Microbiol, 69: 6189-6200.

Stach J.E.M., Maldonado L.A., Ward A.C., Goodfellow M., Bull A.T. (2003b): New Primers Specific for Taxa Assigned to the Class Actinobacteria: Application to Marine and Terrestrial Environments. Environ Microbiol, 5: 828-41.

Stach, J.E.M. and Bull, A.T. (2005): Estimating and Comparing the Diversity of Marine Actinobacteria. Antonie Van Leeuwenhoek, 87: 3-9.

Stritzke K., Schulz, Laatsch H., Helmke E., Beil W. (2004): Novel Caprolactones from a Marine *Streptomycete*. J Nat Prod, 67: 395-401.

Thompson-Bulldis A., Karl D. (1989): Application of a Novel Methods for Phosphorus Determination in the Oligtrophic North Pacific Ocean. Limnol Oceanogr, 43: 1565-1577.

Thornburg C.C., Mark Zabriskie T., McPhail K.L. (2010): Deep-sea Hydrothermal vents: Potential Hot Spots for Natural Products Discovery? J Nat Prod, 73: 489-99.

Tian X.P., Tang S.K., Dong J.D., Zhang Y.Q., Xu L.H., Zhang S., et al. (2009b): *Marinactinospora thermotolerans* gen. nov., sp. nov., a Marine Actinomycete Isolated from a Sediment in the Northern South China Sea. Int J Syst Evol Microbiol, 59: 948-52.

Tian X.P., Zhi X.Y., Qiu Y.Q., Zhang Y.Q., Tang S.K., Xu L.H., et al. (2009a): *Sciscionella* Marina gen. nov., sp. nov., a Marine Actinomycete Isolated from a Sediment in the Northern South China Sea. Int J Syst Evol Microbiol, 59: 222-8.

Tickel, C. (1997): The Value of Biodiversity. In: Ormond, R.F.G., Gage, J.D. Angel, M.V. (Eds.), Marine Biodiversity: Patterns and Processes. Cambridge University Press, Cambridge, pp. xiii-xxii.

Torsvik V., Goksoyr J., Daae F.L. (1990): High Diversity of DNA of Soil Bacteria. Appl Environ Microbiol, 56: 782-7.

UNEP. (2009): Marine Litter: A Global Challenge, Nairobi, UNEP.

Waldichuk, M. (1985): Biological Availability of Metals to Marine Organisms. Marine Pollution Bulletin, 16: 7-11.

Walker W.A. and Coe J.M. (1989): Survey of Marine Debris Ingestion by Odontocete Cetaceans, in Proceedings of the 2nd International Conference on Marine Debris, R.S. Shomura and M.L. Godfrey, Eds., Vol. 1, pp. 747-774.

Wang L., Lee F.S.C., Wang X., Yin Y., Li J. (2007): Chemical Characteristics and Source Implications of Petroleum Hydrocarbon Contaminants in the Sediments Near Major Drainage Outfalls Along the Coastal of Laizhou Bay, Bohai Sea, China. Environ Monit Assess, 125: 229-37.

Webster N.S., Wilson K.J., Blackall L.L., Hill R.T. (2001): Phylogenetic Diversity of Bacteria Associated with the Marine Sponge *Rhopaloeides Odorabile*. Appl Environ Microbiol, 67: 434-444.

White P.M., Duane J.R., Wolf C., Thoma G.J., Reynolds C.M. (2006): Phytoremediation of Alkylated Polycyclic Aromatic Hydrocarbons in a Crude Oil-contaminated Soil. Water Air Soil Pollut, 169: 207-20.

Wu Z., Xie L., Xia G., Zhang J., Nie Y., Hu J., Wang S., Zhang R. (2005): A New Tetrodotoxin Producing Actinomycete, *Nocardiopsis dassonvillei*, Isolated from the Ovaries of Pufferfish *Fugu rubripes*. Toxicon, 45: 851-859.

Xiao J., Luo Y., Xie S., Xu J. (2011): *Serinicoccus profundi* sp. nov., a Novel Actinomycete Isolated from Deep-sea Sediment and Emended Description of the Genus *Serinicoccus*. Int J Syst Evol Microbiol, 61: 16-9.

Yi H., Schumann P., Sohn K., Chun J. (2004): *Serinicoccus marinus* gen. nov., sp nov., a Novel Actinomycete with L-ornithine and L-serine in the peptidoglycan.. Int J Syst Evol Microbiol, 54: 1585-1589.

Zahner H., Fiedler H.P. (1995): Fifty Years of Antimicrobials: Past Perspectives and Future Trends. In: Hunter P.A, Darby G.K, Russell N.J, Editors. The Need for New Antibiotics: Possible Ways Forward. Fifty-third Symposium of the Society for General Microbiology Bath. Cambridge, UK: Cambridge University Press, p. 67-84.

Zhang H., Zhang W., Jin Y., Jin M., Yu X. (2008): A Comparative Study on the Phylogenetic Diversity of Culturable Actinobacteria Isolated from Five Marine Sponge Species. Antonie Van Leeuwenhoek, 93: 241-8.

CHAPTER 8

Vaccine
A Fish Health and Diseases Management Approach for Sustainable Aquaculture

Dharmendra Kumar Meena, *India*; **Pronob Das,** *India*
B.K Behera, *India* **Kanti Meena,** *India*; **Sekar, M.,** *India*
A.K. Prusty, *India*; **Md. Shahbaz Akthar,** *India*
Satendra Kumar, *India*

ABSTRACT

The intensive farming of finishes and shellfishes has led to an imbalance of optimal culture conditions, which shows increased susceptibility to infectious disease. Increased incidence of microbial diseases in aquaculture system is the major obstacle in the success of the industry. Use of antibiotics has attracted lot of criticism due to the issues like antibiotic residues, bacterial drug resistance and toxicity. In this present scenario, vaccination would be the best alternative to combat bacterial and viral disease for the sustainable aquaculture In addition to optimizing husbandry and general management practices, vaccine use, although still limited, is becoming more widespread in certain sectors of aquaculture for disease prevention. In this paper scope, limitations, applications, ethics in vaccination, commercialization, future perspective on fish vaccines development and research have been discussed.

Key words: Antibiotics, Bacterins, Fin fish, Oncogene, Oil adjuvants.

Introduction

Vaccination is an easy, effective and preventive method of protecting fish from diseases. Vaccination is a process by which a protective immune response is induced in an animal by administration of vaccines. Vaccines are preparations of antigens derived from pathogenic organisms, rendered non-pathogenic by various means, which will stimulate immune system of the animal to increase the resistance to the disease on natural encountered with pathogens. Once stimulated by a vaccine, the antibody-producing cells, called B lymphocytes, remain sensitized and ready to respond to the agent should it ever gain entry to the body A vaccine is any biologically based preparation intended to establish or to improve immunity to a particular disease or group of diseases. Vaccines have been used for many years in humans, terrestrial livestock, and companion animals against a variety of diseases.

Vaccines work by exposing the immune system of an animal to an "antigen" a piece of a pathogen or the entire pathogen, and then allowing time for the immune system to develop a response and a "memory" to accelerate this response in later infections by the targeted disease-causing organism. Vaccines are normally administered to healthy animals prior to a disease outbreak. One analogy used for vaccines is that of an insurance policy (Komar *et al.* 2004). A vaccine, if effective, can help prevent a future disaster from being a major economic drain. But vaccines, like insurance, have a premium, or cost. The producer must weigh the cost in materials and labor against the risk and cost of a disease outbreak to determine whether vaccination is warranted. When actual vaccine effectiveness is also unknown, this makes decision-making even more difficult. Consultation with a fish veterinarian or other fish health specialist will be helpful when examining cost vs. benefit of a particular vaccine. Disease is one of the most important limiting factors in aquaculture. Optimal husbandry and general management including bio-security, nutrition, genetics, system management and water quality are critical for maximizing aquatic animal health. However, all facilities are vulnerable to disease outbreaks because many pathogenic disease-causing organisms e.g., bacteria, viruses, fungi, and parasites are opportunistic and present in the environment, or may be found on some fish that are not showing signs of disease (carriers).

In many cases, when fish are no longer eating, treatment options become much more limited and treatment may no longer be effective. It makes sense, then, that prevention of disease is preferable to disease treatment (Grisez and Tan 2005). Vaccines and immunostimulants are the two historical approaches for disease prevention that have been used in other animal industries. Both the approaches have been used successfully in some aquaculture industries, and should be considered as fish health management options.

Collaborative Steps for Developing Vaccine in Aquaculture Sector for Fish Disease

Food and nutritional security is being addressed at the global level through aquaculture in both cold and warm waters. Aquaculture is considered one of the most rapidly growing food producing sectors in the world since capture fishery has stagnated. According to global statistics (FAO, 2010), close to 90 per cent of aquaculture takes place in Asia, China being the leader, followed by India. The major problem faced by aquaculture globally is the mass mortalities due to diseases. In spite of this, it may sound strange that with the exception of Japan, there are no commercial fish vaccines produced in Asia, while the European and American aquaculture has at least a dozen commercial vaccines to prevent disease. One of the consequences of lack of vaccines in Asian aquaculture has been the indiscriminate use of antimicrobial agents leading to unacceptable levels of residues and emergence of antibiotic resistant bacteria.

The need for supporting research that can lead to development of vaccines for aquaculture was recognized by the Department of Biotechnology (DBT), Government of India a decade ago and DBT rightly considered collaboration with Norway that has the experience of minimizing antibiotic use in salmon aquaculture through vaccination. India-Norway Platform on Fish Vaccines was developed after a series of discussions between Indian and Norwegian scientists who met in Delhi first and then in Oslo to develop this collaborative programme. To improve the chances of success and move towards commercial vaccines, Pharmaq, the Norwegian company that has experience in vaccine development and commercialization is involved as a partner in this platform.

Research on vaccine development for cultivable freshwater and marine finfish species to protect them against major aquaculture pathogens. New Norwegian-Indian research collaboration aims to develop new vaccines for fish and shrimps. Together with the Norwegian College of Fishery Science, Nofima, the Norwegian School of Veterinary Science, Bodø Regional College and the vaccine company PHARMAC AS, the Institute of Marine Research has been awarded NOK 44 million for a major Norwegian-Indian research project that aims to develop new vaccines for fish and shrimp. The project will run for four years and the consortium will collaborate with seven extremely competent Indian research institutions. The cooperative project aims to identify and characterise antigens in important disease-producing organisms (bacteria and viruses) in fish and shrimp and to develop effective preventive treatments for them. The project expects to supply new vaccine concepts for the Norwegian and Indian aquaculture industries.

The Immune System and Viruses

The cooperative project that has just been funded is a continuation of a project on which we have been working here at the Institute of Marine Research, in which we have been looking at how the halibut's immune system reacts to infections", says scientist Audun H. Nerland.Researchers are already well under way with mapping the immune system in halibut and cod and have done a great deal of work on nodaviruses, which have posed a challenge to aquaculture in both India and Norway.

By vaccinating fish and studying the reaction of the immune system, they have been able to develop vaccines by employing molecular biological methods. The experience gained in the course of this work will be important for the Norwegian-Indian cooperative project which is now being launched, and which will focus on salmon, halibut, cod and shrimp.

Disease at the Root of Serious Losses

Viruses are the cause of the most costly diseases in Norwegian and Indian aquaculture today, and they can neither be prevented nor treated with antibiotics. This means that it is vital to develop vaccines, and the cooperative project will develop such vaccines for diseases of fish that are causing problems in Norway and India, with particular focus on infectious pancreatic necrosis (IPN) and viral nervous necrosis (VNN) which is caused by nodavirus, in fish, and white-spot syndrome virus in shrimp. The project will also develop vaccines against pathological variants of the Aeromonas, Edwardsiella and Vibrio bacteria.

Bacterial Diseases

Nofima (formerly Fiskeriforskning) and the Norwegian College of Fishery Science have for many years undertaken joint projects to develop vaccines against bacterial diseases in cod in close collaboration with vaccine producer PHARMAQ AS. In the new Norwegian-Indian research project, scientists will continue R & D work on vaccines against atypical furunculosis, which is an increasing problem in cod farms. The bacterial disease francisellosis was discovered in cod a few years ago and has rapidly developed into a serious problem for cod farming. The development of a vaccine against the disease is still in the start phase. However, this project enables the effort in this field to be increased.

India is a major fish farming nation, but the lack of vaccines causes major financial loses," says Nofima Scientist Vera Lund. "Our research collaboration will focus on the development of vaccines against bacterial diseases that are important in both countries. In Indian fish farming, vibriosis and furunculosis are important diseases in carp and sea perch respectively," says Lund. "We will be able to draw reciprocal benefits from each others' knowledge and expertise about disease-causing bacteria and vaccine development and, in doing so, contribute to increased survival rates and minimal use of antibiotics.

Norwegian-Indian Collaboration

The Norwegian side of the project is being financed by the Research Council of Norway and will be shared by research teams at Fiskeriforskning (now known as Nofima) in Tromsø, the Institute of Marine Research in Bergen, the Norwegian School of Veterinary Science in Oslo, Bodø Regional College and PHARMAQ in Oslo for a period of four years. The Norwegian College of Fishery Science at the University of Tromsø is responsible for the project. The Indian research institutes are extremely competent in developing vaccines for human medicine, but have little experience of the development and use of vaccines in aquaculture. The Norwegian and Indian research groups will therefore complement each other, and the exchange of knowledge between the two areas will be an important part of the collaboration. PHARMAQ AS is the only industrial partner in the project, and this company will contribute its expertise in vaccine development in cooperation with the Indian and Norwegian participants. The project is receiving a similar amount of financial support from the Indian authorities.

Rationale of vaccine being used in aquaculture

- Vaccines are not the same as antibiotics and generally will not be effective for stopping a disease outbreak once it has begun.
- Vaccines are used to prevent a specific disease outbreak from occurring and are not a therapy.
- Its efficiency exists for a longer duration with one or more treatments.
- No toxic side effects and healthy fish have better growth performance.
- No accumulation of toxic residues
- Pathogen will not develop resistance.
- Theoretically it can control any bacterial and viral disease.
- No environmental impact.

Properties of an ideal vaccine

- The vaccine used should be safe and non toxic to the animal.
- The vaccine should have high immunogenicity.
- The vaccine should protect the animal for a longer period. In fish, duration of one year or life long protection can be said to be commercially effective for a vaccine preparation.
- The vaccine should have wide spectrum approach against the pathogens to get 100 per cent protection.

- It should be applied to a large number of fish.
- It should be readily licensed and registered It should be cost effective and easily applicable to a wide variety of fish species.
- Vaccine used should be environmental friendly.

Classification of Vaccines

I. Conventional vaccines

Conventional vaccines include those vaccines which has been developed and commercialized for regular use by the consumers, researchers. Of the types currently in use, the most common are described below.

1. *Bacterins (Killed vaccine):* These vaccines are comprised of killed micro-organisms these are previously virulent micro-organisms which have been killed with chemicals or heat. Bacterins stimulate the antibody-related portion of the immune response (Ex: humoral immune response).
2. *Inactivated vaccine:* It is a culture of an infectious agent on a medium and then deactivated using heat or formaldehyde. Viruses are metabolically inserted and they cannot be killed.
3. *Live Attenuated vaccine:* These vaccines are comprised of live micro-organisms (bacteria, viruses) that have been grown in culture and no longer have the properties that cause significant disease. Live attenuated vaccines will stimulate additional parts of the immune system e.g. cell-mediated, as well as a humoral antibody response. They typically provoke more durable immunological responses and are the preferred type for healthy adults
4. *Toxoid vaccine:* comprised of toxic compounds that have been inactivated, so they no longer cause disease rather than the micro-organism itself e.g. the tetanus toxoid vaccine used in human.
5. *Subunit vaccine:* These are made from a small portion of a micro-organism rather than the entire micro-organism that ideally will stimulate an immune response to the entire organism Rather than introducing an inactivated or attenuated micro-organism to an immune system which would constitute a "whole-agent" vaccine, a fragment of it can create an immune response.

II. Unconventional vaccine

These types of vaccines include recombinant vector vaccines, DNA vaccines, *T-ell receptor* peptide vaccines.

1. *Recombinant Vector:* These combines to the parts of disease-causing micro-organisms with those of weakened microorganisms, and by combining the physiology of one micro-organism and the DNA of the other,

immunity can be created against diseases that have complex infection processes. Recombinant vector vaccines allow a weak pathogen to produce antigen.

2. *DNA vaccination:* DNA vaccines are composed of a circular portion of genetic material that can, after being incorporated into the animal, produce a particular immune-stimulating portion of a pathogen. DNA vaccine works by insertion and expression, triggering immune system recognition of viral or bacterial DNA into animal cells. Some cells of the immune system that recognize the proteins expressed will mount an attack against these proteins and cells expressing them. Because these cells live for a very long time, if the pathogen that normally expresses these proteins is encountered at a later time, they will be attacked instantly by the immune system. One advantage of DNA vaccines is that they are very easy to produce and store. DNA vaccination is still experimental.
3. T-cell receptor peptide vaccines are under development for several diseases. These peptides have been shown to modulate cytokine production and improve cell mediated immunity

III. Miscellaneous (diversified) vaccines

These are the vaccine which have been commercialized in other countries like USA, Japan and China but not have been developed in India. Now the formation of an apex regulatory body for vaccines application is on the way to its development in countries like India.

1. Licensed (Commercial)

Commercial vaccines are produced by a manufacturer for a specific fish species or species group and for a specific disease. Commercial vaccines (and other products considered under the umbrella term, "biologics," meaning of biological origin) are regulated and licensed by the USDA-APHIS Center for Veterinary Biologics (CVB).

2. Autogenous

Autogenous vaccines are made from a particular pathogen (commonly a specific bacterium) that has been isolated from diseased fish at a specific facility. Although autogenous vaccine production also must follow strict guidelines, there is more flexibility with use of these products. Autogenous vaccines are restricted to use by or under the direction of a licensed veterinarian within the context of a veterinarian-client-patient relationship.

Method of Vaccine Administration

Vaccines are administered to fish in one of three ways: by mouth, by immersion, or by injection. Each has its advantages and disadvantages. The most effective method will depend upon the pathogen and its natural route of infection, the life stage of the fish, production techniques, and other logistical considerations. A specific route of administration or even multiple applications using different methods may be necessary for adequate protection.

1. *Oral administration:* It results in direct delivery of antigen via the digestive system of the fish. It is the easiest method logistically because feeding is a normal, ongoing part of the production schedule. Stress on the fish is minimal, and no major changes in production are required. Prior to feeding, vaccine is mixed, top-dressed, or bio- encapsulated into the feed. To reduce leaching into the water and/or to provide some protection against breakdown of the vaccine by the fish's digestive processes, a coating agent is often used. For small fish (e.g., 1-5 g or less), bio encapsulation may be a preferred method of oral delivery. Live food (rotifers, brine shrimp) is added to a concentrated vaccine solution, and allowed to take up vaccine. This live food is then fed to fry or small fingerlings. Although oral vaccine is the most preferred method, it conveys relatively short immunity compared to the other methods such that additional vaccination may be required. In addition, because of the problems involved with getting the vaccine intact through the intestine and adequately stimulating the immune system, there are few commercial oral vaccines available (Komar *et al.* 2004).

2. Immersion vaccination permits immune cells located in the fish's skin and gills to become directly exposed to antigens. These immune cells may then mount a response e.g., antibody production, thus protecting the fish from future infection. Other types of immune cells in the skin and gills carry antigens internally, where a more systemic response will also develop. Immersion vaccination occurs by dip or by bath. Dips are short, typically 30 seconds, in a high concentration of vaccine. Baths are of longer duration-an hour or more- and in a much lower concentration of vaccine. In practice, dips are logistically more practical for large numbers of small (1-5g) fish. Unfortunately, protection using immersion methods may not last long and a second vaccination may be required (Komar *et al.* 2004) because smaller, younger fish may have immature immune systems and because this is a more indirect route.

3. Injection vaccination allows direct delivery of a small volume of antigen into the muscle (intramuscular injection) or into the body cavity (intracoelomic, intraperitoneal) injection), allowing for more direct stimulation of a systemic immune response. Injection vaccines normally include an oil-based or water-based compound, known as an adjuvant, that serves to further stimulate the immune system. Injection is effective

for many pathogens that cause systemic disease; and protection 6 months to a year is much longer than by other methods. Every fish in the population is injected, giving more assurance to the producer. Another advantage is that multiple antigens (for different diseases) can be delivered at the same time. However, vaccination by injection is logistically the most demanding of all three methods. Fish must be anesthetized to minimize stress. Injection requires more time, labor, and skilled personnel. The correct needle size is important. The vaccine may incite a more severe reaction if it is injected into the wrong portion of the fish. And finally, smaller-sized fish (under 10 g) may not respond well to this method (Komar *et al.* 2004).

Availability and Status of Vaccine Application in Aquaculture

There are a number of vaccines commercially available in different countries other than USA (Biering *et al.* 2005; Hastein *et al.* 2005). Ultimately, commercial vaccine availability is a matter of economics. Manufacturers of these vaccines must first decide whether or not the U.S. market will be economically beneficial to them. Next, they must submit their vaccine(s) to the USDA-APHIS-CVB for official licensing, and this can be a lengthy process. After all licensing, testing, and other requirements are completed, the vaccine would be available for U.S. producers.

However a number of vaccines are not currently available in the U.S. but have been, or are registered and commercially available in other countries. For the prevention of bacterial diseases, vaccines include those for streptoccocosis (caused by *Streptococcus iniae* and related bacteria); pasteurellosis (*Photobacterium damsela* subsp. *piscicida*); warmwater vibriosis (*V. alginolyticus*, *V. harveyi*, *V. vulnificus*, and *V. parahaemolyticus*); and lactococcosis (*Lactococcus garvieae*). Vaccines for the prevention of viral diseases include those for koi herpesvirus (CyHV-3); infectious pancreatic necrosis (IPN); infectious hematopoietic necrosis (IHNV); viral hemorrhagic septicemia (VHS); salmon pancreatic disease (SPD); grass carp aquareovirus (GCR); and iridovirus in *Seriola spp.* (Grisez and Tan 2005; Hastein *et al.* 2005).

Within the genus *Vibrio*, the species causing the most economically serious diseases in marine culture are *Vibrio anguillarum*, *V. ordalii*, *V. salmonicida* and *V. vulnificus* biotype- II. *Vibrio anguillarum* is the responsible agent of the classical vibriosis which affects salmonid and non-salmonid fish with a world wide distribution. However, different polyvalent oiladjuvanted vaccines, including different combinations of *V. anguillarum* with other pathogens, such as *V. ordalii*, *V. salmonicida*, *Aeromonas salmonicida*, *Moritella viscosa* and infectious pancreatic necrosis virus, are also available on the market to be used for salmonids by the ip route (Toranzo *et al.*, 1997; Greger and Goodrich, 1999).

In the case of strictly marine fishes, such as turbot (*Scophthalmus maximus*) or sea bass (*Dicentrarchus labrax*), *V. anguillarum* vaccines are being employed by bath in 1-2 g fish, with two immersions in the vaccine bath being necessary after a monthly interval. In contrast to *V. anguillarum*, *V. ordalii* is antigenically homogeneous with no serotypes being detected. Although some cross-reactions exist between *V. ordalii* and *V. anguillarum* serotype O2, both species do not have identical antigenic properties (Mutharia *et al.*, 1992).

In fact, commercial bacterins including *V. anguillarum* serotype O1 and *V. ordalii* as antigens elicit very poor protection against infections by *V. anguillarum* serotype O2 (Toranzo *et al.*, 1997). *Vibrio salmonicida* is the etiological agent of the "cold water diseases" or "Hitra diseases" which affect only salmonids and cod (*Gadus morhua*) cultured in Canada and Nordic countries of Europe (mainly Norway and the UK) (Egidius *et al.*,1986; Sorum *et al.*, 1990). As stated above, salmonids in Nordic countries are systematically vaccinated with polyvalent bacterins containing at least two pathogenic vibrios, *V. anguillarum* and *V. salmonicida* (Toranzo *et al.*, 1997). *Vibrio vulnificus* comprises two biotypes. Whereas biotype 1 is an opportunistic human pathogen causing disease generally associated with handling or ingestion of raw shellfish, the strains of biotype 2 are virulent for eels (Tison *et al.*, 1982; Biosca *et al.*, 1991; Dalsgaard *et al.*, 1998).

Although these strains can belong to distinct serotypes, only serovar E behaves as a primary pathogen for eels (*Anguilla anguilla* and *A. japonica*). However, a triple exposure to the vaccine in a short space of time (approximately 1 month) by prolonged immersion was needed to ensure an acceptable level of protection. Since no cross-protection between serotypes exists, vaccinated eels with *V. vulnificus* serovar E can be infected by other less frequent serovars of the pathogen which act as secondary pathogens (Fouz and Amaro, 2003).

Vaccines have been used in food fish, in particular the salmon industry, for approximately 30 years, and are believed to be one of the main reasons that salmon production has been so successful. Vaccination of salmon also dropped the industry's use of antibiotics to a mere fraction of its original use (Sommerset *et al.* 2005). In Norway, for example, in 1987, before widespread use of vaccines, approximately 50,000 kg of antibiotics was used. By 1997, when vaccines had become more routine, antibiotic usage had dropped to less than 1000-2000 kg (Sommerset *et al.* 2005).

Table 8.1: Commonly used Vaccines for Aquaculture Application

Vaccines	Fish Species	Disease	References
1	2	3	4
Aeromonas	Atlantic salmon	Furunculosis	H. Shieh 1985; 2006
salmonicida Bacterin *Vibrio anguillarum*-Ordalii-*Yersinia ruckeri* Bacterin	Rainbow trout	Vibriosis, yersiniosis (enteric red- mouth disease)	Raida et al. 2008; 2009
Yersinia ruckeri Bacterin	Salmonids	Yersiniosis (enteric red-mouth disease)	Stevenson 1997
Vibrio salmonicida Bacterin	Salmonids	Vibriosis	Hjeltnes *et al.* 1989
Edwardsiella ictaluri Bacterin	Channel Catfish	Enteric septicaemia	Shoemaker *et al.* 1997; Klesius *et al.* 2004
DNA vaccine	Common carp	Spring viraemia of carp	Kanellos *et al.* 2006
Biofilm and free-cell vaccines of *Aeromonas hydrophila*	Indian major carps and common carp	Dropsy	Azad *et al.* 2000
Streptococcus agalactiae (groupB) vaccine	Tilapia spp.	Streptococcosis	Klesius *et al.* 1999; Evans *et al.* 2005; Pretto-Giordano *et al.* 2010.
Betanodavirus	Grouper	Betanodavirus disease	Kai *et al.* 2008.
DNA vaccine	Sea bass	Vibriosis	Kumar *et al.* 2007.
Beta glucan	Nile tilapia	*Streptococcus iniae infection*	Whittington *et al.* 2005.
β-hydroxy-β-methylbutyrate	Nile tilapia	*Streptococcus iniae infection*	Whittington *et al.* 2003.
Inositol	Nile tilapia	*Streptococcus iniae infection*	Peres *et al.* 2004.
Attenuated siderophore deficient and *aro*-A deletion mutant strains	Striped bass hybrids	Pasteurellosis	Hawke *et al.*, 2002
Attenuated and stable *aroA* auxotrophic *A. salmonicida* mutant strains	Goldfish, carps	Furunculosis	Vaughan *et al.*, 1993

(Contd…)

1	2	3	4
A-layer and O-antigen deficient *A. salmonicida* vaccines	Goldfish, carps	Furunculosis	Thornton *et al.*, 1991, 1994
Aeromonas salmonicida baterin	Salmonids	Furunculosis	Austin *et al.*, 1996; Bernoth, 1997; Ellis, 1997; Hiney and Oliver, 1999)
Oil-based *M.viscosa* multivalent vaccines	Atlantic salmon	Winter ulcer	Greger and Goodrich, 1999
Commercial ERM vaccines with sarovar (O1a and O2b)	Salmonids	Yersiniosis	Newman, 1993; Stevenson, 1997; Romalde, 1992
AQUAVAC-ESCO	Channel catfish	Enteric septicaemia of catfish	Klesius and Shoemaker, 1998
Flexibacteriosis vaccine ("FM 95")	Turbot	Marine flexibacteriosis	Santos *et al.*, 1999
Oil-adjuvanted *F. psychrophilum* ip vaccines		Cold water disease or rainbow trout fry syndrome (RTFS)	LaFrentz *et al.*, 2002
No vaccines	Ictalurids, eels, salmonids, cyprinids	Columnaris disease or saddleback disease	Newman, 1993; Bernardet, 1997
Aqueous and non-mineral oil-adjuvanted *P.anguilliseptica* bacterins	Turbot	Sekiten-bio" or "red spot disease	Romalde *et al.*, 2003
L. garvieae and *S. parauberis* bacterins	yellowtail and turbot	Streptococcosis	Toranzo *et al.*, 1995b; Romalde *et al.*, 1999b; Ooyama *et al.*, 1999
Renogen	Atlantic salmon	Bacterial kidney disease	Salonius et al., 2003
Renogen	Pacific salmon	Piscirickettsiosis	Salonius *et al.*, 2003

Requisites to Develop New Vaccines

A number of factors and a certain amount of information are necessary to facilitate vaccine development and their more beneficial applications in aquaculture sector.

1. *Sound under standing of fish shell fish farming practices:* Husbandry practices should be well understood, and relatively intensive culture of a fish

with good management is ideal for economic aquaculture production. There should be a good understanding of what organism causes the disease under study, and under what conditions.

2. *Knowledge of biology of pathogens and antigens:* In some cases, if scientific resources are available, the biological structure of relevant antigens (parts of the pathogen that incite the best immune response) can be determined and used. The vaccine should be administered in a way that will stimulate the proper immune response and should mimic how the pathogen infects the fish naturally.
3. *Knowledge of fish immunology:* It is very fundamental thing to keep the well sighted knowledge of the fish species' immune system development that will also help to identify how early the fish can be vaccinated and when during the production cycle the vaccine should be administered. (Grisez and Tan 2005). Association between plasma antibody response and protection in rainbow trout *Oncorhynchus mykiss* vaccinated against *yersinia rukeri* was also performed very recently (Raida *et al.* 2011)

Timing of Vaccinations

Vaccines are not the same as antibiotics and generally will not be effective for stopping a disease outbreak once it has begun. Vaccines are used to prevent a specific disease outbreak from occurring and are not a therapy. Vaccines rely upon a healthy immune system to work properly.

Ethics in Fish Vaccination

1. Do not expect vaccines to eradicate disease. If vaccines against a particular disease are used routinely on the farm, evidence of this disease will largely disappear. However, this does not mean that the organism which causes the disease has been eradicated. In fact, it is still present and capable of infecting susceptible unvaccinated fish.
2. Do not let vaccines solve your husbandry problems. Events or practices such as overstocking, undue stress, or poor water quality can cause breakdowns in vaccine protection.
3. Only vaccinate healthy fish. The performance of vaccines is very dependent on the health status of the fish at the time of vaccination. Vaccines cannot be expected to give good or longterm protection if the fish are sick, in poor condition, or they are carriers of pathogens when vaccinated.
4. Allow sufficient time for immunity to develop. Immunity takes time to develop and thus vaccinated fish are not immediately protected. Thus, vaccinated fish must be maintained during this time in the less stressful conditions as possible. The time of the development of immunity is dependent mainly upon the surrounding water temperature (i.e. at 10°C it takes 15-20 days).

5. Strictly follow the recommendations of vaccine usage when immunizing fish. Do not try to shorten the recommended time of exposure to the vaccines; do not modify the dilution or dose recommended; do not overload the net when fish are vaccinated by dip immersion; do ensure that the water used to dilute the vaccine is a similar temperature to that in which the fish are being held; do not use the vaccine after the expiry data.

Economic Aspect for Developing Fish Vaccines

All sustainable industries producing live stock intensively rely on effective vaccination programmes. However, vaccines are not "cure all" remedies but are an integral part of comprehensive health management programmes. Most producers do not realise the true economic value of vaccines. However, fish vaccines are normally more cost effective than other investments related to growing fish commercially. When producers have to choose between vaccines, they must bear in mind that small improvements in vaccine efficacy far outweigh any economic benefits related to large differences in vaccine price.

The following parameters of economic importance must be considered in the implementation of vaccination strategies against particular diseases:

1. Expected/historical mortality of fish due to the diseases
2. Degree/duration of disease protection provided by vaccines
3. Expected/historical drug cost needed to treat against the disease(s) when not vaccinated.

In addition, there are other economic aspects (potential benefits and/or costs) that must be taken into account when vaccinating fish:

1. Potential benefits
   (i) Increased appetite and growth in vaccinated compared to non-vaccinated fish because of the better food conversion rates in vaccinated fish.
   (ii) Potential of growing vaccinated fish at higher densities because disease is not a limiting factor in the population.
   (iii) Reduction of drug use and, therefore, the incidence of appearance of bacterial drug resistance, as well as drug residues in the final product.
   (iv) Improvement of industry image for the sanitary quality of the fish produced, as well as from the environmental safety stand point.
2. Potential costs
   (i) Post-vaccination mortality as a result of: Fish are latent carriers of pathogen which "emerges". Fish are weakened by improper handling or rearing practices.

(ii) Decrease in growth caused by side effects such as those produced by some adjuvanted.

Factor Affecting Vaccines Efficacy

Just as with any other fish health management tool or technique, vaccines are not a universal preventative. Excellent husbandry, including good biosecurity and genetics, optimal nutrition, appropriate densities, life stage considerations, and system management including water quality/chemistry are all important for minimizing disease in general, as well as for maximizing vaccine effectiveness. Good biosecurity, including appropriate quarantine and adequate sanitation and disinfection, will minimize the potential for introduction of unwanted pathogens and reduce loading of opportunistic pathogens. Making sure the fish are as healthy as possible, given production parameter constraints, will go far toward preparing fish for vaccination and boosting their immune systems. Following factor to be taken under consideration during vaccination.

1. *Proper disease diagnosis:* It is very critical factor affecting vaccines efficacy. Producers should work with an aquatic veterinarian or other fish health professional, and with a fish disease diagnostic laboratory to determine the major contributing factors to a disease outbreak. This will facilitate vaccine development and feasibility. Some diseases will have primarily environmental (water quality, handling) components that may not require a vaccine. Some diseases will have a specific pathogen, such as a specific strain of bacteria, for which a legal, commercial vaccine may or may not be available.

2. *Timing of disease out breaks:* Determining when in the production cycle fish get sick (for ongoing diseases) and at what stage fish can be successfully vaccinated may require some additional diagnostics and experiments. This step is also necessary for proper vaccine use.

3. *Method of vaccine administration:* The various methods of administration (injection, immersion, or oral) have different advantages and disadvantages; the choice of which one to use will depend upon the situation.

4. *Environmental factor:* Water temperature during the immunization process will determine how quickly immunity will develop. Any stress during this time period will also hinder development of immunity. For warm water species, 1-3 weeks may be required.

5. *Type of species:* Cold water species like trout, salmon are supposed to take more time fro immunity development while warm water species, may require 1-3 weeks.

Present Status of Development of Fish Vaccines

During the last two decades vaccination has become as an important method for prevention of infectious diseases in farmed fish, mainly salmonid species. So far, most commercial vaccines have been inactivated vaccines administered by injection or immersion. Bacterial infections caused by Gram-negative bacteria such as *Vibrio* sp., *Aeromonas* sp., and *Yersinia* sp. have been effectively controlled by vaccination. With furunculosis, the success is attributed to the use of injectable vaccines containing adjuvants. Vaccines against virus infections, including infectious pancreatic necrosis, have also been used in commercial fish farming. Vaccines against several other bacterial and viral infections have been studied and found to be technically feasible. The overall positive effect of vaccination in farmed fish is reduced mortality. However, for the future of the fish farming industry it is also important that vaccination contributes to a sustainable biological production with negligible consumption of antibiotics.

Future Prospectus

Under specified conditions, autogenous vaccines may also be used for animal populations that are close to the facility for which the autogenous vaccine was originally manufactured. Autogenous vaccines have been developed and used successfully in ornamental fish aquaculture (Russo *et al.* 2006a and Russo *et al.* 2006b). There should some strategic manipulation and research so that these types of vaccine may be applied in culture fisheries. How ever, some work has been done on virus-like particles (VLPs) expressing human ONCOGENE c-myc for non-infective infectious pancreatic necrosis (IPNV) in salmonid fishes (Dhar *et al.* 2006). Antigenicity of infectious pancreatic necrosis virus capsid protein VP2 virus-like particles expressed in yeast (Thomas *et al.* 2007). Robert *et al.* (2007) used real-time reverse transcriptase-polymerase chain method for quantitative detection of infectious pancreatic necrosis virus in rainbow trout (*Oncorhynchus mykiss*). There is great scope in developing the standard methodology for production and scientific utilization of DNA vaccine, Recombinant vector vaccines, T-cell receptor peptide vaccines where as some new area may be of great interest from vaccination point of view.

1. To achieve progress in fish vaccinology, an increase in the co-operation between basic and applied science (i.e., between the immunologist/ microbiologist and the vaccinologist) is needed.
2. Since there is not always correlation between the major antigens expressed *in vitro* and those expressed *in vivo*, the development of more effective vaccines for the diseases in aquaculture should rely in the identification of the important immunogens expressed by the pathogens *in vivo*, and the selection of *in vitro* conditions that maximize their expression.

3. Improvement in oral immunization with biodegradable microparticle-based vaccines to be used for booster vaccination.
4. Development of new non-mineral oil adjuvants lacking side effects.
5. Development of polyvalent vaccines and standardization of a vaccination calendar appropriate for each economically important fish species.
6. Investigation of the mechanisms of immunoglobulin transfer from pre-spawning females to offspring as a useful way of protecting fish against pathogens which affect early life stages.

Thrust Areas

Manufacturers and researchers must run numerous experimental trials when developing and testing vaccines for commercial production. During these trials, vaccinated and unvaccinated groups of fish are challenged infected in the laboratory with a given pathogen to determine the effectiveness of a given vaccine. Researchers must have a good understanding of the disease and the fish species, and should be able to grow the disease organism easily.

An autogenous vaccine or bacterin for a facility with a specific disease problem can be manufactured much more rapidly than a commercial vaccine or bacterin can be developed and licensed. Autogenous vaccines for a specific pathogen causing disease in a specific facility can be developed based on their requisites. Briefly, the facility must work with a veterinarian or a qualified fish health specialist; the pathogen of concern in most cases, bacteria must be identified and cultured from diseased fish at the facility; and then, using that particular isolate/strain of pathogen, the autogenous product can be produced by the veterinarian following appropriate guidelines. This process may take several months or longer, depending upon the situation. Additional rules regarding use of this autogenous product, including length of time for use and how many times the product can be reissued, must also be followed. Bottom line, as much information as possible is needed to ensure that other factors that contribute to disease are minimized and that vaccination occurs at the best time during production for logistical reasons and effectiveness. Following are few area in which more research and attention is needed

1. To standardize methodology for identification and isolation of bacterial proteins that are involved in complement inhibition that would neutralize the key bacterial virulence mechanism.
2. Development of alternative cost effective vaccine most vaccines are created using inactivated or attenuated compounds from micro-organisms where as synthetic vaccines are composed mainly or wholly of synthetic peptides, carbohydrates or antigens. So researcher must look forward to explore new sources for vaccine development.

3. Standardization of vaccine dose and method of administration.
4. Development of wide spectrum vaccine.
5. Establishment of regulatory apex body or authority to take over the stock of situation of vaccine applications and their development.

Conclusion

A number of vaccines have been in use by the salmonid industry for decades. However, commercial vaccine development for other aquaculture sectors, including producers of warm water fish, is still quite limited in the India. Greater demand by producers and increased levels of research and interest by manufacturers is helping to make vaccination a more viable option. Currently, vaccines are available for some economically important bacterial and viral diseases. Vaccines for protection against parasitic and fungal diseases have not yet been developed. There are virtually no antimicrobial agents available for treatment of molluscan or crustacean diseases and alternative control measures are therefore required. Alternatives to the use of antimicrobial agents include good husbandry, adequate feed composition, vaccines, biological control and movement restrictions through legislation. Further research is required in areas such as vaccine development, immunostimulants and the use of probiotics.

Vaccination should be considered part of a comprehensive fish health management scheme, and not the only solution for a disease problem. Vaccination is intended for disease prevention, and not for disease treatment, and can be thought of as "insurance." To ensure that vaccination will work, producers must weigh carefully the many factors that determine whether a given vaccine will be effective in a given situation (the particular pathogen and disease, the fish species and age, fish production methods, vaccine route of administration, and economics).

Autogenous vaccines are manufactured from specific pathogens (e.g., bacteria or viruses) isolated from sick fish. This type of vaccine can help prevent recurrent disease problems, and should be considered a management option. Producers considering incorporating vaccines into their management schemes should work closely with a fish veterinarian or other fish health specialist. Commercial vaccines may or may not be adequate, and autogenous vaccines may be required for a given situation. However, since less research will have been carried out with autogenous vaccines, their effectiveness will be more variable and, ideally, small-scale trials should be run at the facility before these vaccines are put into widespread use.

REFERENCES

Austin, B., Altwegg, M., Gosling, P.J. and Joseph, S.W. (eds), 1996. *"The Genus Aeromonas"*. John Wiley and Sons, Ltd., Chichester, UK.

Azad, I. S., K. M. Shankar, C. V. Mohan and B. Kalita. 2000. Uptake and Processing of Biofilm and Free-cell Vaccines of Aeromonas Hydrophila in Indian Major Carps and Common Carp following Oral Vaccination Antigen Localization by a Monoclonal Antibody. Diseases of Aquatic Organisms 43: 103-108.

Bernadet, J.F., 1997. Immunization with Bacterial Antigens: Flavobacterium and Flexibacter Infections. In: R. Gudding, A. Lillehaug, P.J. Midtlyng and F. Brown (eds). *Fish Vaccinology*. Karger, Basel, Switzeland, p. 179-188.

Bernoth, E.M., 1997. Furunculosis: The History of the Disease and of Disease Research. In: E.M. Bernoth, A.E. Ellis, P.J. Midtlyng and P. Smith (eds.). *Furunculosis. Multidisciplinary Fish Disease Research.* Academic Press, UK. p. 1-20.

Biering, E., S. Villoing, I. Sommerset and K. E. Christie. 2005. Update on Viral Vaccines for Fish. *Progress in Fish Vaccinology. Developments in Biologicals*, P.J. Midtlyng, (ed.): 121: 97-113.

Biosca, E.G., Amaro, C., Esteve, C., Alcaide, E. and Garay, E., 1991. First Record of *Vibrio vulnificus* biotype 2 from Diseased European eel, *Anguilla anguilla*, L. *J. Fish Dis.*, 14, p. 103-109.

Dalsgaard, I., Hoi, L., Siebeling, R.J. and Dalsgaard, A., 1998. Indole-positive *Vibrio vulnificus* isolated from Outbreaks on a Danish eel Farm. *Dis. Aquat. Org.*, 35, pp. 187-194.

Dhar, A.K., R. Bowers, C. Rowe and F. C. Thomas Allnutt. 2006. Formation of Non-infective Infectious Pancreatic Necrosis (IPNV) Virus-like Particles (VLPs) Expressing Human ONCOGENE c-myc. Presented in World Aquaculture Society Meeting in Florence, Italy, May 09-13.

Egidius, E., Wiik, R., Andersen, K., Holff, K.A. and Hjeltness, B., 1986. *Vibrio salmonicida* sp. nov., A New Fish Pathogen. *Int. J. Syst. Bacteriol.*, 36, p. 518-520.

Ellis, A.E., 1997. Immunization with Bacterial Antigens: Furunculosis. In: R. Gudding, A. Lillehaug, P.J.Midtlyng and F. Brown (eds). *Fish Vaccinology*. Basel, Karger, p. 107-116.

Evans, J., P. Klesius, C. Shoemaker and B. Fitzpatrick. 2005. Streptococcus Agalactiae Vaccination and Infection Stress in Nile Tilapia, Oreochromis niloticus. Journal of Applied Aquaculture 16(3): 105-115.

Fouz, B. and Amaro, C., 2003. Isolation of a New Serovar of *Vibrio vulnificus* Pathogenic for Eels Cultured in Freshwater Farms. *Aquaculture*, 217, p. 677-682.

Greger, E. and Goodrich, T., 1999. Vaccine Development for Winter Ulcer Disease, *Vibrio viscosus*, in Atlantic Salmon, *Salmo salar* L. *J. Fish Dis.*, 22, p. 193-199.

Grisez, L and Z. Tan. 2005. Vaccine Development for Asian Aquaculture. Pages V: 483-494 In: *Diseases in Asian Aquaculture*, P. Walker, R. Lester. and M. G. Bondad-Reantaso (eds),. Fish Health Section, Asian Fisheries Society, Manila.

Hastein, T., R. Gudding and O. Evensen. 2005. Bacterial Vaccines for Fish Nan update of the Current Situation Worldwide. *Progress in Fish Vaccinology. Developments in Biologicals*, P. J. Midtlyng, (ed), 121: 55-74.

Hawke, J.P., Miller, R.A. and Thune, R.L., 2002. Virulence of Siderophore Deficient and *aro*A Deletion Mutants of *Photobacterium damselae* subsp. *piscicida* in a hybrid striped bass (*Morone saxatilis* x *M.chrysops*) Infection Model. In: *4th International Symposium on Aquatic Animal Health.* New Orleans, LA, USA. p. 127.

Hiney, M. and Oliver, G., 1999. Furunculosis (*Aeromonas salmonicida*). In: P.T.K. Wo, and D.W. Bruno (eds). *Fish Diseases and Disorders*, Vol. 3. CAB Intern. Publ., UK. p. 341-426.

Hjeltnes, B., K. Andersen and E. Hans-Magne. 1989 (online 2003). Vaccination Against Vibrio salmonicida: The Effect of Different Routes of Administration and of Revaccination. Aquaculture. 83(1-2): 1-6.

Kai, Y-H. and S-C. Chi. 2008. Efficacies of Inactivated Vaccines Against Betanodavirus in Grouper Larvae (Epinephelus coioides) by Bath Immunization. Vaccine 26(11): 1450-1457.

Kanellos, T., I. D. Sylvester, F. D'Mello, C. R. Howard. A. Mackie. P. F. Dixon, K-C. Chang, A. Ramstad. Paul. J. Midtlyng and P. H. Russell. 2006. DNA Vaccination can Protect Cyprinus Carpio Against Spring Viraemia of Carp Virus. Vaccine 24 (23): 4927-4933.

Klesius, P.H., J.J. Evans and C.A. Shoemaker. 2004. Warm Water Fish Vaccinology in Catfish Production. Animal Health Research Reviews 5(2): 305-311.

Klesius, P.H. and Shoemaker, C.A., 1998. Development and Use of Modified Live *Edwardsiella ictaluri* Vaccine Against Enteric Septicemia of Catfish. In: R.D. Schultz (ed). *Advances in Veterinary Medicine*,Vol. 41. Academic Press, Ltd (UK). p. 523- 537.

Klesius, P.H., C.A. Shoemaker and J.J. Evans. (1999). Efficacy of a killed Streptococcus iniae vaccine in tilapia (Oreochromis niloticus) in Bulletin of the European Association of Fish Pathologists 19(1): 39-41.

Komar, C., W. J. Enright, L. Grisez and Z. Tan. 2004. Understanding Fish Vaccination. *AQUA Culture AsiaPacific Magazine* November/December 2004: 27-29.

Kumar, S.R., V. Parameswaran, V.P. Ahmed, S.S. Musthaq and A.S. Hameed. 2007. Protective Efficiency of DNA Vaccination in Asian Seabass Lates Calcarifer Against Vibrio anguillarum. Fish & shellfish immunology 23(2): 316-326.

LaFrentz, B.R., LaPatra, S.E., Jones, G.R., Congleton, J.L., Sun, B. and Cain, K.D., 2002. Characterization of Serum and Mucosal Antibody Responses and Relative per cent Survival in Rainbow Trout *Oncorhynchus mykiss* (Walbaum), following Immunization and Challenge with *Flavobacterium psychrophilum. J. Fish Dis.*, 25, p. 703-713.

Mutharia, L.W., Raymond, B.T., Dekievit, T.R. and Stevenson, R.M.W., 1992. Antibody Specificities of Polyclonal Rabbit and Rainbow Trout Antisera Against *Vibrio ordalii* and Serotype O2 strains of *Vibrio anguillarum. Can. J. Microbiol.*, 39, pp. 492-499.

Newman, S.G., 1993. Bacterial Vaccines of Fish. *Ann. Rev. Fish Dis.*, 3, pp. 145-186.

Ooyama, T., Kera, A., Okada, T., Inglis, V. and Yoshida, T., 1999. The Protective Immune Response of Yellowtail *Seriola quinqueradiata* to the Bacterial Fish Pathogen *Lactococcus garvieae*. *Dis. Aquat. Org.*, 37, pp. 121-126.

Peres, H., C. Lim and P. H. Klesius. 2004. Growth, Chemical Composition and Resistance to Streptococcus iniae Challenge of Juvenile Nile tilapia (Oreochromis niloticus) Fed Graded Levels of Dietary Inositol. Aquaculture 235: 423-432.

Pretto-Giordano, L.G., E.E. Muller, P. Klesius and V.G.D. Silva. 2010. Efficacy of an Experimentally Inactivated Streptococcus Agalactiae Vaccine in Nile tilapia (Oreochromis niloticus) reared in Brazil. Aquaculture Research 41(10): 1539-1544.

Raida, M.K., J. Nylen, L. Holten-Andersen and K. Buchmann. 2011. Association Between Plasma Antibody Response and Protection in Rainbow rout (*Oncorhynchus mykiss)* Immersion Vaccinated Against *Yersinia ruckeri.*, PLoS One: 6(6): e18832. doi:10.1371/journal.pone.0018832.

Raida, M.K., K. Buchmann. 2008. Development of Adaptive Immunity in Rainbow Trout, *Oncorhynchus mykiss* (Walbaum) Surviving an Infection with *Yersinia ruckeri*. Fish & Shellfish Immunology 25: 533-541.

Raida, M. K., K. Buchmann. 2009. Innate Immune Response in Rainbow Trout (*Oncorhynchus mykiss*) Against Primary and Secondary Infections with *Yersinia ruckeri* O1. Developmental and Comparative Immunology 33: 35-45.

Robert, M. Bowers., Scott, E. LaPatra. Krista, N. Kaizer. and A.K. Dhar. 2007. A Real-time Reverse Transcriptase-polymerase Chain Method for Quantitative Detection of Infectious Pancreatic Necrosis Virus in Rainbow Trout (Oncorhynchus mykiss).World Aquaculture Society Meeting in San Antonio, Texas, Feb 26-March 02.

Romalde, J.L., 1992. *Yersinia ruckeri*: Estudio epidemiológico y del mecanismo de virulencia. PhD Thesis.Universidad de Santiago de Compostela, Spain.

Romalde, J.L., Magariños, B. and Toranzo, A.E., 1999b. Prevention of Streptococcosis in turbot by intraperitoneal vaccination: A review. *J. Appl. Ichthyol.*, 15, pp. 153-158.

Romalde, J.L., Ravelo, C., López-Romalde, S., Magariños, B., Barja, J.L. and Toranzo, A.E., 2003. Vaccination Strategies to Prevent Important Emerging Diseases for Aquaculture in Spain. In: *Abstracts 3rd. International Symposium on Fish Vaccinology*, Bergen, Norway. p. 38.

Russo, R., H. Mitchell and R. P. E. Yanong. 2006a. Characterization of *Streptococcus iniae* Isolated from Ornamental Cyprinid Fishes and Development of Challenge Models. *Aquaculture* 256: 105-110.

Russo, R., R. P. E. Yanong and H. Mitchell. 2006b. Dietary beta-glucans and nucleotides Enhance Resistance of Red-tail Black shark (*Epalzeorhynchus bicolor*, fam. Cyprinidae) to *Streptococcus iniae* Infection. *Journal of the World Aquaculture Society* 37: 298-306.

Salonius, K., Siderakis, C.V. and Griffiths, S.G., 2003. Further Characterization of *Arthrobacter davidanieli* and use as a live vaccine to immunize against intracellular Pathogens of Salmonids. In: *Abstracts 3rd.International Symposium on Fish Vaccinology*, Bergen, Norway. p. 41.

Santos, Y., Pazos, F. and Barja, J.L., 1999. *Flexibacter maritimus*, Causal Agent of Flexibacteriosis in Marine Fish. In: G. Olivier (ed.). *ICES Identification Leaflets for Diseases and Parasites of Fish and Shellfish*, No. 55. International Council for the Exploration of the Sea, Copenhagen, Denmark.

Shieh, H. S. 1985. (Online 2006). Vaccination of Atlantic Salmon, (*Salmo salar)* L., Against Furunculosis with Protease of an Avirulent Strain of *Aeromonas salmonicida.* Journal of Fish Biology 27(1): 97-101.

Shoemaker, Craig and Klesius, Philip. 1997. Protective Immunity Against Enteric Septicemia of Channel Catfish Following Controlled Exposure to Live Edwardsiella ictaluri. Veterinary Immunology and Immunopathology (ARS, Publication).

Sommerset, I., B. Krossoy, E. Biering and Frost, P. 2005. Vaccines for Fish in Aquaculture. Expert Review of Vaccines 4(1): 89-101.

Sorum, H., Hvaal, A.B., Heum, M., Daae, F.L. and Wiik, R., 1990. Plasmid Profiling of *Vibrio salmonicida* for Epidemiological Studies of Cold-water Vibriosis in Atlantic Salmon (*Salmo salar*) and Cod (*Gadus morhua*). *Appl. Environ. Microbiol.*, 56, p. 1033-1037.

Stevenson, R.M. 1997. Immunization with Bacterial Antigens: Yersiniosis. Development in Biological Standardization 90: 117-24.

Thomas Allnutt, F. C., Robert. M. Bowers, Christopher, G. Rowe, Vikram, N. Vakharia, Scott, E. LaPatra. and Arun, K. Dhar. 2007. Antigenicity of Infectious Pancreatic Necrosis virus Capsid Protein VP2 virus-like Particles Expressed in Yeast. Presented in World Aquaculture Society Meeting in San Antonio, Texas, Feb 26-March 02.

Thornton, J.C., Garduño, R.A. and Kay, W.W., 1994. The Development of Live Vaccines for Furunculosis Lacking the A-layer and O-antigen of *Aeromonas salmonicida. J. Fish Dis.*, 17, pp. 195-204.

Thornton, J.C., Garduño, R.A., Newman, S.G. and Kay, W.W., 1991. Surface Disorganized, Attenuated Mutants of *Aeromonas salmonicida* as Furunculosis Vaccines. *Microb. Path.*, 11, pp. 85-89.

Tison, D.L., Nishibuchi, M., Greenwood, J.D. and Seidler, R.J., 1982. *Vibrio vulnificus* Biotype 2: New Biogroup Pathogenic for Eels. *Appl. Environ. Microbiol.*, 44, pp. 640-646.

Toranzo, A.E., Devesa, S., Romalde, J.L., Lamas, J., Riaza, A., Leiro, J. and Barja, J.L., 1995b. Efficacy of Intraperitoneal and Immersion Vaccination Against *Enterococcus* sp. Infection in Turbot. *Aquaculture,* 134, pp. 17-27.

Toranzo, A.E., Santos, Y. and Barja, J.L., 1997. Immunization with Bacterial Antigens: *Vibrio* Infections. In:R. Gudding, A. Lillehaug, P.J. Midtlyng and F. Brown (eds), *Fish Vaccinology*. Karger, Basel,' Switzerland. pp. 93-105.

Vaughan, L.M., Smith, P.R. and Foster, T.J., 1993. An Aromatic-dependent Mutant of the Fish Pathogen *Aeromonas salmonicida* is attenuated and is Effective as a live Vaccine Against the Salmonid Disease, Furunculosis. *Infect. Immun.*, 61, pp. 2172-2181.

Whittington, R., Lim C., and P.H. Klesius. 2005. Effect of Dietary β-glucan Levels on the Growth Response and Efficacy of *Streptococcus iniae* Vaccine in Nile tilapia, (Oreochromis niloticus). Aquaculture 248: 217-225.

Whittington, R., Shoemaker, C.A. Lim, C. and P.H. Klesius. 2003. Effects of Dietary β-hydroxy-β-methylbutyrate on Growth and Survival of Nile Tilapia, (Oreochromis niloticus), Vaccinated Against Streptococcus iniae. Journal of Applied Aquaculture 14: 25-36.

CHAPTER 9

A Sustainable Eco-friendly Biotechnological Solution for Environmental Protection

Vibha Bhardwaj, *India;* **Mayank Dave,** *India*
Neelam Garg, *India*

ABSTRACT

Biodiversity is the foundation of life on earth. It underpins the functioning of ecosystems from which we derive essential products and services such as oxygen, food, fresh water and medicines. Healthy biodiversity is essential for human wellbeing, sustainable development and poverty reduction. Biodiversity is the variability among living organisms and the ecological complexes of which they are part, including diversity within and between species and ecosystems. Conservation and sustainable use of biodiversity is fundamental to ecologically sustainable development. Biodiversity is part of our daily lives and livelihood. The human activities which have adversely affected the environment, are leading to loss of the planet's biodiversity.

The maintenance of biodiversity is important on many grounds ranging from aesthetic considerations to its usefulness, particularly for biotechnology. The benefits that we gain from biodiversity go far beyond the mere provision of raw materials for biotechnology. Biodiversity data has proved very important for discovery of novel products and their technical applications. Microbial diversity was the least understood component of biodiversity. Microbes have astronomical abundance on a global scale.

The vast majority of microbial diversity remains to be discovered. Microbes are one of the biota communities, which are very interesting to be studied in order to find out their existence and uses. They have an important role to the subsistence on earth, because they mediate many critical ecosystem processes using their enzymatic system. The fastest growing segments are enzymes for feed and fuel production. Moreover, most substrates are plant based and microbes on plants have been the main enzyme discovery focus. More than 98 per cent industrial enzymes being used are found in nature as extracellular proteins. Despite the ecological importance, majority of the enzymes used in industry are also microbial in origin because these enzymes are relatively more stable than the one derived from plants and animals.

Protease,pectinase,lipase,cellulase are the microbial enzymes which are extensively used in industries such as textiles, paper and pulp industry, food, beverages, waste water treatment. Microorganisms are ubiquitous. So, as everything {microbes} is everywhere, ecosystem functions will rarely, if ever, be limited by lack of microbial diversity. Threats to biodiversity are numerous and human activity is responsible for most of them. The main threats are habitat loss and degradation, introductions of invasive alien species, over-exploitation of natural resources, pollution and diseases and human induced climate change. Most people appreciate the beauty of natural world, but awareness of biodiversity, how seriously it is threatened, and the implications for human wellbeing, is alarmingly low. from time immemorial, nature has fed us, cured us, and protected us. But today the roles have switched. We need to feed nature, we need to cure it and protect it if we want to secure a healthy and prosperous future for our children.

Key words: Biodiversity, sustainable development, enzymes, pectinase, microbial diversity.

Introduction

The environment is man's greatest gift. The environment could be looked at as the basis for man existence. The misuse or misappropriation of the constituents of the environment could hamper the health, socioeconomy and peace of nation. This may lead to state or national security.Thus,it is essential that man should design a way for its sustainability. This can only be achieved through formulation and development of adequate and dynamic environmental protection policy which will engender environmental sustainability. The Environmental Sustainability as an off shoot of the principle of Sustainable development emphasizes the need to meet the needs and aspiration of the present without compromising the needs of the future. It can only be midwife by the nation with the support of its citizenry. Sustainable development entails the harmonization of population growth with utilization and exploitation of natural resources through redirection and reorientation of research and development as well as institutional changes. The variety of life forms and its many processes constitute biodiversity. Humanity is dependent on biodiversity for all its requirements. Presently great concern has been voiced for the present state of biodiversity. Though the concept of biodiversity has been known to man since times he observes the living beings around him, however this word appeared as a catch word of conservationists and biologists towards the twentieth of centuary.In 1992, the Earth summit at Rio in Brazil laid clear stress on biological diversity and the need to preserve it.

Presently, the term microbe is used to include a wide variety of microorganisms, viz. algae, bacteria, fungi {including yeasts ,lichens forming species and slime moulds}, viruses {including phages and viroids}. The microbes are known to have occupied niches on earth as 3.5 billion years ago but as per the available data presently less than 5 per cent of the fungi, bacteria and viruses have been named {Hawksworth,1996}. There is however a misconception about the role, range and ecological requirements of microbes all over the world. Generally, it is believed that microbes are 'omnipresent' occupying special ecological niches and also entering into different types and levels of associations with other organizations.

Though they are believed to be 'omnipresent' yet have not been studied very systematically not their distribution has ever been properly quantified. Their role in natural processes, their habitat, and range are not investigated in detail and properly. It has now been realized microbes are not 'present everywhwre'but have preferences for specific ecological niches and specific associations, symbiotic or otherwise, with other groups of organisms. it is only during the last one decade that significance of microbial diversity has received adequate attention. Previously ,'microorganism', was merely a synonym of bacterium. With the recognition of significance of biodiversity, that world over, the initial concept has been modified and enlarged to include three main components of biodiversity: diversity within species is the *genetic diversity*, between species is the species or *taxonomic or organism cal diversity*, and of ecosystem is the ecological or *habitat diversity*.

Microbes play very important role in biogeochemical cycles. They are both beneficial and adversary of plants, animals and human beings. They have applications in agriculture, industry, medicines and management of environment. A large number of biotechnological processes are based on microbes. In spite of their ubiquitous processes and important role they played in natural and human made ecosystems, the microbial diversity has been explored less in comparison to plant and animal diversity. This is because of microbial population vary from one place to another with the variation in temperature,pH,relative humidity and moisture content, soil composition and organic substrate. The microscopic size and lack of specialized techniques to detect and isolate the complete microbial flora of a particular place is another reason for lesser information on microbial diversity.

The potential of the so-called "white biotechnology" as an ecological advantageous and moreover economical beneficial technology is beyond all question. Caused of the ever growing costs for energy and polluted waste water, enzymatic technologies will stay in the focus of science and technique, and their relevance will increase significantly in the future. Enzymes, biological catalysts with high selectivities, have been used in the food industry for hundreds of years, and play an important role in many other industries (washing agents, textile manufacturing, pharmaceuticals, pulp and paper). Currently, enzymes are becoming increasingly important in sustainable technology and green chemistry. In the opinion of many experts and based on different studies, by 2010, 20 per cent of all chemical products in a dimension of 300 billion US dollar will be produced using biotechnology. This would represent a tenfold increase compared to 2001. Micro-organisms are considered to be prospective enzyme producing sources. They have a number of advantages: through the application of selection methods increase of biosynthesis via the conditions of cultivation , in-depth interaction on various substrates, wide spectrum of enzyme complex and their application in gene engineering via gene cloning.

Enormous quantities of industrial waste residues are generated throughout the world from processing raw agricultural materials for foods. These, in turn, impose a high BOD burden on the environment when dumped. Thus industrial residues from the processing of sugarcane, orange, coffee and rice present suitable feed stocks for bioconversion into chemicals, including enzymes by fermentation processes, there by adding value to what normally constitute a waste product Citrus fruits constitute an important group of fruit crops produced all over the world.

Brazil is the world's largest producer of oranges, and exports frozen orange juice concentrates. India is also a major producer of citrus fruits. These are produced all over India, but the major producers are the states of

Maharashtra, Tamil Nadu, Andhra Pradesh, Himachal Pradesh, Punjab and Haryana. Oranges of Nagpur are famous for their size and aroma. Citrus fruits are utilized mostly for table purposes, but a significant portion is processed into various products, such as squash single strength juices, juice concentrates, marmalades, pickles *etc.*

The family of citrus fruits consists of Oranges, Kinnow, Khatta, Lime, Lemon (Galgal), Grapefruit, Malta, Mausami, Sweet orange etc. These all are known to contain appreciable amounts of pectin. Pectic substances are present in the primary plant cell wall and the middle lamella. Besides these, other fruits like Mango (*Mangifera indica*), Avocado Pear (*Avocado avocado*), Guava (*Psidium guajava*), Banana (*Musa sapientum*), Papaya (*Carica papaya*), Cashew Apple (*Anacardium occidentale*), Garden-egg (*Solanum nigrum* Linn.), Star Apple (*Crysophylum albidium*), and Tomato (*Lycopersicum esculentum*) also contain substantial amounts of pectin having a high gelling grade. Sugar beet pulp, a by-product of sugar extraction, also contains pectin .Fruit processing industries produce a large amount of waste material in the form of peel, pulp, seeds, etc. Some fresh orange peel is, however, used in shredded form in the preparation of orange-marmalade. This waste material presents considerable disposal problems and ultimately leads to pollution. Dried citrus peel is rich in carbohydrates, proteins and pectin; the fat content, however, is low. Various microbial transformations have been proposed for the utilization of food processing waste for producing valuable products like biogas, ethanol, citric acid, chemicals, various enzymes, volatile flavouring compounds, fatty acids and microbial biomass . Citrus peel contains an appreciable amount of pectin and thus can be used as a substrate for the production of pectinolytic enzymes by micro-organisms. Pectin acts as the inducer for the production of pectinolytic enzymes by microbial systems .The advantage of using micro-organisms for the production of enzymes is that these are not influenced by climatic and seasonal factors, and can be subjected to genetic and environmental manipulations to increase the yield. Highly productive strains of micro-organisms are required at the industrial level to reduce the production costs.

Different types of micro-organisms have been exploited for the production of enzymes. Pectinolytic enzymes have been reported to be produced by a large number of bacteria and fungi such as *Bacillus* spp., *Clostridium* spp., *Pseudomonas* spp., *Aspergillus* spp., *Monilla laxa, Fusarium spp., Verticillium* spp., *Penicillium* spp., *Sclerotinia libertiana, Coniothyrium diplodiella, Thermomyces lanuginosus, Polyporus squamosus, etc*. Pectic enzymes are widely distributed in nature. They mainly occur in plants, bacteria, fungi, yeasts, insects, nematodes and protozoa. Pectic substance is a generic name used for the compounds that are acted upon by the pectinolytic enzymes. These are negatively charged acidic glycosidic macromolecules and have high molecular weight. These are present in the plants as the major component of middle lamella between the cells in the form of calcium pectate and magnesium pectate. Pectinase is an enzyme that breaks down pectins. Pectic substances are glycosidic macromolecules with high molecular weight. They form the major components of the middle lamella and primary plant cell wall. Pectic substance consists of protopectins, pectinic acids, pectins and pectic acids. The main chain of pectin is partially methyl esterified 1, 4-D-galacturonan. Demethylated pectin is known as pectic acid (pectate) or polygalacturonic acid.

Pectic substances are naturally degraded by pectinases. The classification of pectic enzymes is based on their attack on the galacturonan backbone of the pectic substance molecule. Basically, there are three types of pectic enzymes; de-esterifying enzymes (pectin esterase), depolymerizing enzymes and protopectinases.

Pectin esterases catalyze the hydrolysis of methyl to produce pectic acid and methanol. Depolymerizing enzymes consist of hydrolases and lyases. Lyases are also called transeliminases, which split the glycosidic bonds of either pectate (polygalacturonate) or pectin (polymethylgalacturonate).

Pectinases are produced by a large number of organisms, such as bacteria, fungi, actinomycetes and yeast. Pectinases have been used in processes and industries where the elimination of pectin is essential; fruit juice processing, coffee and tea processing, macerating of plants and vegetable tissue, degumming of plant fibers, treatment waste water, extracting vegetable oil, bleaching of paper, adding poultry feed and in the textile, alcoholic beverages and food industries.

Pectinolytic enzymes are commonly used during processing of fruits and vegetables for juices and wine. The pectic substances account for about 0.5-4 per cent of the weight of fresh material. The raw pressed juice is rich in insoluble particles mainly made up of pectic substances. When the tissue is ground, the pectin is found in the liquid phase (soluble pectin) causing an increase in viscosity and the pulp particles. It is difficult to extract this juice by pressing or using other mechanical methods. With the addition of pectinases the viscosity of the fruit juice drops, the press ability of the pulp improves, the jelly structure disintegrates and the fruit juice is easily obtained with higher yields, Pectinase are produced during the natural ripening process of same fruits. This can also increase the volume of juice (increase the yield), lowers the viscosity of juice, and reduces the cloudiness of juices, which is caused by suspended pieces of cell wall. Pectinase group of enzymes include polygalacturanases, pectin methyl esterase, pecin lyases. These pectinases enzymes act in different ways and on the pectins. Pectinase are extensively used in fruits juices processing (extraction and clarification) vegetable oil extraction, processing of alcoholic beverages and a variety of applications in food industries. Pectinase have an optimum temperature and pH at which they are most active.

The commercial Pectinase might typically be activated at 45° to 55°C and well work at a pH of 4 to 5. Pectinolytic micro-organism are widely distributed in soil, spoiled fruits, vegetables, decayed leaves and wood and can also be seen in water samples taken from decaying coconut husks, especially in Coastal areas. Intestinal flora of humans also includes pectinolytic micro-organism, mainly bacteria, since pectin the dietary fibre is the substrate for them. Traditionally, commercial source of pectin have been citrus peel and apple pomace. Citrus peel has often been the preferred material for pectin manufacture due to its high pectin content and good colour properties. Most recently other sources of pectin are sugar beet pectin, sunflower pectin. The amount of pectin from different sources varies considerably.

Apple pomace → 10-15%   Citrus peel → 25-35%

Sugar beet → 10-20%   Sunflower → 15-25%

Pectin was first isolated in 1820and shown to be the key substances in making jams and jellies. Jam and jellies have been produced for many years, at least since the 18th century. Pectinases are a heterogeneous group of enzymes that degrade pectin. These are widely used in the food industry for the production and clarification of fruit juices, to improve the cloud stability of fruit and vegetable juices and nectars, for depectinization in order to produce high density fruit juice concentrates, and for haze removal from wines. Pectic enzyme preparations are also used for the production of low methoxy pectin for diabetic foods, in the degumming of natural fibres in the textile industry, and in making commercial softwoods, such as Sitka and Norway spruce, more permeable to preservatives.

Purified pectinases have also been developed specifically for use in plant protoplast culture studies. When used with cellulase, purified pectinases have been found to be very useful for generating good yields of viable protoplast in several plant systems, *e.g.* corn, soybean, red beet, sunflower, tomato, citrus etc. Commercial enzymes are generally obtained from fungal sources since the pH optima of these enzymes are in the range found naturally in materials to be processed and the enzymes are secreted into the culture media, making the downstream processing easier. Keeping in view the importance of enzyme pectinases in the food processing industry and the problems associated with the disposal of food processing industry waste, the present study was undertaken with the objectives of Isolation and screening of Pectinase producing micro-organism.

Materials and Methods

Isolation of Pectinase Producing Micro-organism

Samples from waste, soil etc. will be collected from different places. For isolation of bacteria, suspension of samples will be prepared in sterile distilled water, which will then be plated on modified pectin agar medium .Isolates A loop of the homogenate was then streaked onto nutrient medium and incubated at 30°C for 24 to 72h. All morphological contrasting colonies were purified by repeated streaking. Pure cultures were sub-cultured onto slants media.

Construction of Galacturonic Acid Standard Curves

A stock solution (10.000 mg/ml) of the standard g Galacturonic acid supplied by Sigma was prepare in acetate buffer (0.2 M) at pH 5. The stock solution was used for making of different concentrations. After preparing of the require dilutions, only 1.0 ml of each dilution was transferred to determine of the amount of reducing sugar according to Miller. A standard curve was constructed relating all different sugar concentrations applied against their corresponding to optical density at 540nm. The obtained standard curve was used forestimating the polygalacturonase activities in terms of mg/ml and then units (U). One unit is defined as the amount of enzyme protein (mg) required to exert free galacturonic acid, from pectin of time under 35°C for 1 hour in acetate buffer (0.2 M) at pH 5.0

Screening of Isolates for Efficient Pectinase Producer

Isolates will be tested qualitatively by growing the culture on modified pectin agar medium followed by observing zone of hydrolysis around pectinase producing colonies. After the colonies reached around 3 mm, iodine-potassium iodide solution (1.0g iodine, 5.0g potassium iodide and 330ml H_2O) was added to detect clearance zones. Pectinase producing isolate will be selected and maintain on nutrient agar for further studies.

Production Media

Basal Medium: The basal medium (BM) was prepared according to Vincent. It contained of the following (g/l): Sucrose, 10; KNO, 0.6 ; KHPO, 1; MgSO4 , 0.25 and CaCl , 0.1 wa s found mos t convenient for the production of different enzymes. It was modified to include the following constituents: (g/l) NaNO, 2; KHPO, 0.5; KCl, 0.5 and yeast extract, 1. These previous ly mentioned contents were dissolved in citrate phosphate buffer at pH 7.

Characterization of Bacterial Isolate

Morphological, cultural and chemical characteristic of the selected isolates will be studied according to standard techniques.

Qualitative Screening

Qualitative Screening Test Media , Methods, and Conditions (First Survey)

Pectinolytic Enzyme Production Medium: This medium consists of part (A) and part (B). Part (A) conta ined (g/l): NaNO, 2; KH PO , 1; KCl , 0.5; MgSO .7H O, 0.5; Yeast extract, 1. These contents were dissolved in 40 ml distilled water. Th e pH was adjusted at pH 7 by NaOH (5%, w/v) .Part (B) contained (g/l): Pectin, 5 , dissolved in 10 ml. of distilled water. The two parts (A) and (B) were autoclaved for 20 minutes at 1.5 atmospheric pressure and mixed together after autoclaving. This medium was inoculated with bacterial isolates. This medium was incubated at 37°C for 96 hours, then assayed for pectinolytic productivity and activity were tested in the pectinase assay medium.

Qualitative Screening Test Media, Methods and Conditions (Second Survey)

Petinoytic Enzyme Production Medium (Pepm) : This medium contained the main ingredients of BM supplemented with c itrus peels mixture (2% w/v) separately. The pH of this medium was adjusted at 7 by dissolve its contents in citrate-phosphate buffer (pH 7) . It was autoclaved at 1.5 atmospheric pressure for 20 minutes. This medium was inoculated with bacterial isolates under study. This medium was inocubated at 37°C for 96 hours, then assayed for pectinolytic productivity.

Enzyme Assay

Enzyme assay was based on the determination of reducing sugars produced as a result of enzymatic hydrolysis of pectin by dinitrosalicylic acid reagent (DNS) method . For this, to 0.2 ml of 1 per cent pectin solution, 2.0 ml of sodium citrate buffer of pH 5.0 and 1.0 ml of enzyme extract was added. The reaction mixture was incubated at 35°C±1°C for 25 min After 25 min, 1.0 ml of this reaction mixture was withdrawn and added to test-tubes containing 0.5 ml of 1M sodium carbonate solution. To each test-tube, 3.0 ml of DNS reagent was added and the test-tubes were shaken to mix the contents. The test-tubes were heated to boiling on the boiling water-bath for 10-15 min. Then these were cooled and 20 ml of distilled water was added to the contents of each tube and the absorbance was measured at.570 nm using Spectronic 20+ D. The enzyme and substrate blanks were run parallel. The standard curve was prepared for reducing sugars with glucose. One enzyme unit ofendopolygalacturonase is the number of µM of reducing sugars measured interms of glucose, produced as a result of the action of 1.0 ml of enzyme extract in 1 minute at 35°C ± 1°C.

Effect of Various Parameters for Production of Enzyme

Effect of various process parameters, such as substrate mesh size, substrate state, substrate concentration, temperature of incubation, time of incubation and the size of inoculum will be studied.

Different Inoculum Sizes: Different inoculum sizes of the most potent bacterial isolate (prepared by harvesting 5 slants in 100 ml sterile saline solution under aseptic conditions) are used. The following inoculum sizes were applied viz., 1, 2, 5, 10, 15, 20, and 24 ml per each flask (250 ml). At the end of incubation periods, polygalacturonase productivity was determined for each flask after incubation period as the previously mentioned.

Different Substrate Concentrations: Different concentrations of substrate (g/flask, 25 ml, w/v) were applied viz ., 0.1, 0.3, 0.5, 0.75, 1.0, 1.25, 1.5, 2.0, 5.0, 10 and 15). At the end of incubation period, enzyme productivity were assayed.

Different Incubation Periods: The most potent bacterial isolate was allowed to grow on the waste and incubated for 6, 12, 24, 48, 72, 96, 120, 144, 168 and 192 hours respectively.

Different pH Values: The production medium for most potent isolate were prepared as previously mentioned . Th e pH was adjusted at different pH values viz , by using boric acid -borax buffer and (3, 5, 5.5, 6, 6.2, 6.4, 6.6 and 7.0) by using citrate-phosphate buffer. Inoculation and incubation conditions were carried as previously mentioned.

Different Temperatures: The most potent bacterial isolate was allowed to grow on the grounded citrus peels (PP) medium at different temperatures viz., 10, 15, 30, 37, 40, 45, 55, 65 and 75°C respectively for 96h.

Different Nitrogen Sources: Prodution medium was supplemented with different nitrogen sources at an equimolecular amount of nitrogen that present in sodium nitrate (0.2%, w/v) in basal medium. Peptone, gelatin, and case in were introduced as organic nitrogen source at the level of 2 per cent and the control was devoid from any nitrogen source. The applied nitrogen sources were ammonium sulphate, ammonium molybdate, ammonium chloride, ammonium oxalate, ammonium citrate , ammonium tartrate, ammonium nitrate, diammonium hydrogen phosphate, potassium nitrate , gelatin, peptone, casine and urea . All other factors (temperature, pH, substrate concentration and carbon sources) were carried out as previously mentioned.

Different carbon sources: Different carbon sources were introduced in to the production medium atan equimolecular amount located at 1 per cent (w/v) glucose.Parallel experiment was made with no sugar as a control. The carbon sources were represented by xylose, arabinose, glucose, galactose, mannose, fructose, trehalose, lactose, maltose , sucrose , starch, cellulose and pectin. Starch, cellulose and pectin was in troduced at the level of 1 per cent (w/v). In all cases, other previously mentioned optimal conditions were taken into consideration.

Different Vitamin Requirements: Different vitamins viz , ascorbic acid, riboflavin, vitamin B6 and folic acid were added separately to the medium specialized for polygalacturonase production at 100, 250, 500, and 1000 ppm while the control was applied free from any vitamin. Inoculation, incubation conditions, and measurement of enzyme productivity were performed as previously mentioned.

Different Aeration Conditions: This experiment was carriedout to investigate the effect of different aeration conditions on polygalacturonase productivity. It was performed by using four different volumes viz , 100, 250, 500 and 1000 ml for agricultural waste as substrate. Each flask contained 25 ml of the medium in case of potato peels production medium for polygalacturonase. The enzyme productivity was assayed as previously mentioned.

Results

Selection of strains with pectinolytic activity: 168 bacterial strains able to grow on medium containing citrus pectin as the only carbon source were isolated. The strains were classified as very good producers of pectin depolymerizing enzymes when presented clear halos around colonies of at least 1.5 cm, good producers when the halos were of at least 1 cm, weak producers when halos were at least 0.5 cm and poor producers when no pectinolytic activity and no clear lysis zones were observed.

Parameters Controlling the Polygalacturonase (PG) Productivity

Different Inoculum Size: Different volumes of bacterial suspension were used as an inocul a sizes to inoculate flasks (250 ml) containing the inoculum size used were 1, 2, 5, 10, 20 and 24 ml. Each one ml of the heavy bacterial cell suspension contained about 30 x 10 CFU. The optimal inoculum sizes need to produce the highest yield of polygalacturonase were 3.0 ml and 0.5ml. At this particular inoculum size, the highest yield of polygalacturonase was 155 U/ml. Inoculum size above the previously optimal recorded value gave value gradually decreasing as compared to that of the optimum one.

Different Substrate Concentrations: The maximum polygalacturonase productivity 190 U/ml was obtained in presence of 1.25g/25 ml on pectin at 37°C for 24h.

Different Incubation Periods: Effect of different incubation periods on the polygalacturonase productivity under solid state fermentation conditions was tested at time intervals of 6, 12, 24, 48, 72, 96, 120, 144, 168 and 192 hours. The level of polygalacturonase increased gradually with increasing the incubation period up to a maximum of 24 h.

Different Initial PH Values: The polygal acturonase productivity reached its m axim um at initial p H 4 .0 and 9.. Since the enzym e yield reached up to 177.5 U/ml., below and above this optimal pH value, the enzyme productivity gradually decreased.

Different Incubation Temperatures: The polygal acturonase productivity reached its optimal value 160 U/ml at an incubation temperature at 45°C.

Different Nitrogen Sources: Effect of different organic as well as inorganic nitrogen sources on polygalacturonase productivity were studied.Different nitrogen sources were applied as equimolecular amount located in sodium nitrate. The maximum value of polygalacturonase productivity reached upto 183U/ml in the presence of potassium nitrate.

Different Carbon Sources: The effect of different carbon sources were introduced into the applied production medium of polygalacturonase productivity under SSF condition were studied. It was clear that all the different carbon sources exhibited various degree slower than control Sucrose was the best carbon source for polygalacturonase production where the productivity reached up to 180 U/ml.

Different Vitamins: All of the tested vitamins exert suppressive effects on polygalacturonase productivity at concentrations 100, 250, 500 and 1000 ppm 10.

Different Aeration Conditions: 500 ml flask volume was more favorable for polygalacturonase productivity, where it reached upto 200 U/ml.

Discussion

Enzyme production is a growing field of biotechnology and the world market for enzyme is1.5 billion and it is anticipated to double by the year 2008.The majority of the industrial enzymes are of microbial origin. In the present study, eighty five isolates were isolated from different places. These isolates were grown at different temperature and pH to be able to produce a polygalacturonase which favourable to be used as additive for clarification of juice. A screening of pectinolytic productivities of the isolates showed that many of them gave good pectinolytic productivities. The nature of solid substrate is the most important factor in solid state fermentation. This, not only supplies the nutrient to the culture but also serve as anchorage for the growth of microbial cell.

The selection of substrate SSF depends upon several factors mainly with the cost of availability and this may involve the screening of several agro-industrial residue. An optimum substrate provides all necessary nutrients to the micro organism for optimum function. However, some of the nutrients may be available in suboptimal concentrations or even not present in the substrate. In such cases, it would be necessary to supplement them externally.

Indeed 30-40 per cent of the production cost for industrial enzymes is accounted for the cost of the culture medium. In order to reduce medium costs we screened different low cost substrate and in the course of this we identified citrus peel for cost effective production of the enzyme under study. SSF is receiving a renewed surge of interest, primarily because increased productivity and prospect of using a wide agro industrial residue as substrate. From industrial point of view, in order to achieve production of low cost of enzymes, these isolates under study were allowed to grow.

The selection of the substrate for the process of enzyme biosynthesis was based on the following factors i.e.

1. They represent the most cheapest agro-industrial waste.
2. They are available at any time of the year.
3. Their storage represents no problem in comparison with other substrate.
4. They resist any drastic effect due to exposure to other environmental conditions e.g. temperature variation in the weather from season to season and from day to night.

SSF are usually simple and can use waste of agro-industrial substrates for enzyme production . The minimal amount of water allows the production of metabolites, less time consuming and less expensive.

Higher production of pectinase in SSF process may be due to the reason that solid substrate not only supplies the nutrient to the microbial culture growing in it, but also serves as anchorage for the cell allowing them to utilize the substrate effectively. The environmental conditions in SSF conditions can stimulate the microbe to produce the extra cellular enzymes with different properties other than those of enzymes produced by same organism under the conditions performed in submerged fermentation. In this field many workers dealt with the main different factors that effects the enzyme productions such as temperature, pH, aeration, addition of different carbon and nitrogen sources .Although such factors were previously studied. Still we need for more investigation seems to be continuously required to give a chance to isolate more.

The present work is to determine the optimum conditions for the enzyme. On the other hand, the economic feasibility of the microbial enzymes production application generally depends on the cost of its production processes. In order to obtain high and commercially viable yields of pectinases enzyme, it is essential to optimise the fermentation medium used for growth and enzyme production. Optimal parameters of the pectinases enzyme biosynthesis from microbial origin, varied greatly, with the variation of the producing strain, environmental and nutritional conditions.

REFERENCES

Ahlawat, S., B.Battan, S.S Dhiman , J.Sharma and R.P Mandhan, 2007. Production of the Thermostable Pectinase and Xylanase for Their Potential Application Bleaching of Kraft pulp. *J.Ind. Microbiol Biotechnol*, 34; pp. 763-770.

Beg Q.K., B.Bhushan, M.Kapoor and G.S.Hoondal ,2000a. Enhanced Production of a Thermostable Xylanase from Streptomyes sp QG-11-3 and its Application in Biobelaching of Eucalyptus kraft Pulp. *Enzyme Microbio. Biotechnol* 2000, 27; pp. 459-66.

Beg. Q.K., B.Bhushan, M.Kapoor, G.S. Handal, 2000b. Production and Characterization of Thermostable Xylanase & Pectinase from Streptomyces sp QG-11-3 *J.Ind microbiol Biotechanol* 2000, 24: 396-402.

D.R.Kashyap , S.K.Soni, R.Tiwari, Enhanced Production of Pectinase by Bacillus sp DT7 using Solid State Fermentation, *Bioresource Technol.* 88[2003] pp. 251-254.

G.S.Hoondal, R.P. Tiwari,R.Tiwari, N.Dahiya, Q.K. Beg, Microbial Alkaline Pectinases and Their Industrial Applications. A Review, *App microbiol. Biotechnol.* 59 [2002] 409-418.

J.W. Cao, W.H. Sun, Y.pan, S.Y.Chen, High Producers of Polygalacturonase Selected from Mutants Resistant to Rifampin in Alkalophilic Bacillus sp. NTT33, *Enzyme Microbio Technol.* 27 [2000] 545-548.

Kapoor, M, Q.K. Beg B.Bhusan, K.S. Dadhich and G.S. Hundal, 2000. Production and Partial Purification and Characterization of a Thermo-alkali Stable Polygalacturonase from Bacillus sp MG-CP-2 *Process Biocham,* 36; 467-473.

Kashyap, D.R, S.K.Soni and R.Tiwari, 2003.Enhanced Production of Pectinase by Bacillus sp DT7 Using Solid, State Fermentation. *Bioresource. Technol*, 88; 51-254.

Kashyap, D.R., Vohra, P.K, Chopra. S and Tiwari, R. Applications of Pectinase in the Commercial Sector *Review Bioresource Technal*, 77, 215-227 [2001].

Miller, G.L Use of Dinitrosalicylic Acid Reagent for Determination of Reducing Sugars. Anal. Chem., 31, 426-429 [1959].

M.Kapoor, R.C.Kuhad, Improved Polygalacturonase Production from Bacillus sp. M.G-CP-2 Under Submerged [smf] and Solid State [ssf] Fermentation, letl. *appl. Microbiol* 34 [2002] 317-322.

O.Sunnotel, P.nigan, Pectinolytic Activity of Bacteria Isolated from Siol and Two Fungal Strains during Submerged Fermentation *World J.Microbiol Biotechnol.* 18[2002] 835-839.

Q.K.Beg, B.Bhushan, M.Kapoor, G.S.Hoondal, Production and Characterization of Thermostable Xylanase 7 Pectinase from Streptomyces sp. QG-11-3-J. *Ind microbiol. BIO-technol.* 24 [2000] 396-402.

Q.K.Beg, B.Hushan, M.Kapoor , G.S. Hoondal, Effect of Amino Acids on Production of Xylanase and Pectinase from Streptomyces sp. QG-11-3, *World J.Microbiol Biotechnol.* 16[2000] 211-213.

R.C Kuhad, M.Kapoor, R.Rustagi, Enhanced Production of an Alkaline Pectinase from Streptomyes sp. RCK- SC by whole Cell Immobilization and Solid State Cultivation, World *J.Microbiol Biotechnol.* 20[2004] 257-263.

R.S Jayani, S.Saxena, R .Gupta, Microbial Pectinolytic Enzymes: A Review, Process Biochem.40 [2005] 2931-2944. S.N. Gummadi, T.Panda, Purification and Biochemical Properties of Microbial Pectinase- A Review, *Process Biochem.* 38[2003] 987-996.

Sakai, T., T.Sakamoto, J.Haellert and E.Vandamme 1993 a. Pectin, Pectinase and Protopectinase, Production, Properties and Applications *Adv.Apple. microbiol,* 25; 213-294.

Sharma, D.C. and T. Satyanarayana, 2005. A Marked Enhancement in the Production of a Highly Alkaline and Thermostable Pectinase by Bacillus Pumilus dcsrl in Submerged Fermentation by Using Statistical Methods. *Bioresou. Technol.,* 97; 727-733 [2006].

S.N. Gummadi, T.Panda, Purification and Biochemical Properties of Microbial Pectinase — A Review, *Process Biochem.* 38[2003] 987-996.

S.N.Gummadi, D.S.Kumar, Microbial Pectic Transeliminases, Biatechnol. Lett. 27[2005]451-458.

Soares, M.M.C.N silva R, Carmona, E.C and Gomes, E [2001], Pectinolytic Enzymes Production by Bacillus Species and Their Potential Application on Juice Extraction. World *J.Microbiol. Biotechinol,* 17, 79-82.

Z.M.Li, Z.H.Bai, B.G. Zhang, H.J.Xie, Q.B.Hu, C.B.Hao, W.T. Xue , H.X. Zang, Newly Isolated, Bacillus Gibsonii S-2 Capable of Using Sugar Beet Pulp for Alkaline Pectinase Production, *world J.Microbiol .Biotechanol* 21[2005] 1483-1486.

M.M. Alexander and G.A. Sulebele, "Characteristics of Pectins from Indian Citrus Peels", *J. Food Sci. Technol.* 17 (4), 180-182 (1980).

I. Alkorta, C. Garbisu, M.J. Llama and J.L. Serra, "Industrial Applications of Pectic Enzymes: A Review", *Process Biochem.* 33(1), 21-28 (1998).

M.K. Dhingra and O.P. Gupta, "Evaluation of Chemicals for the Pectin Extraction from Guava (*Psidium guajava* L.) Fruits", *J. Food Sci. Technol.* 21, 173-175 (1984).

S. Kumar, A.K. Goswami and T.R. Sharma, "Changes in Pectin Content and Polygalacturase Activity in Developing Apple Fruits", *J. Food Sci. Technol.* 22, 282-283 (1985).

L. Phatak, K.C. Chang and G. Brown, "Isolation and Characterization of Pectin in Sugar-beet Pulp", *J. Food Sci.* 53 (3), 830-833 (1988).

Y.D. Hang, C.Y. Lee and E.E. Woodams, "A Solid State Fermentation System for the Production of Ethanol from Apple Pomace", *J. Food Sci.* 47, 1851-1852 (1982).

Y.D. Hang and E.E. Woodams, "A Solid State Fermentation of Apple Pomace for Citric Acid Production", *J. Appl. Microbial. Biotech.* 2, 283-287 (1986).

Y.D. Hang, "Production of Fuels and Chemicals from Apple Pomace". *Food Technol.* 41, 115-117 (1987).

Y.D. Hang and E.E. Woodams, "Production of Fungal Polygalacturonase from Apple Pomace", *Food Sci. Technol.* 27, 194-196 (1994).

Y.D. Hang and E.E. Woodams, "Microbial Production of Citric Acid by Solid Fermentation of Kiwifruit Peel", *J. Food Sci.* 52, 226-227 (1998).

J.N. Nigam, "Continuous Ethanol Production from Pineapple Cannery Waste", *J. Biotechnol.* 72, 197-202 (1999).

C. Krishna, "Production of Bacterial Cellulase by Solid State Bioprocessing of Banana Wastes", *Bioresource Technol.* 69, 231-239 (1999).

P. Christen, A. Bramorski, S. Revah and C.R. Soccol, "Characterization of Volatile Compounds Produced by *Rhizopus* Strains Grown on Agro-industrial Solid Wastes", *Bioresource Technol.* 71, 211-215 (2000).

M. Stredansky, E. Conti, S. Stredanska and F. Zanetti, "-Linolenic Acid Production with *Thamnidium elegans* by Solid-state Fermentation on Apple Pomace", *Bioresource Technol.* 73, 41-45 (2000).

M.H. Choi, G.E. Ji, K.H. Koh, Y.W. Ryu, D.H. Jo and Y.H. Park, "Use of Waste Chinese Cabbage as a Substrate for Yeast Biomass Production", *Bioresource Technol.* 83, 251-253 (2002).

G. Aguilar and C. Huitr´on, "Conidial and Mycelial-bound Exo-pectinase of *Aspergillus* sp.", *FEMSMicrobiology Letters* 108, 127 (1993).

J.T.P. B¨oing, "Enzyme Production", In: (G. Reed, ed) *Prescott and Dunn's Industrial Microbiolog*, 4th ed (CBS Publishers and Distributors, Delhi, 1987) pp. 678-681.

S. Solis, M.E. Flores and C. Huitr´on, "Isolation of endo Polygalacturonase hyperproducing mutants of *Aspergillus* spp.CH-Y-1043", *Biotechnology Letters* 12 (10), 751-756 (1990).

J. Fredurek and Z. Ilczuk, "Synthesis of Pectinolytic Enzymes by Forced Heterokaryons of *Aspergillus niger* in Submerged Culture", *Acta. Alimenta. Pol.* 9, 101-107 (1983).

J.V. Bhat, N.P. Jayasankar, A.D. Agate and M.H. Bilimoria, "Microbial Degradation of Pectic Substances", *J. Sci. Ind. Res.* 27, 196-203 (1968).

S. Solis, M.E. Flores and C. Huitr´on, "Protoplasts from Pectinolitic Fungi: Isolation Regeneration and Pectinases Production", *Lett. Appl. Microbiol.* 23, 31-35 (1996).

M. Berovic and H. Ostroversnik, "Production of *Aspergillus niger* Pectinolytic Enzymes by Solid State Bioprocessing of Apple Pomace", *J. Biotechnol.* 53, 47-53 (1997).

V. Puchart, P. Katapodis, P. Biely, L. Kremnick´y, P. Christakopoulos, M. Vr¢sansk´a, D. Kekos, B.J. Macris and M.K. Bhat, "Production of xylanases, Mannanases, and Pectinases by the Thermophilic Fungus *Thermomyces lanuginosus*", *Enz. Microb. Technol.* 24, 355-361 (1999).

M.G. Antov and D.M. Peri¢cin, "Production of pectinases by *Polyporus squamosus* in aqueous two-phase system", *Enz. Microb. Technol.* 28, 467-472 (2001).

F.M. Rombouts and W. Pilnik, "Enzymes in Fruit and Vegetable Juice Technology", *Process Biochem.* 13 (8), 9-13 (1978).

J.W. Bauman, "Applications of Enzymes in Fruit Juice Technology", In: (G.G. Birch, N. Blakebrough and K.J. Parker, eds) *Enzyme and Food Processing* (Applied Science Publishers, London, 1981) pp. 129-147.

A. Kilara, "Enzymes and Their Uses in the Processed Apple Industry: A Review", *Process Biochem.* 17 (4), 35-41 (1982).

M. Corredig and L. Wicker, "Juice Clarification by Thermostable Fractions of Marsh Grapefruit Pectinmethylesterase", *J. Food Sci* 67 (5), 1668-1671 (2002).

W.M. Fogarty and C.T. Kelly, "Pectic Enzymes", In: (W.M. Fogarty, ed) *Microbial Enzymes and Biotechnology* (Applied Science Publishers, London, 1983) pp. 131-182.

G.L. Miller, "Use of Dinitrosalicylic Acid Reagent for Determination of Reducing Sugar", *Anal. Chem.* 31, 426-428 (1959).

CHAPTER 10

Fatty Acids of Some Microalgae in Aquatic Environments
Biological Implications and Biotechnological Potentials

Nermin Adel El Semary; *Egypt*

ABSTRACT

Fatty acids play multiple biological roles in algal cells and their environments. They consitute essential components of cellular membranes within the cells. They also act as precursors of hormones and a source of energy. Within algal environments, they play an essential role in aquatic food chain, especially ω3 fatty acids, which are known to be limiting for zooplankton nutrition. They also play a role in succession of algal species in aquatic niches. They protect some of the algae from their competitors due to their cyto-toxic effect on membranes. Several algal taxa show variation in their fatty acid composition. Consequently, this can be used as a chemotaxonomic marker for different algal taxa. On the biotechnological front, algae rich in polyunsaturated fatty acids can serve as a renewable source of these important nutritional elements.They derive their importance from the fact that those fatty acids are not produced by many animals and therefore are needed in their dietary intake. Also several fatty acids have many pharmaceutical applications and can be used as remedies for some physical ailments. Fatty acids can also exert antimicrobial action against different microbial pathogens and their membrane permeability due to their hydrophobic nature makes them plausible components for antimicrobial drug preparations.

Key words: antimicrobial, chemotaxonomic marker, species succession, stress tolerance, zooplankton nutrition.

Introduction

Fatty acids are natural compounds formed by condensation of malonyl-coenzyme A units by the catalytic activity of fatty acid synthetase complex (Christie, 1989). In general, fatty acids contain even numbers of carbon atoms in straight chains, with a carboxyl group at one end. They can be saturated (lacking double bond) or unsaturated (possessing one or more double bonds) (Christie, 1989). When there is a single double bond, the fatty acid is called monounsaturated e.g., oleic acid 18:1(*n*-9). Polyunsaturated fatty acids on the other hand, possess more than a double bond possibly up to six (Christie, 1989). Fatty acids play multiple biological roles in the cell as they consitute essential components of cellular membranes. They also act as precursors of hormones and a source of energy (Madigan *et al.*, 2000). Fatty acids play a role in the structural modification of certain cells. For example, the polyunsaturated fatty acids are the major constituents of the glycolipid envelope of the heterocyst (modified cell for nitrogen fixation) in heterocystous cyanobacteria (Campell *et al.*, 1997).

Biological Implications of Fatty Acids

Fatty Acids As Limiting Resources for Zooplankton Nutrition

Some fatty acids are essential dietary components of many animals. Polyunsaturated fatty acids including linoleic acid (18:2ω6) and ω3 fatty acids such as linolenic acid (18:3ω3), EPA (eicosapentaenoic acid; 20:5ω3), and DHA (docosahexaenoic acid; 22:6ω3) are considered to be limiting dietary elements for zooplankton nutrition (Richmond, 1990). This stems from the fact that those fatty acids are important for many physiological processes and most zooplanktons lack the ability to synthesise (ω3-fatty acids) by themselves (Brett and Müller-Navarra, 1997). Nevertheless, saturated fatty acids are also important for zooplankton nutrition due to their high energy content (DeMott and Müller-Navarra, 1997).

Fatty Acids As Determinants of Species Succession in Aquatic Environments

Fatty acids play an important role in the succession of certain phytoplankton species in aquatic environments (Cembella, 2003). For example, Sushchik *et al.* (2004) associated essential ù3fatty acids in a setston of a Siberian water body to phytoplankton species composition. They found that total diatoms were related to the polyunsaturated eicosapentaenoic fatty acid, whereas two of the four dominant cyanobacteria species, *Anabaena flos-aquae* and *Planktothrix agardhii* were strongly associated with linolenic fatty acid. No such correlation was found for *Aphanizomenon flos-aquae* and *Microcystis aeruginosa*.

The role played by fatty acids in determining the succesion of algal species might be widely attributed to the toxic effect of these acids as a mechanism of protecting their producers against other algae (Wu *et al.*, 1998; 2006). This toxic effect is attributed to the hydrophobic nature of fatty acids that enables them to form micelles in water; those micelles penetrate through the rivals' membranes and iduce toxic effects (Perez and Martin, 2001). The thickness of the target organism's mucilage layer determines the susceptibility to fatty acid toxic effect with those possessing a thin layer being more vulnerable than those with thick layer (Chiang *et al.*, 2004; Wu *et al.*, 2006). The proposed scenario on how fatty acids drastically affects cellular membrane starts with Ca^{2+} channel activation, causing Ca^{2+} influx and the activation of both calmodulin and the enzyme phospholipase A2. This consequently leads to the hydrolysis of the membrane and the immedaite leakage of K^+ (Igarashi *et al.*, 1999). Potassium laekage can be used as an indicator of the degree of membranes' damage (Wu *et al.*, 2006).

Wu *et al.* (2006) also suggested that membrane susceptability of target rivals increases if exposed to external fatty acids that form part of their plasma membranes as they might interact more easily with plasma membranes and result in a change in membrane conformation. Concerning interaction with other microorganisms, Mundt *et al.* (2003) suggested that some unsaturated fatty acids synthesized by cyanobacteria are involved in defense reactions against other mircoorganisms in their vicinity. They suggested that fatty acids are able to change the permeability of the cell membrane through interacting with proteins and lipids of the membrane, inhibiting special enzymes or by forming a layer around the cells.

Fatty Acids Role in Stress Tolerance

Cyanobacteria counteract stressful conditions such as drought mainly through increasing the unsaturation of fatty acids in their memberanes and interaction with sugars such as trehalose and sucrose to minimise loss of water (Singh *et al.*, 2002). Increasing the membranes' fluidity also plays a major role in salt stress through:

1. Depressing the activities of K+ and Na+ channels.
2. Activating the Na+/H+antiport system thus protecting photosynthetic systems.
3. Affecting the activities of several membrane-bound enzymes.

4. Stimulating the synthesis of the Na+/H+ antiporter(s) and/ or H+ ATPase(s) leading to increased density in the membrane, thus resulting in a decrease in the concentration of Na+ in the cytosplasm, thus protecting photosystems against salt induced inhibition (Singh *et al.*, 2002).

Also unsaturation of fatty acids at low temperature as a mechanism of protecting proteins essential for photosynthetic membranes where acyl groups function to anchor those proteins to membranes (Singh *et al.*, 2002).

Fatty Acids Composition As A Chemotaxonomic Marker

Fatty acid composition has long been a useful tool in studying the taxonomy and evolution of prokaryotes. For example, Nichols *et al.* (1965) used this chemotaxonomic marker to establish link between cyanobacteria and cholorplasts. They demonstrated that in cyanobacteria, unsaturated fatty acids are synthesized by aerobic desaturation similar to eukaryotic chloroplasts. In most eubacteria however, the synthesis of monounsaturated fatty acids proceeds anaerobically, and polyunsaturated fatty acids are absent (Henderson *et al.*, 1993). Nevertheless, several unicellular cyanobacteria possessed monounsaturated fatty acids, thus resembling other eubacteria by lacking polyunsaturated fatty acids (Kenyon, 1972).

However, some exceptions still exist. For example, the simple cyanobacterium *Gloeobacter violaceus* possessed polyunsaturated fatty acids (Maslova *et al.*, 2004). Concerning the cyanobacterial filamentous strains, they mostly contain high amounts of di- and tri-unsaturated fatty acids (Sato and Murata 1982), with a few exceptions (Kenyon *et al.* 1972). However, the lack of polyunsaturated fatty acids may be wide-spread not only among the unicellular cyanobacteria but also among the filamentous ones (Oren *et al.*, 1985). Lack of polyunsaturated fatty acids was also associated with some benthic cyanobacteria showing a strong hydrophobic behaviour such as *Oscillatoria. Limnetica* and *Phormidium* from Wadi Natrun, Egypt. Other cyanobacterial species such as *Microcoleus* sp. and *A. halophytica* possessed a high degree of cell surface hydrophobicity that allows them to aggregate and form benthic mats (Oren *et al.*, 1985).

Regarding individual groups of cyanobacteria, Caudales *et al.* (1992) indicated that the heterocystous *Nostoc* and *Anabaena* genera could be differentiated based on their cellular fatty acid contents. Other studies indicated that fatty acid could be used as a biochemical marker for 28 bloom-forming cyanobacterial strains (Li *et al.*, 1998). Gugger *et al.* (2002) examined fatty acid composition of 22 cyanobacterial strains belonging to different genera and confirmed that analysis of fatty acid content could be used to complement other approaches to establish a polyphasic classification of cyanobacteria. At the genus level, Liu *et al.* (2004) analyzed 16 *Nostoc* strains belonging to 5 species, and suggested that profiling fatty acids could be a useful approach in the taxonomic study of the genus.

The quantity rather than the quality of fatty acid composition of cyanobacteria can be affected by several environmental factors such as temperature, photonfluence rate, composition of aerating gas and growth medium investigation. Nevertheless, the fatty acid data should always be treated with caution where it must be taken into consideration the relationship between the characteristics of fatty acid composition fixed by evolution and the changes caused by adaptation to a particular environment (Maslova *et al.*, 2004). Concerning the fatty acid composition of some chlorophytes , it is very rich in palmitic acid (16:0), linolenic acid (18:3ω3), 18:1ω9/12 (18:lω9: oleic acid), but very poor in EPA. DHA was not detected in any of the samples (Ahlgren *et al.* 1992).

Biotechnological Potentials of Fatty Acids from Microalgae

Use of Fatty Acids as Therapeutics and Dietary Supplements

Certain fatty acids such as gamma linoleic acid act as a precursor in the synthesis of prostaglandin E_1 (PGE_1) and in the synthesis of eicosapentaenoic acid (EPA), the precursor of the series-3 prostaglandins, the series-5 leukotrienes and the series-3 thromboxanes (http://www.flexyx.com/S/Star%20GLA%20(GNC).html). Polyunsaturated fatty acids namely eicosanoids, have anti-thrombogenic, anti-inflammatory effects and some have anticancereous effects (Das *et al.*, 1995 and Fan *et al.*, 1998). Moreover, some fatty acids are being used for prevention of restenosis after coronary angioplasty (Dehmer *et al.*, 1988).

Use of Fatty Acids As Antimicrobial Compounds

The antimicrobial action of fatty acids has been investigated in eukaryotic algae by Harder and Oppermann (1953) who found activity against Gram+ and Gram– bacteria in the culture media of *Stichococcus bacillaris* Nägeli and *Protosiphon botryoides* (Kützing) and proposed fatty acids as active components. Rossell and Srivastava (1987) also reported the antimicrobial action of fatty acids from brown algae. Ohta *et al.* (1995) found that extracts from *Chlorococcum* strain HS-101 and *Dunaliella primolecta* strongly inhibited the growth of a strain of methicillin-resistant *Staphylococcus aureus* (MRSA) where one of the bioactive compounds in both strains was γ-linolenic acid. They also found that other unsaturated fatty acids had antimicrobial activity against MRSA, including α-linolenic acid, eicosapentaenoic acid and docosahexaenoic acid (DHA, C22:6). They suggested that α-linolenic acid should be given as a dietary supplement to patients infected with hospital bug. Safonova and

Reisser (2005) showed that antimicrobial effect may be either constitutive (always expressed in the algal culture medium), or induced; (when algae are in contact with bacteria).

Improving Culture Conditions for Fatty Acids Production

It is crucially important to select for the optimum growth conditions that allow for the full biotechnological exploitation of algal's ability to produce essential fatty acids. In that regard, Ohta *et al.* (1995) reported that fatty acid production of antimicrobial effect by *Chlorococcum* strain increased significantly when the concentration of $MgSO_4$ and K_2HPO_4 was supplied at a higher concentration than their standard concentration in BG-11 medium. Qiang *et al.* (1997) investigated the growth conditions favourable to the production of eicosapentaenoic acid (EPA) and γ-linolenic acid (GLA) in semi-continuous outdoor cultures of *Monodus subterraneus* and *Spirulina platensis.* In *Mondus. subterraneus*, the highest EPA cell content was attained at density corresponding to highest biomass per culture volume. In *S. platensis*, high density was associated with a decrease in total fatty acid content, but the relative abundance of GLA increased. Fatty acid desaturation seemed to be associated with an increase in culture density of *S. platensis*, resulting in an increase in the proportion of the fatty acids 16:1 and GLA and a decrease in 16:0 and 18:2. Therefore, Qiang *et al.* (1997) suggested that very high culture densities in enclosed reactors represent an optimal condition for improving productivity of certain polyunsaturated fatty acids.

Conclusion

Fatty acids from microalgae have many biological implications and biotechnological potentials. The fact that some fatty acids are on high demand, despite being of limited availability, makes the use of microalgae as a renewable source for those fatty acid an ecomomically-favourable option.

REFERENCES

Ahlgren, G., Gustafsson, I.-B., Boberg, M., Fatty acid Content and Chemical Composition of Freshwater Microalgae, Journal of Phycology, 28 (1992), 37-50.

Brett, M.T., Müller-Navarra, D. C., The Role of Highly Unsaturated Fatty Acids in Aquatic Food web Processes, Freshwater Biology, 38(1997), 483-499.

Das, U.N., Prasad V.V., Reddy, D. R., Local Application of Gamma-linolenic Acid in the Treatment of Human Gliomas. Cancer Letters, 94 (1995) 147-155.

Fan, Y.Y., Chapkin, R. S., Importance of Dietary Gamma-linolenic Acid in Human Health and Nutrition, Journal of Nutrition, 128 (1998), 1411-1414.

Caudales, R., Wells, J. M., Differentiation of the Free-living *Anabaena* and *Nostoc* Cyanobacteria on the Basis of Fatty Acid Composition, International Journal of Systematic Bacteriology, 42 (1992), 246-251.

Cembella, A.D., Chemical Ecology of Eukaryotic Microalgae in Marine Ecosystems. Phycologia, 42(2003), 420-447.

Christie, W.W., Gas Chromatography and Lipids, Published by the Oily Press, Bridgwater, UK, (1989).

Chiang, I.Z., Huang, W.Y., Wu, J.T., Allelochemicals of *Botryococcus braunii* (Chlorophyceae), Journal of Phycology, 40 (2004), 474-480.

Dehmer, G.J., Popma, J.J., van den Berg, E.K., Eighhom, E.J., Prewitt, J,B., Campbell, W.B., Jennings, L., Willerson, J.T., Schmitz, J.M., Reduction in the Rate of Early Restenosis After Coronary Angioplasty by a Diet Supplemented with n-3 Fatty Acids. New England Journal of Medicine, 319 (1988), 733-740.

DeMott, W. R., Müller-Navarra, D. C., The Importance of Highly Unsaturated Fatty Acids in Zooplankton Nutrition: Evidence from Experiments with *Daphnia,* a Cyanobacterium and Lipid Emulsions, Freshwater Biology, 38 (1997), 649-664.

Gugger, M., Lyra, C., Suominen, I., Tsitko, I., Humbert, J., Salkinoja- Salonen, M.S., Cellular Fatty Acids as Chemotaxonomic Marker of the Genera *Anabaena, Aphanizomenon, Microcystis, Nostoc* and *Planktothrix* (Cyanobacteria), International Journal of Systematic and Evolutionary Microbiology, 52 (2002), 1007-1011.

Harder, R., Oppermann, A. Über antibiotische Stoffe bei den Grünalgen *Stichococcus bacillaris* und *Protosiphon botryoides*. Archiv für Mikrobiologie, 19 (1953), 398-401.

Henderson, R.J., Millar, R.M., Sargent, J.R., Jostensen, J.P. Trans Monoenoic and Polyunsaturated Fatty Acids in Phospholipids of a *Vibrio* Species of Bacterium in Relation to Growth Conditions, Lipids, 28 (1993), 389-396.

Igarashi, T., Aritake, S., Yasumoto, T., Mechanisms Underlying the Hemolytic and Ichthyotoxic Activities of Maitotoxin, Natural Toxins, 7 (1999) 71-79.

Kenyon, C.N., Fatty Acid Composition of Unicellular Strains of Blue-green Algae, Journal of Bacteriology, 109 (1972), 827- 834.

Kenyon, C.N., Rippka, R. and Stanier, R.Y., Fatty Acid Composition and Physiological Properties of some Filamentous Blue-green Algae. Archiv für Mikrobiologie, 83(1972), 216-236.

Li, R., Yokota, A., Sugiyama, J., Watanabe, M., Watanabe, M. M., Chemotaxonomy of Planktonic Cyanobacteria Based on Non-polar and 3-hydroxy Fatty Acid Composition, Phycological Research, 46 (1998), 21-28.

Liu, X., Chen, F., Jiang, Y., Differentiation of *Nostoc flagelliforme* and its Neighbouring Species Using Fatty Acid Profile as a Chemotaxonomic Tool, Current Microbiology, 47 (2004), 467-474.

Li, R., Watanabe, M. M., Fatty Acid Composition of Planktonic Species of *Anabaena* (Cyanobacteria) with Coiled Trichomes Exhibited a Significant Taxonomic Value. Current Microbiology, 49(2004), 376-380.

Madigan, M.T., Martinko, J. M., Parker, J., Brock Biology of Microorganisms, Prentice-Hall International Ltd., London, U.K., (2000).

Maslova, I.P., Mouradyan, E.A., Lapina, S.S., Klyachko-Gurvich, G.L., Los, D.A., Lipid Fatty Acid Composition and Thermophilicity of Cyanobacteria. Russian Journal of Plant Physiology, 51 (3) (2004), 353-360.

Mundt, S., Kreitlow, S. Jansen, R., Fatty Acids with Antibacterial Activity from the Cyanobacterium *Oscillatoria redekei* HUB 051, Journal of Applied Phycology, 15 (2003), 263-267.

Nichols, B.W., Harris, R.V. James, A.T., The Lipid Metabolism of Blue-green Algae. Biochemistry and Biophysics Research Communication. 20(1965), 256-262.

Ohta, S., Shiomi, Y., Kawashima, A., Aozasa, O., Nakao, I., T., Nagate, T., Kitamura, K., Miyata, H., Antibiotic Effect of Linolenic Acid from *Chlorococcum* Strain HS-IO1 and *Dunaliella primolecta* on Methicillin-resistant *Staphylococcus aureus*. Journal of Applied Phycology, 7 (1995), 121-127.

Oren, A., Fattom, A., Padan, E., Tietz, A., Unsaturated Fatty Acid Composition and Biosynthesis in *Oscillatoda limnetica* and other Cyanobacteria. Archives of Microbiology, 141 (1985), 138-142.

Perez, E., Martin, D.F., Critical Micelle Concentrations of Allelopathic Substances Produced by *Nannochloris oculata* which Affect a Red Tide Organism *Gymnodinium breve*. Cytobios, 106 (2001), 163-170.

Qiang, H., Zhengyu, H., Cohen, Z., Richmond, A., Enhancement of Eicosapentaenoic Acid (EPA) and ã-linolenic Acid (GLA) Production by Manipulating Algal Density of Outdoor Cultures of *Monodus subterraneus* (Eustigmatophyta) and *Spirulina platensis* (Cyanobacteria). European Journal of Phycology, 32(1997), 81-86.

Richmond, A., Large Scale Microalgal Culture and Applications, *In* Progress in Phycological Research, 7(1990), pp.1-62. Biopress, Bristol.

Sato, N., Murata, N., Lipid Biosynthesis in the Blue-green Alga, *Anabaena variabilis*. II. Fatty Acids and Lipid Molecular Species, Biochimica et Biophysica Acta, 710 (1982), 279-289.

Singh, S.C., Sinha, R.P., Häder, Donat-P., Role of Lipids and Fatty Acids in Stress Tolerance in Cyanobacteria. A Review Article. Acta Protozoologica, 41 (2002), 297-308.

Sushchik, N., Gladyshev, M. I., Makhutova, O. N., Kalachova, G.S., Kravchuk, E.S., Ivanova, E. A., Associating particulate essential fatty acids of the ω3 Family with Phytoplankton Species Composition in a Siberian Reservoir. Freshwater Biology, 49 (2004), 1206-1219.

Wu, J.T., Kuo-Huang, L.L., Lee, J. Algicidal Effect of *Peridinium bipes* on *Microcystis aeruginosa*. Current Microbiology, 37(1998), 257-261.

Wu, Jiunn-Tzong, Chiang, Yin-Ru, Huanga, Wen-Ya and Jane, Wann-Neng, Cytotoxic Effects of Free Fatty Acids on Phytoplankton Algae and Cyanobacteria, Aquatic Toxicology, 80 (2006), 338-345.

Website: http://www.flexyx.com/S/Star%20GLA%20(GNC).html.

CHAPTER 11

Genetic Engineering and Applications

Aakansha Goswami, *India*; **B. Singh,** *India*
Gayatri Bhadana, *India*; **Sandhya Sharma,** *India*
Jaswant Ray, *India*

Introduction

Genetic engineering, also called genetic modification, is the direct manipulation of an organism's genome using modern DNA technology. It involves the introduction of foreign DNA or synthetic genes into the organism of interest. The introduction of new DNA does not require the use of classical genetic methods, however traditional breeding methods are typically used for the propagation of recombinant organisms. An organism that is generated through the introduction of recombinant DNA is considered to be a genetically modified organism. The first organisms genetically engineered were bacteria in 1973 and then mice in 1974. Insulin-producing bacteria were commercialized in 1982 and genetically modified food has been sold since 1994.

The most common form of genetic engineering involves the insertion of new genetic material at an unspecified location in the host genome. This is accomplished by isolating and copying the genetic material of interest using molecular cloning methods to generate a DNA sequence containing the required genetic elements for expression, and then inserting this construct into the host organism. Other forms of genetic engineering include gene targeting and knocking out specific genes via engineered nucleases such as zinc finger nucleases or engineered homing endonucleases.

Genetic engineering techniques have been applied in numerous fields including research, biotechnology, and medicine. Medicines such as insulin and human growth hormone are now produced in bacteria, experimental mice such as the oncomouse and the knockout mouse are being used for research purposes and insect resistant and/or herbicide tolerant crops have been commercialized. Genetically engineered plants and animals capable of producing biotechnology drugs more cheaply than current methods (called pharming) are also being developed, and in 2009 the United States FDA approved the sale of the pharmaceutical protein antithrombin produced in the milk of genetically engineered goats.

Genetic engineering alters the genetic makeup of an organism using techniques that introduce heritable material prepared outside the organism either directly into the host or into a cell that is then fused or hybridized with the host. This involves using recombinant nucleic acid (DNA or RNA) techniques to form new combinations of heritable genetic material followed by the incorporation of that material either indirectly through a vector system or directly through micro-injection, macro-injection and micro-encapsulation techniques. Genetic engineering does not include traditional animal and plant breeding, in vitro fertilisation, induction of polyploidy, mutagenesis and cell fusion techniques that do not use recombinant nucleic acids or a genetically modified organism in the process. Cloning and stem cell research, although not considered genetic engineering, are closely related and genetic engineering can be used within them. Synthetic biology is an emerging discipline that takes genetic engineering a step further by introducing artificially synthesized genetic material from raw materials into an organism.

If genetic material from another species is added to the host, the resulting organism is called transgenic. If genetic material from the same species or a species that can naturally breed with the host is used the resulting organism is called cisgenic. Genetic engineering can also be used to remove genetic material from the target organism, creating a gene knockout organism. In Europe genetic modification is synonymous with genetic engineering while within the United States of America it can also refer to conventional breeding methods. Within the scientific community, the term genetic engineering is not commonly used; more specific terms such as transgenic are preferred.

Probably the most important scientific event of the 20th century was the 1953 discovery, by James Watson and Francis Crick, of the structure of the DNA molecule which is the basis of heredity. Darwin had shown how species might have changed over eons by slow, random natural processes. Watson and Crick gave us the key to moving evolution along much faster, to suit our own purposes. (Whether the biological world is governed by God's plan or Darwin's is a matter which continues to divide people, but nothing in this report should require you to change your own view!)

A DNA molecule is like a string of letters, using a four letter alphabet, easily copied when living cells reproduce. The sequences of letters make sentences, which we call genes. These sentences are the instructions for making and operating a living cell. There are two kinds of sequences. One kind of gene gives a cell the necessary instructions for making one of the various kinds of protein, used for structures, enzymes, signals, all the basic mechanisms of life. The other kind of sequence is used as a control mechanism so that a cell can tell when to make which proteins and when to do something else. By 1966, scientists had learned the language of protein-making gene sequences. This language is the same for all forms of life. That means that a human gene sentence for making insulin, a kind of protein, could be transferred to, say, a yeast cell, and then the yeast cell could equally well make human insulin.

The other gene sequences, the control sequences, are like switches that turn other genes on or off. A control sequence could have different results in different organisms, just as an electrical switch can produce a different result in a car or in an oil burner. In particular, it could control a completely different protein-making gene. Some control genes are used to turn another gene on, and others are used to turn another gene off, and some control genes turn other control genes on or off.

In a simple case, suppose a cell needs protein A, but not too much. If the gene that tells the cell to make protein A is turned on, eventually the control gene will sense that there is lots of protein A available, so it will turn off the protein making gene. Later when the supply of protein A has diminished, the control gene will relent and let the protein making gene turn back on.

There are more complicated control arrangements. For example, the gene which makes insulin is turned on in pancreas cells but not in liver cells.

To understand the connection between a gene and its function requires lots of scientific work, enough to keep biologists busy for a very long time. Even in the simplest cases, one first needs to know what sequence of letters make up the protein-making gene, and what sequences make up the control genes which turn it on or off, as well as where they are situated on the chromosome; one needs to know what signals activate the control genes; then one needs to know the chemical reactions in which the protein molecule takes part, and finally one needs to know how those chemical reactions relate to some activity of the cell. Each different organism has tens of thousands of different genes and makes a huge number of proteins. Life is enormously complex.

Slowly but surely, more and more secrets of living things are being uncovered. Hundreds of genes are now understood completely. There are many more genes which have been discovered and associated with some function, but not yet understood very well. It is now possible to transfer a gene from the DNA of one species to the DNA of another species. For cases in which scientists know exactly what a gene does and exactly how it does it, it is now possible to express that function in another species. That is genetic engineering.

Process

I. Isolating the gene

First, the gene to be inserted into the genetically modified organism must be chosen and isolated. Presently, most genes transferred into plants provide protection against insects or tolerance to herbicides. In animals the majority of genes used are growth hormone genes. Once chosen the genes must be isolated. This typically involves multiplying the gene using polymerase chain reaction (PCR). If the chosen gene or the donor organism's genome has been well studied it may be present in a genetic library. If the DNA sequence is known, but no copies of the gene are available, it can be artificially synthesized. Once isolated, the gene is inserted into a bacterial plasmid.

II. Constructs

The gene to be inserted into the genetically modified organism must be combined with other genetic elements in order for it to work properly. The gene can also be modified at this stage for better expression or effectiveness. As well as the gene to be inserted most constructs contain a promoter and terminator region as well as a selectable marker gene. The promoter region initiates transcription of the gene and can be used to control the location and level of gene expression, while the terminator region ends transcription. The selectable marker, which in most cases confers antibiotic resistance to the organism it is expressed in, is needed to determine which cells are transformed with the new gene. The constructs are made using recombinant DNA techniques, such as restriction digests, ligations and molecular cloning.

III. Gene targeting

The most common form of genetic engineering involves inserting new genetic material randomly within the host genome. Other techniques allow new genetic material to be inserted at a specific location in the host genome or generate mutations at desired genomic loci capable of knocking out endogenous genes. The technique of gene targeting uses homologous recombination to target desired changes to a specific endogenous gene. This tends to occur at a relatively low frequency in plants and animals and generally requires the use of selectable markers. The frequency of gene targeting can be greatly enhanced with the use of engineered nucleases such as zinc finger nucleases, engineered homing endonucleases, or nucleases created from TAL effectors. In addition to enhancing gene targeting, engineered nucleases can also be used to introduce mutations at endogenous genes that generate a gene knockout.

IV. Transformation

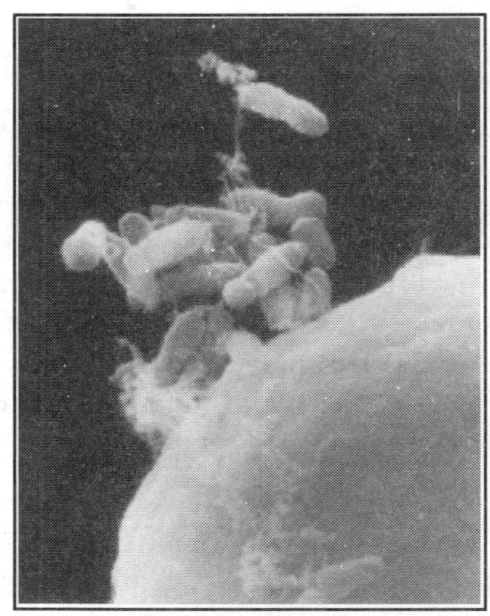

A. tumefaciens attaching itself to a carrot cell

About 1 per cent of bacteria are naturally able to take up foreign DNA but it can also be induced in other bacteria. Stressing the bacteria for example, with a heat shock or an electric shock, can make the cell membrane permeable to DNA that may then incorporate into their genome or exist as extrachromosomal DNA. DNA is generally inserted into animal cells using microinjection, where it can be injected through the cells nuclear envelope directly into the nucleus or through the use of viral vectors. In plants the DNA is generally inserted using *Agrobacterium*-mediated recombination or biolistics.

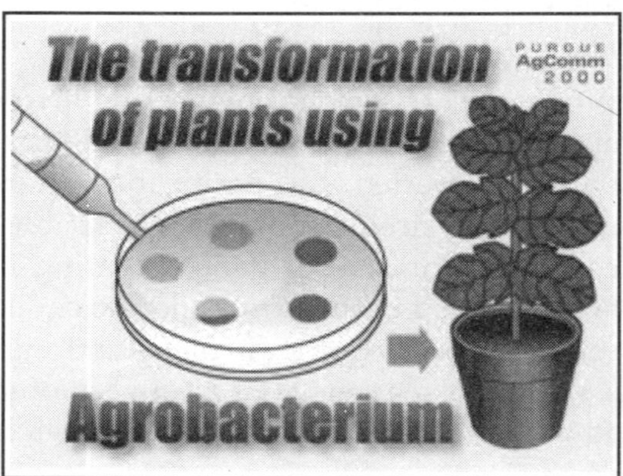

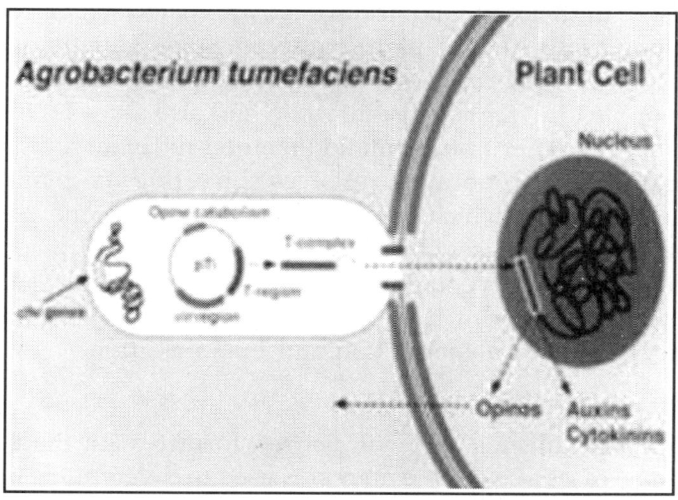

In *Agrobacterium*-mediated recombination the plasmid construct must also contain T-DNA. *Agrobacterium* naturally inserts DNA from a tumor inducing plasmid into any susceptible plant's genome it infects, causing crown gall disease. The T-DNA region of this plasmid is responsible for insertion of the DNA. The genes to be inserted are cloned into a binary vector, which contains T-DNA and can be grown in both *E. Coli* and *Agrobacterium*. Once the binary vector is constructed the plasmid is transformed into *Agrobacterium* containing no plasmids and plant cells are infected. The *Agrobacterium* will then naturally insert the genetic material into the plant cells.

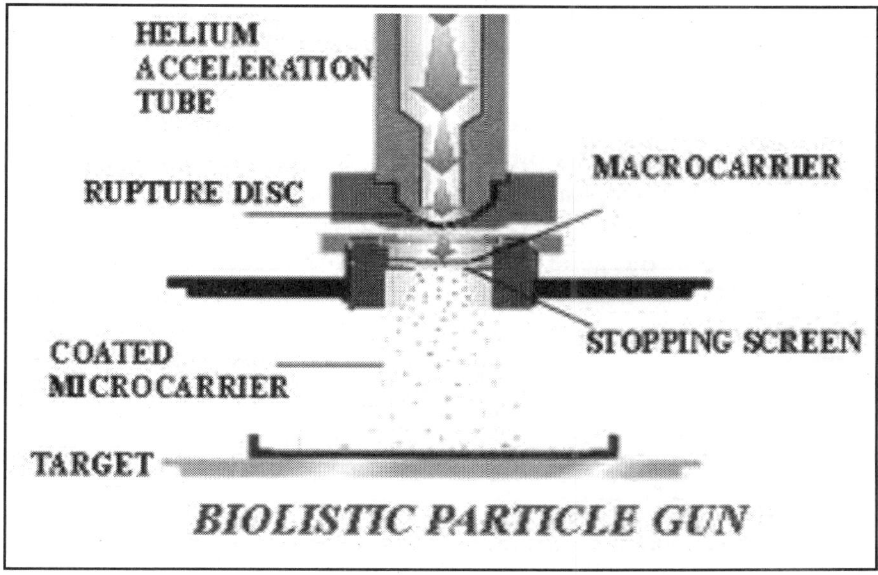

In biolistics particles of gold or tungsten are coated with DNA and then shot into young plant cells or plant embryos. Some genetic material will enter the cells and transform them. This method can be used on plants that are not susceptible to *Agrobacterium* infection and also allows transformation of plant plastids. Another transformation method for plant and animal cells is electroporation. Electroporation involves subjecting the plant or animal cell to an electric shock, which can make the cell membrane permeable to plasmid DNA. In some cases the electroporated cells will incorporate the DNA into their genome. Due to the damage caused to the cells and DNA the transformation efficiency of biolistics and electroporation is lower than agrobacterial mediated transformation and microinjection.

V. Selection

Not all the organism's cells will be transformed with the new genetic material; in most cases a selectable marker is used to differentiate transformed from untransformed cells. If a cell has been successfully transformed with the DNA it will also contain the marker gene. By growing the cells in the presence of an antibiotic or chemical that selects or marks the cells expressing that gene it is possible to separate the transgenic events from the non-transgenic. Another method of screening involves using a DNA probe that will only stick to the inserted gene. A number of strategies have been developed that can remove the selectable marker from the mature transgenic plant.

VI. Regeneration

As often only a single cell is transformed with genetic material the organism must be regrown from that single cell. As bacteria consist of a single cell and reproduce clonally regeneration is not necessary. In plants this is accomplished through the use of tissue culture. Each plant species has different requirements for successful regeneration through tissue culture. If successful an adult plant is produced that contains the transgene in every cell. In animals it is necessary to ensure that the inserted DNA is present in the embryonic stem cells. When the offspring is produced they can be screened for the presence of the gene. All offspring from the first generation will be heterozygous for the inserted gene and must be mated together to produce a homozygous animal.

VII. Confirmation

The finding that a recombinant organism contains the inserted genes is not usually sufficient to ensure that the genes will be expressed in an appropriate manner in the intended tissues of the recombinant organism. To examine the presence of the gene, further analysis frequently uses PCR, Southern hybridization, and DNA sequencing, which serve to determine the chromosomal location and copy number of the inserted gene. To examine expression of the trans-gene, an extensive analysis of transcription, RNA processing patterns, and the expression and localization of the protein product(s) is usually necessary, using methods including northern hybridization, quantitative RT-PCR, Western blot, immunofluorescence and phenotypic analysis. When appropriate, the organism's offspring are studied to confirm that the trans-gene and associated phenotype are stably inherited.

Impact of Genetic Modification on Agriculture

Genetic modification may be a tool that can be used in order to help bring on many advances in the field of agriculture. The creation of genetically modified plants may help bring about increased plant production, better harvests and better quality crops. This may sound very beneficial to a whole lot of people all over the world. With the need for increased harvests to feed a rapidly growing world population, genetic modification may truly be looked upon as a very useful field to explore for solutions to such problems.

Although the technology of genetic modification may have been developed for more than three decades now, the impact that it may have on the world has not yet been fully grasped. True, genetic modification in agriculture will greatly help in improving strains of plants to be more disease and pest resistant, better able to withstand extreme weather patterns as well as provide increased harvests. But the science itself behind genetic modification may be something that might require further study and research.

The science of altering the DNA of an organism is the basis of genetic modification. That is where problems lie. Simply by changing an organism's genetic make-up or structure, scientists are introducing a modified organism into the environment that may have serious implications later on. What these implications may be, most scientists may not know for sure if more extensive studies are made. And that is where more problems crop up and may already have cropped up in some parts of the world.

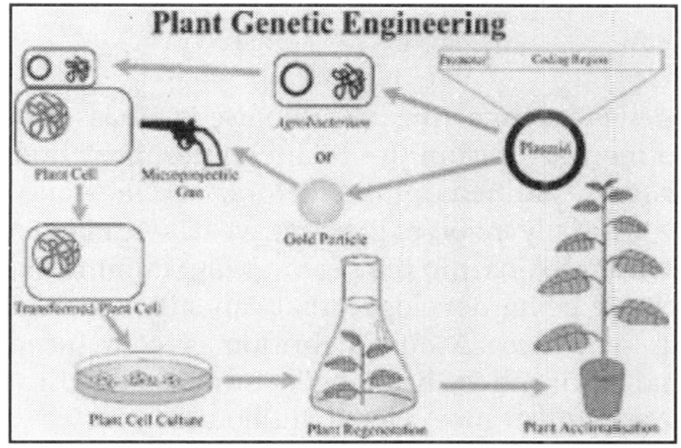

Quite a number of biotechnology firms today seem to be quite active in coming up with a number of genetically modified crops almost every year. Their research in developing such GM plants may truly be considered as aggressive in its approach. But the problem is that less work and research are being done in assessing a new GM plant's probable impact on the natural environment. Many biotech firms are more focused in introducing new GM plants into the market in order to gain more revenue for the company that some may have already neglected how such crops may affect the world in the future.

A genetically modified organism such as those being done on GM crops should be considered alien to the natural environment. And because such plants have been genetically altered and modified to form new and different functions, how the environment would react to them and vice versa would be something that may need further study. How a genetically modified plant engineered to make its own insecticide would truly be some cause for concern since it may also affect other plants and animals around it if introduced into the natural environment.

That is just one example of how GM plants have become a cause of concern in the world today. What might be required is that some biotech firms need not be too aggressive in their approach to introduce new GM plants in the market just for profit. If not, then biotech firms should also provide the same aggressiveness in letting such GM plants undergo further extensive studies to look upon their probable impact to our natural environment before they ever decide to release them for use. Care and concern for the world and the environment would be a nice trait for many biotech companies to have. Who knows, it might prove to be more beneficial in the long run.

Applications

Genetic engineering has applications in medicine, research, industry and agriculture and can be used on a wide range of plants, animals and micro organism.

(a) Medicine

In medicine genetic engineering has been used to mass-produce insulin, human growth hormones, follistim (for treating infertility), human albumin, monoclonal antibodies, antihemophilic factors, vaccines and many other drugs. Vaccination generally involves injecting weak live, killed or inactivated forms of viruses or their toxins into the person being immunized. Genetically engineered viruses are being developed that can still confer immunity, but lack the infectious sequences. Mouse hybridomas, cells fused together to create monoclonal antibodies, have been humanised through genetic engineering to create human monoclonal antibodies.

Genetic engineering is used to create animal models of human diseases. Genetically modified mice are the most common genetically engineered animal model. They have been used to study and model cancer (the oncomouse), obesity, heart disease, diabetes, arthritis, substance abuse, anxiety, aging and Parkinson disease. Potential cures can be tested against these mouse models. Also genetically modified pigs have been bred with the aim of increasing the success of pig to human organ transplantation.

Gene therapy is the genetic engineering of humans by replacing defective human genes with functional copies. This can occur in somatic tissue or germline tissue. If the gene is inserted into the germline tissue it can be passed down to that person's descendants. Gene therapy has been used to treat patients suffering from immune deficiencies (notably Severe combined immunodeficiency) and trials have been carried out on other genetic disorders. The success of gene therapy so far has been limited and a patient (Jesse Gelsinger) has died during a clinical trial testing a new treatment. There are also ethical concerns should the technology be used not just for treatment, but for enhancement, modification or alteration of a human beings' appearance, adaptability, intelligence, character or behaviour. The distinction between cure and enhancement can also be difficult to establish. Transhumanists consider the enhancement of humans desirable.

(b) Research

Human cells in which some proteins are fused with green fluorescent protein to allow them to be visualized. Genetic engineering is an important tool for natural scientists. Genes and other genetic information from a wide range of organisms are transformed into bacteria for storage and modification, creating genetically modified bacteria in the process. Bacteria are cheap, easy to grow, clonal, multiply quickly, relatively easy to transform and can be stored at -80°C almost indefinitely. Once a gene is isolated it can be stored inside the bacteria providing an unlimited supply for research.

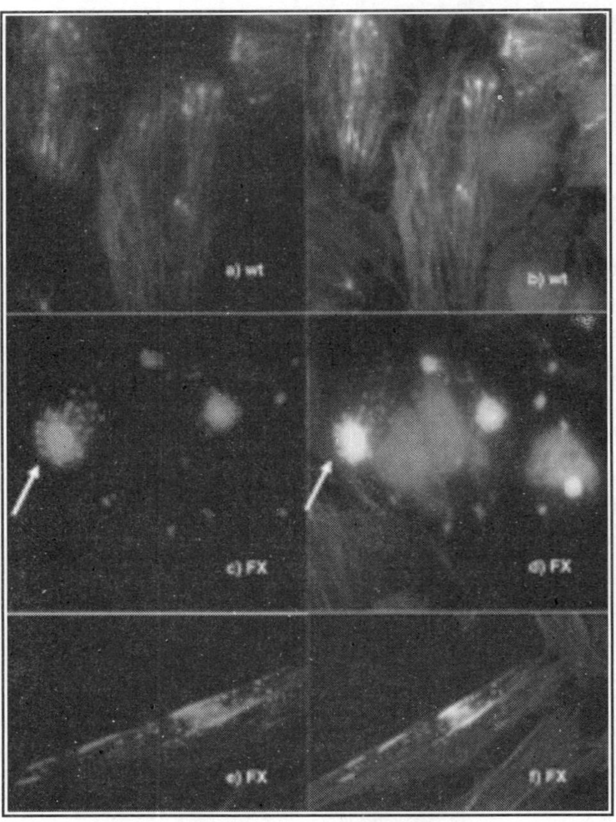

Organisms are genetically engineered to discover the functions of certain genes. This could be the effect on the phenotype of the organism, where the gene is expressed or what other genes it interacts with. These experiments generally involve loss of function, gain of function, tracking and expression.

- **Loss of function experiments**, such as in a gene knockout experiment, in which an organism is engineered to lack the activity of one or more genes. A knockout experiment involves the creation and manipulation of a DNA construct *in vitro*, which, in a simple knockout, consists of a copy of the desired gene, which has been altered such that it is non-functional. Embryonic stem cells incorporate the altered gene, which replaces the already present functional copy. These stem cells are injected into blastocysts, which are implanted into surrogate mothers. This allows the experimenter to analyze the defects caused by this mutation and thereby determine the role of particular genes. It is used especially frequently in developmental biology. Another method, useful in organisms such as Drosophila (fruit fly), is to induce mutations in a large population and then screen the progeny for the desired mutation. A similar process can be used in both plants and prokaryotes.

- **Gain of function experiments**, the logical counterpart of knockouts. These are sometimes performed in conjunction with knockout experiments to more finely establish the function of the desired gene. The process is much the same as that in knockout engineering, except that the construct is designed to increase the function of the gene, usually by providing extra copies of the gene or inducing synthesis of the protein more frequently.
- **Tracking experiments**, which seek to gain information about the localization and interaction of the desired protein. One way to do this is to replace the wild-type gene with a 'fusion' gene, which is a juxtaposition of the wild-type gene with a reporting element such as green fluorescent protein (GFP) that will allow easy visualization of the products of the genetic modification. While this is a useful technique, the manipulation can destroy the function of the gene, creating secondary effects and possibly calling into question the results of the experiment. More sophisticated techniques are now in development that can track protein products without mitigating their function, such as the addition of small sequences that will serve as binding motifs to monoclonal antibodies.
- **Expression studies** aim to discover where and when specific proteins are produced. In these experiments, the DNA sequence before the DNA that codes for a protein, known as a gene's promoter, is reintroduced into an organism with the protein coding region replaced by a reporter gene such as GFP or an enzyme that catalyzes the production of a dye. Thus the time and place where a particular protein is produced can be observed. Expression studies can be taken a step further by altering the promoter to find which pieces are crucial for the proper expression of the gene and are actually bound by transcription factor proteins; this process is known as promoter bashing.

(c) Industrial

By engineering genes into bacterial plasmids it is possible to create a biological factory that can produce proteins and enzymes. Some genes do not work well in bacteria, so yeast, a eukaryote, can also be used. Bacteria and yeast factories have been used to produce medicines such as insulin, human growth hormone, and vaccines, supplements such as tryptophan, aid in the production of food (chymosin in cheese making) and fuels. Other applications involving genetically engineered bacteria being investigated involve making the bacteria perform tasks outside their natural cycle, such as cleaning up oil spills, carbon and other toxic waste.

(d) Agriculture

Bt-toxins present in peanut leaves (bottom image) protect it from extensive damage caused by European corn borer larvae (top image). One of the best-known and controversial applications of genetic engineering is the creation of genetically modified food. There are three generations of genetically modified crops. First generation crops have been commercialized and most provide protection from insects and/or resistance to herbicides. There are also fungal and virus resistant crops developed or in development. They have been developed to make the insect and weed management of crops easier and can indirectly increase crop yield.

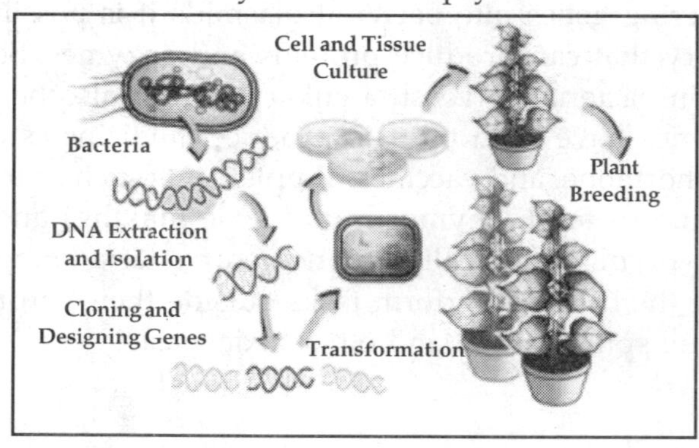

The second generation of genetically modified crops being developed aim to directly improve yield by improving salt, cold or drought tolerance and to increase the nutritional value of the crops. The third generation consists of pharmaceutical crops, crops that contain edible vaccines and other drugs. Some agriculturally important animals have been genetically modified with growth hormones to increase their size while others have been engineered to express drugs and other proteins in their milk.

The genetic engineering of agricultural crops can increase the growth rates and resistance to different diseases caused by pathogens and parasites. This is beneficial as it can greatly increase the production of food sources with the usage of fewer resources that would be required to host the world's growing populations. These modified crops would also reduce the usage of chemicals, such as fertilizers and pesticides, and therefore decrease the severity and frequency of the damages produced by these chemical pollution.

Ethical and safety concerns have been raised around the use of genetically modified food. A major safety concern relates to the human health implications of eating genetically modified food, in particular whether toxic or allergic reactions could occur. Gene flow into related non-transgenic crops, off target effects on beneficial organisms and the impact on biodiversity are important environmental issues. Ethical concerns involve religious issues, corporate control of the food supply, intellectual property rights and the level of labeling needed on genetically modified products.

(e) Other uses

In materials science, a genetically modified virus has been used to construct a more environmentally friendly lithium-ion battery. Some bacteria have been genetically engineered to create black and white photographs while others have potential to be used as sensors by expressing a fluorescent protein under certain environmental conditions. Genetic engineering is also being used to create BioArt and novelty items such as blue roses, and glowing fish.

Some Fruit Possibilities

This section is not about reality, but speculation. What might genetic engineering bring us in the future?

As we've seen above, there are many opponents of the technology who imagine all sorts of catastrophes. In the hands of true mad scientists, biotechnology could be used for great evil. New bacteria or viruses could be developed, capable of causing diseases which medicine could not treat. Modern nations have abandoned germ warfare with the possible exception of a few rogue states, but what is to prevent an individual or a terrorist organization from such a course?

The future could also bring us improvements in our lives, or in how our technologies impact the other beings who share our planet.

In the waters off the coast of North America there is a peculiar animal called a horseshoe crab (Limulus polyphemus). Horseshoe crabs are regularly captured and their blood is used to make a substance used to sterilize medical supplies. There are certain bacteria, called gram negative bacteria, hard to detect, but which will cause clotting in a mixture of biological chemicals called Limulus Amebocyte Lysate (L.A.L.), found only in the horseshoe crab's blood. Horseshoe crabs are not yet considered an endangered species, but their numbers have declined precipitously in recent years. Obviously the crabs would be better off if we could copy their genes into a convenient plant or yeast and make whatever L.A.L. we need without bothering them anymore.

We make many useful things like plastics from oil. Someday, there won't be much oil left in the ground and we will need to use substitutes for energy and for chemical feedstocks. There is no reason why plastics could not be made by plants if we could somehow engineer their genes to control the necessary chemical pathways. In fact, plants ought to be able to make petroleum.

Bayberries are a wild shrub, usually growing near the ocean, which bear waxy berries. They are used to make candles which burn with a delightful fragrance. Paraffin candles are much less expensive. They're made from petroleum. Why could not the genes that let the bayberry make wax be transferred into a more convenient crop plant?

Many of our medical drugs are now produced by genetically engineered bacteria or yeasts, but could instead be produced by genetically engineered plants. In fact, they could even be produced in the parts of plants which are now unused, like stalks of corn or wheat. One scientist is even working on a way to deliver edible vaccines in bananas.

There are endangered species whose decline has nothing to do with human exploitation. Two such are the American chestnut and the American elm. Before the twentieth century, chestnut trees were one of the keystone species of America's eastern forests. They were then decimated by a fungus. Many of these chestnut trees are still alive as roots, which still send up saplings, but they never grow to maturity before the fungus reinfects them. Elm trees, once the most popular shade tree lining streets of American small towns, are highly susceptible to a different fungus, carried by a beetle. Few elm trees have survived. But scientists in Scotland have transferred genes into elm trees that should make them immune to the Dutch elm fungus. Why couldn't we transfer genes that would enable the chestnut to thrive again, so that in a hundred years this species could again enrich our forests?

Blue jeans are made from two plants. Cotton provides the fiber and indigo provides the color. Why not engineer the cotton plant with some indigo genes so that it produces navy blue cotton?

Can we get wool from a plant? Can we get silk from a plant?

Citrus fruits are grown in Florida and California, where the weather is warm. Could they be engineered to grow in Maine or Minnesota?

These are imaginary applications, and you can probably think of many others. But there are reasons why at least some of them won't happen soon. First, we have not learned enough, in most cases, to successfully transfer whole complexes of genes and make them function. We could feasibly identify every gene that helps the horseshoe crab make Limulus Amebocyte Lysate, and every protein involved, but that would not be enough. We need to know the whole complex synthesis pathway, and how each chemical involved would interact with other processes in the target species.

Second, there's simple economics. Private companies do most of the genetic engineering. They need to be motivated by a prospect of large future profits. They are in no hurry to develop products for a niche market. Such products are developed, instead, by university researchers, but they usually can't get the capital necessary to comply with all the safety regulations.

Third, as long as the movement to frustrate genetic engineered agriculture remains effective, investors will seek other directions, and young scientists will choose to work on less controversial research

1. What is Genetic Engineering?

Genetic engineering involves taking genes from one species and inserting them into another. For example, genes from an arctic flounder which has "antifreeze" properties may be spliced into a tomato to prevent frost damage.

The genetic engineering is a set of laboratory techniques for isolating genes from organisms, cutting and rejoining it to make new combinations, multiplying copies of the recombined genetic material and transferring it into organisms. It is also called recombinant DNA technology because it recombines genes within an organism as well as those from other organisms.

"Genetic engineering" means the technique by which heritable material, which does not usually occur or will not occur naturally in the organism or cell concerned, generated outside the organism or the cell is inserted into said cell or organism. It shall also mean the formation of new combinations of genetic material by incorporation of a cell into a host cell, where they occur naturally (self cloning) as well as modification of an organism or in a cell by deletion and removal of parts of the heritable material.

2. What is Genetic Modification?

The genetic modification involves modifying an organism genetic make up by the introduction of a gene or genes into its cells in a way that follows the transfer of the genes to successive generation.

3. What is a genetically modified organism (GMO)?

GMO is the broad term used to identify organisms in which the genetic material has been altered by use of molecular techniques, which does not occur naturally. It also known as genetically engineered organisms or transgenic organisms.

REFERENCES

"Application of Some Genetically Engineered Bacteria". Retrieved 9/7/2010.

"Artificial Genes". TIME. 15 November 1982. Retrieved 17 July 2010.

Arnold, Paul (2009). "History of Genetics: Genetic Engineering Timeline".

"Background: Cloned and Genetically Modified Animals". Center for Genetics and Society. 14 April 2005.

Barbara Hohn, Avraham A Levy and Holger Puchta (2001). "Elimination of Selection Markers from Transgenic Plants". *Current Opinion in Biotechnology* 12 (2): 139-143. doi:10.1016/S0958-1669(00)00188-9. PMID 11287227.

Behrooz Darbani, Safar Farajnia, Mahmoud Toorchi, Saeed Zakerbostanabad, Shahin Noeparvar and C. Neal Stewart Jr. (2010). "DNA-Delivery Methods to Produce Transgenic Plants". Science Alert.

Berg, P.; Mertz, J. (2010). "Personal Reflections on the Origins and Emergence of Recombinant DNA Technology". *Genetics* 184 (1): 9-17. doi:10.1534/genetics.109.112144. PMC 2815933. PMID 20061565.

Bruening G. and Lyons J.M. (2000). "The case of the FLAVR SAVR tomato". *California Agriculture* 54 (4): 6-7. doi:10.3733/ca.v054n04p6.

Capecchi, M. R. (2001). "Generating Mice with Targeted Mutations". *Nature Medicine* 7 (10): 1086-1090. doi:10.1038/nm1001-1086. PMID 11590420.

Chen I, Dubnau D (2004). "DNA Uptake During Bacterial Transformation". *Nat. Rev. Microbiol.* 2 (3): 241–9. doi:10.1038/nrmicro844. PMID 15083159.

Christian M, Cermak T, Doyle EL, *et al.* (July 2010). "TAL Effector Nucleases Create Targeted DNA Double-strand Breaks". *Genetics* 186 (2): 757-61. doi:10.1534/genetics.110.120717. PMC 2942870. PMID 20660643.

C. Neal Stewart, J (April 2006). "Go with the Glow: Fluorescent Proteins to Light Transgenic Organisms". *Trends in Biotechnology* 24 (4): 155-162. doi:10.1016/j.tibtech.2006.02.002. PMID 16488034.

David M. Suter, Michel Dubois-Dauphin, Karl-Heinz Krause (2006). "Genetic Engineering of Embryonic Stem Cells". *Swiss Med Wkly* 136 (27-28): 413-415. PMID 16897894.

Debora MacKenzie (18 June 1994). *Transgenic tobacco is European first*. New Scientist.

Ernesto Andrianantoandro, Subhayu Basu, David K Kariga & Ron Weiss (16 May 2006). "Synthetic Biology: New Engineering Rules for An Emerging Discipline". *Molecular Systems Biology* 2 (2006.0028): 2006.0028. doi:10.1038/msb4100073. PMC 1681505. PMID 16738572.

Food and Agricultural Organisation of the United Nations. "The Process of Genetic Modification".

Goeddel, David; Dennis G. Kleid, Francisco Bolivar, Herbert L. Heyneker, Daniel G. Yansura, Roberto Crea, Tadaaki Hirose, Adam Kraszewski, Keiichi Itakura, AND Arthur D. Riggs (January 1979). "Expression in Escherichia coli of chemically synthesized genes for human insulin". *PNAS* 76 (1): 106-110. Bibcode 1979PNAS...76..106G. doi:10.1073/pnas.76.1.106. PMC 382885. PMID 85300.

Hershey A, Chase M (1952). "Independent Functions of Viral Protein and Nucleic Acid in Growth of Bacteriophage" (PDF). *J Gen Physiol* 36 (1): 39-56. doi:10.1085/jgp.36.1.39. PMC 2147348. PMID 12981234.

The European Parliament and the Council of the European Union (12 March 2001). *Directive on the Release of Genetically Modified Organisms (GMOs) Directive 2001/18/EC ANNEX I A*. Official Journal of the European Communities. p. 17.

Van Eenennaam, Alison. "Is Livestock Cloning Another Form of Genetic Engineering?". agbiotech.

Jacobsen, E.; Schouten, H. J. (2008). "Cisgenesis, a New Tool for Traditional Plant Breeding, Should be Exempted from the Regulation on Genetically Modified Organisms in a Step by Step Approach". *Potato Research* 51: 75-88. doi:10.1007/s11540-008-9097-y.

James H. Maryanski (19 October 1999). "Genetically Engineered Foods". Centre for Food Safety and Applied Nutrition at the Food and Drug Administration.

Stableford, Brian M. (2004). *Historical Dictionary of Science Fiction literature*. p. 133. ISBN 9780810849389.

Jackson, DA; Symons, RH; Berg, P (1 October 1972). "Biochemical Method for Inserting New Genetic Information into DNA of Simian Virus 40: Circular SV40 DNA Molecules Containing Lambda Phage Genes and the Galactose Operon of Escherichia coli". *PNAS* 69 (10): 2904–2909. Bibcode 1972PNAS...69.2904J. doi:10.1073/pnas.69.10.2904. PMC 389671. PMID 4342968.

Stanley N. Cohen and Annie C. Y. Chang (1 May 1973). "Recircularization and Autonomous Replication of a Sheared R-Factor DNA Segment in Escherichia coli Transformants — PNAS". Pnas.org. Retrieved 17 July 2010.

Jaenisch, R. and Mintz, B. (1974). "Simian Virus 40 DNA Sequences in DNA of Healthy Adult Mice Derived from Preimplantation Blastocysts Injected with Viral DNA". *Proc. Natl. Acad. Sci.* 71 (4): 1250-1254. Bibcode 1974PNAS...71.1250J. doi:10.1073/pnas.71.4.1250. PMC 388203. PMID 4364530.

US Supreme Court Cases from Justia & Oyez (16 June 1980). *Diamond V Chakrabarty*. 447. Supreme.justia.com. Retrieved 17 July 2010.

James, Clive (1996). "Global Review of the Field Testing and Commercialization of Transgenic Plants: 1986 to 1995". The International Service for the Acquisition of Agri-biotech Applications. Retrieved 17 July 2010.

James, Clive (1997). "Global Status of Transgenic Crops in 1997". *ISAAA Briefs No. 5.*: 31.

Genetically Altered Potato Ok'd For Crops Lawrence Journal-World - 6 May 1995.

Global Status of Commercialized Biotech/GM Crops: 2009 ISAAA Brief 41-2009, 23 February 2010. Retrieved 10 August 2010.

Gibson, D.; Glass, J.; Lartigue, C.; Noskov, V.; Chuang, R.; Algire, M.; Benders, G.; Montague, M. et al. (2010). "Creation of a Bacterial Cell Controlled by a Chemically Synthesized Genome". *Science* 329 (5987): 52-6. Bibcode 2010Sci...329...52G. doi:10.1126/science.1190719. PMID 20488990.

Ian Sample (20 May 2010). "Craig Venter Creates Synthetic Life Form". London: guardian.co.uk.

James, Clive (2008). "Global Status of Commercilized Biotech/GM Crops:2008". *ISSA Brief No. 39.*

Townsend JA, Wright DA, Winfrey RJ, *et al.* (May 2009). "High-frequency Modification of Plant Genes Using Engineered Zinc-finger Nucleases". *Nature* 459 (7245): 442–5. Bibcode 2009Natur.459..442T. doi:10.1038/nature07845. PMC 2743854. PMID 19404258.

Shukla VK, Doyon Y, Miller JC, *et al.* (May 2009). "Precise Genome Modification in the Crop Species Zea Mays Using Zinc-finger Nucleases". *Nature* 459 (7245): 437-41. Bibcode 2009Natur.459..437S. doi:10.1038/nature07992. PMID 19404259.

Grizot S, Smith J, Daboussi F, *et al.* (September 2009). "Efficient Targeting of a SCID Gene by an Engineered Single-chain Homing Endonuclease". *Nucleic Acids Res.* 37 (16): 5405-19. doi:10.1093/nar/gkp548. PMC 2760784. PMID 19584299.

Gao H, Smith J, Yang M, *et al.* (January 2010). "Heritable Targeted Mutagenesis in Maize Using a Designed Endonuclease". *Plant J.* 61 (1): 176-87. doi:10.1111/j.1365-313X.2009.04041.x. PMID 19811621.

Li T, Huang S, Jiang WZ, *et al.* (August 2010). "TAL Nucleases (TALNs): Hybrid Proteins Composed of TAL Effectors and FokI DNA-cleavage domain". *Nucleic Acids* Res 39 (1): 359-72. doi:10.1093/nar/gkq704. PMC 3017587. PMID 20699274.

S.C. Ekker (2008). "Zinc Finger-based Knockout Punches for Zebrafish Genes". *Zebrafish* 5 (2): 1121-3. doi:10.1089/zeb.2008.9988. PMC 2849655. PMID 18554175.

Geurts AM, Cost GJ, Freyvert Y, *et al.* (July 2009). "Knockout Rats via Embryo Microinjection of Zinc-finger nucleases". *Science* 325 (5939): 433. Bibcode 2009Sci...325..433G. doi:10.1126/science.1172447. PMC 2831805. PMID 19628861.

Graham Head; Hull, Roger H; Tzotzos, George T. (2009). *Genetically Modified Plants: Assessing Safety and Managing Risk*. London: Academic Pr. pp. 244. ISBN 0-12-374106-8.

Gelvin, S. B. (2003). "Agrobacterium-Mediated Plant Transformation: the Biology behind the "Gene-Jockeying" Tool". *Microbiology and Molecular Biology Reviews* 67 (1): 16-37, table of contents. doi:10.1128/MMBR.67.1.16-37.2003. PMC 150518. PMID 12626681.

John C. Avise (2004). *The Hope, Hype & Reality of Genetic Engineering: Remarkable Stories from Agriculture, Industry, Medicine, and the Environment*. Oxford University Press US. p. 22. ISBN 978-0-19-516950-8.

National Institute of Allergies and Infectious Diseases. "Vaccine Types". National Institute of Health.

Rodriguez, L.; Grubman, M. (2009). "Foot and Mouth Disease Virus Vaccines". *Vaccine* 27 Suppl 4: D90–D94. doi:10.1016/j.vaccine.2009.08.039. PMID 19837296.

Roque AC, Lowe CR, Taipa MA. (2004). "Antibodies and Genetically Engineered Related Molecules: Production and Purification". *Biotechnol Proress* 20 (3): 639-54. doi:10.1021/bp030070k. PMID 15176864.

"Knockout Mice". Nation Human Genome Research Institute. 2009.

"GM Pigs Best Bet for Organ Transplant". Medical News Today. 21 September 2003.

"What is Genetic Engineering? A Simple Introduction". Physicians and Scientists for Responsible Application of Science and Technology.

"Gene Therapy". Oak Ridge National Laboratory. 11 June 2009. Retrieved 9/7/2010.

Sheryl Gay (4 July 2010). "Trials are Halted on a Gene Therapy". *The New York Times*.

Emilie R. Bergeson (1997). "The Ethics of Gene Therapy".

Kathi E. Hanna. "Genetic Enhancement". National Human Genome Research Institute.

"Applications of Genetic Engineering". Microbiologyprocedure. Retrieved 9/7/2010.

"Biotech: What are transgenic organisms?". Easyscience. 2002. Retrieved 9/7/2010.

Savage, Neil (1 August 2007). "Making Gasoline from Bacteria: A Biotech Startup wants to Coax Fuels from Engineered Microbes". Technology Review. Retrieved 9/7/2010.

Jan Suszkiw (November 1999.). "Tifton, Georgia: A Peanut Pest Showdown". *Agricultural Research magazine*. Retrieved 23 November 2008.

Magaña-Gómez JA, de la Barca AM (2009). "Risk Assessment of Genetically Modified Crops for Nutrition and Health". *Nutr. Rev.* 67 (1): 1-16. doi:10.1111/j.1753-4887.2008.00130.x. PMID 19146501.

Aparna Islam (2006). "Fungus Resistant Transgenic Plants: Strategies, Progress and Lessons Learnt". *Plant Tissue Culture and Biotechnology* 16 (2).

"Disease resistant crops". GMO Compass.

Demont, M.; Tollens, E. (2004). "First Impact of Biotechnology in the EU: Bt Maize Adoption in Spain". *Annals of Applied Biology* 145 (2): 197. doi:10.1111/j.1744-7348.2004.tb00376.x.

Deborah B. Whitman (2000). "Genetically Modified Foods: Harmful or Helpful?".

Michelle Marvier (2008). "Pharmaceutical Crops in California, Benefits and Risks. A Review". *Agron. Sustain. Dev.* 28: 1-9. doi:10.1051/agro:2007050.

"Giant GM salmon on the way". BBC News. 11 April 2000.

Emma Young (2003). "GM Cows to Please Cheese-makers". *New Scientist.*

"FDA Approves First Human Biologic Produced by GE Animals". US Food and Drug Administration.

Paulo Rebêlo (15 July 2004). "GM Cow Milk 'Could Provide Treatment for Blood Disease'". SciDev.

Sustaining Life. Oxford University Press, Inc. 2008. ISBN 978-0-19-517509-7.

Carrington, Damien (13 June 2012) GM Crops Good for Environment, Study Finds The Guardian. Retrieved 16 June 2012.

John Pickrell (4 September 2006). "Introduction: GM Organisms". New Scientist.

"20 Questions on Genetically Modified Foods". World Health Organization. 2010.

"Can GM Crops Harm the Environment?". National Environment Research Council (NERC).

"New Virus-built Battery Could Power Cars, Electronic Devices". Web.mit.edu. 2 April 2009. Retrieved 17 July 2010.

"Hidden Ingredient In New, Greener Battery: A Virus". Npr.org. Retrieved 17 July 2010.

Joab Jackson (6 December 2005). "Genetically Modified Bacteria Produce Living Photographs". National Geographic News.

"Researchers Synchronize Blinking 'Genetic Clocks' — Genetically Engineered Bacteria That Keep Track of Time". ScienceDaily. 24 January 2010.

Jessica M. Pasko (3/4/2007). "Bio-artists Bridge Gap Between Arts, Sciences: Use of Living Organisms is Attracting Attention and Controversy". msnbc.

Yukihisa Katsumoto *et. al* (9 October 2007). "Engineering of the Rose Flavonoid Biosynthetic Pathway Successfully Generated Blue-Hued Flowers Accumulating Delphinidin". *Plant and Cell Physiology* 48 (11): 1589–1600. doi:10.1093/pcp/pcm131. PMID 17925311.

Richard Black (6 August 2010). "GM Plants 'Established in the Wild'". BBC.

Index